THE BRAVE LEARNER

"In *The Brave Learner*, Julie captures the essence of learning. Homeschooling is not about the schooling or even the home but rather it's about people—their stories, hopes, needs, opportunities, communities, and future. *The Brave Learner* emphasizes this beautifully by moving between the vision and practice of homeschooling—not an easy transition to make. The book is a worthy read for any parent, whether they homeschool or not."　　　　—Terry Heick, founder of TeachThought

"Julie Bogart's everyday magic is her knack for combining galvanizing inspiration and hands-on practicality. Her writing is frank, funny, and full of charm. Her approach to homeschooling—and to parenting in general—emphasizes a spirit of adventure and camaraderie, placing relationship at the center of a family's educational journey. This is the guidebook I wish I'd had when I was starting out."
—Melissa Wiley, author of *Fox and Crow Are Not Friends*

"Julie Bogart is tireless in providing ingenious and creative help for homeschoolers."　　　　—Peter Elbow, Professor of English Emeritus, University of Massachusetts Amherst

"Breathes fresh life into your homeschool days."
—Ainsley Arment, founder of Wild + Free

"*The Brave Learner* is the book I would have adored as a young parent. Julie's wise advice, genuine humor, and refreshing honesty wrapped me in a spirit of hope and possibility. This is a joyful book brimming with generous, practical ideas about how to live and teach at any age. I only wish I had more children!"
—Amy Ludwig VanDerwater, author of *Forest Has a Song*

"Julie's voice is personable, encouraging, informative, and reassuring. *The Brave Learner* is filled with inspirational and practical tips on helping children thrive whether you're a homeschooling parent or not."
—Charnaie Gordon, creator of Here Wee Read

THE
BRAVE LEARNER

THE
BRAVE LEARNER

* * *

Finding Everyday Magic in
Homeschool, Learning, and Life

* * *

JULIE BOGART

A TarcherPerigee Book

tarcherperigee

An imprint of Penguin Random House LLC
penguinrandomhouse.com

Most TarcherPerigee books are available at special quantity discounts for bulk purchase for sales promotions, premiums, fund-raising, and educational needs. Special books or book excerpts also can be created to fit specific needs. For details, write: SpecialMarkets@penguinrandomhouse.com.

Library of Congress Cataloging-in-Publication Data

Names: Bogart, Julie, author.
Title: The brave learner : finding everyday magic in homeschool,
learning, and life / Julie Bogart.
Description: New York, NY : TarcherPerigee, 2019 |
Includes bibliographical references and index.
Identifiers: LCCN 2018049576| ISBN 9780143133223 (trade pbk.) |
ISBN 9780525505006 (ebk.)
Subjects: LCSH: Home schooling.
Classification: LCC LC40 .B64 2019 | DDC 371.04/2—dc23
LC record available at https://lccn.loc.gov/2018049576

Printed in the United States of America
7 9 10 8 6

Book design by Laura K. Corless

To Noah, Johannah, Jacob, Liam, and Caitrin—
who taught me how to learn

To my mother—
who taught me how to love

There's no place like home.

—DOROTHY, *THE WIZARD OF OZ*

CONTENTS

xv FOREWORD BY SUSAN WISE BAUER

xix INTRODUCTION

PART ONE
THE ENCHANTED LANDSCAPE OF LEARNING

3 **CHAPTER 1**
Enchanted Living
Creating the Context for Magic in Our Homes

11 **CHAPTER 2**
Sparks Fly
Igniting a Passion for Learning

17 **CHAPTER 3**
Magic Doors
Lessons from Monsters and Maps

PART TWO
CASTING THE SPELL: The Superpowers of Brave Learning

33 **CHAPTER 4**
The Four Forces of Enchantment
Surprise, Mystery, Risk, and Adventure

64 **CHAPTER 5**

The Four Capacities for Learning

Curiosity, Collaboration, Contemplation, and Celebration

97 **CHAPTER 6**

The Four Ports of Entry

Mind, Body, Heart, and Spirit

125 **CHAPTER 7**

Applying the Superpowers

Practical Help in Core Subjects

PART THREE
SUSTAINING THE MAGIC

165 **CHAPTER 8**

Liberation from School

To Schedule or Not to Schedule, That Is the Question
(Answers Inside!)

187 **CHAPTER 9**

House-schooling

Recruit Your Home to Help You Educate
(and That Pernicious Topic: Chores)

202 **CHAPTER 10**

The Pixie Dust of Reasonable Expectations

Embracing Our Limits

218 **CHAPTER 11**

Awesome Adulting

Expanding Our Horizons

PART FOUR
BREAKING THE SPELL AND REKINDLING THE MAGIC

235 CHAPTER 12

The Invisible Education
The Power of Family Dysfunction to Sideline Learning

254 CHAPTER 13

The Disenchanting Power of Doing It Right
The Dangers of Ideological Alignment and True Belief-ism
in Home Education

266 CHAPTER 14

Reverse the Curse
How to Rekindle the Magic

275 ACKNOWLEDGMENTS

279 NOTES

283 INDEX

FOREWORD

By Susan Wise Bauer

I've been homeschooling for decades—first as a home-educated student myself, and then as a mother of four home learners (aged, as I write this, eighteen to twenty-eight). For a good bit of that time, I've tried very hard to create a passion for learning in my children. But as I near the end of my homeschool journey, I realize just how impossible that is.

We can't *create* a love for education. Like creativity itself, or the romantic version of love, the passion for learning is a mysterious, internally generated force. We can't instill it from the outside any more than we can control a teenager's first hopeless crush.

All those years of experience have finally taught me that my job, as a parent, as a teacher, isn't to persuade my kids to fall in love with grammar or math, history or science. (Thank goodness, because, as Julie points out with wisdom and much-needed humor, that's just not going to happen.) Instead, our task is to provide the oxygen-rich surroundings that will allow sparking new interests to blaze into full life: a rich, varied, colorful landscape in which our kids can find their own paths forward into meaningful, challenging adult lives.

This is what *The Brave Learner* tackles: the attitudes, approaches, and strategies that we parents can adopt in order to give our children what they *really* need, the "conditions for that magical eruption of passion to occur." It's a much-needed philosophical corrective to our standards-driven, results-oriented educational system, one that too often focuses myopically on test results and successful college application.

There is big thinking here, a philosophy aimed at developing the unique, quirky, sometimes maddening, always magical *people* living in our houses. But there is also practicality—bullet lists, how-tos, and thought experiments, all vital scaffolding for a new application of principles. Julie doesn't just tell you that children should be exposed to different ways of seeing; she suggests investing in binoculars, a jeweler's loupe, 3-D glasses, and a kaleidoscope so that you can physically change the way they see, and draw a connection to perception more generally. She doesn't simply lecture you about how important it is for a teen to develop independence in learning; she gives you a list of learning opportunities to investigate in your own town or city that will put your teenager on the road to independence. She doesn't just advise you to keep "a glorious array of supplies" on hand, to awaken interest in art; she gives you an abundant list of possibilities that you can take down to Staples or Office Depot.

And she doesn't forget that our kids won't always be home with us—and that the season of homeschooling is a short one, compared with our entire life span. When you finish *The Brave Learner*, you'll realize that you haven't just been reevaluating your child's learning style; you've begun to reevaluate yourself as well. As Julie writes, "Knowing who you are and what brings you joy beyond your children provides comfort and optimism at the end of the homeschool odyssey. Not only that, but homeschooling may lead you to the contribution you are destined to make."

This is a valuable handbook on education, one I wish I'd had when my children were young. (Julie's were young at the same time, and the wisdom she's distilled here is hard-won.) Yet it's also more than that. It's a primer on how to be present in the moment, how to find the immediate joys of life in the midst of our daily labors—even in the days (or weeks, or months) when our kids may seem interested in absolutely nothing at all.

This, too, is reality. *The Brave Learner* doesn't back away from it. But Julie offers you the courage to accept it, be at peace, stoke that air up with just a little more oxygen, and wait—in the settled assurance that your kids, and you, will be well.

—Susan Wise Bauer, coauthor of *The Well-Trained Mind*

INTRODUCTION

The whole world is a series of miracles, but we are so used to them we call them ordinary things.

— HANS CHRISTIAN ANDERSEN

Before we begin, pour yourself a cup of coffee or tea. Adjust the reading lamp. Arrange yourself comfortably. I'll wait. Ready?

Let's face the daunting task of educating your children in the glow of soft light and warmth. I invite you to join me on a scavenger hunt for the ordinary magic already at work in your family. In this book, I offer you a kind, gentle approach to parenting and homeschooling your young charges—a plan that facilitates your dreams. Picture your child taking the initiative to study ancient history or Latin grammar or composting a garden. What would it be like not to worry about video games or too much television? Imagine knowing how to turn around a day gone wrong. Pause—see in your mind's eye an eager face, excited to share writing with you; see another face enjoying the effort it takes to master an algebraic equation. Pretend it's the end of a school year—you and your children share happy memories, love being together; academic progress is clear. Wouldn't that feel great?

It's possible to feel this good about your children's education.

I'm here to help you get more of *that* into your daily experience.

Every home educator and parent I've met offers me the same mission statement: "I just want my children to *love* learning." Me too. I have five adult kids I homeschooled for seventeen years with the same fragile aspiration. I felt batted back and forth between curricula, education theories, and homeschool philosophies. I felt too late to every party—as though I would never catch up.

At the heart of each belief system, a love of learning was considered the magical key to unlock the riches of a valuable education. Yet who would define it in a way I could apply it? When I began my homeschooling odyssey, I imagined my "in love with learning kids" would wake up, tumble down the stairs, and dive at the math book, declaring: "I can't wait to work on fractions today!" I bet you're ahead of me—that never happened. Not once.

Over my years of homeschooling, the glittering vision of a "love of learning" shape-shifted multiple times—perhaps it meant that my children's passions would magically teach them grammar; maybe it meant I'd find a trick to get my kids to fall in love with geometry; maybe we needed to start in ancient Greece and work forward until my children became consumed with self-education. I wondered if classical educators had it right or if I ought to go all-in on unschooling (that tempting idea that children can learn all they need to know without formal instruction). I asked myself: What causes kids to put in the hard work of learning what they don't know, because they *want* to know?

Love and learning seem unrelated when we look at traditional school subjects. Exhausted parents living the day-to-day grind of instructing and homework frequently give up trying to make lessons "fun" or "interesting." Education becomes a juggling act: supervising workbook pages by multiple kids at multiple levels while a toddler scrawls permanent marker on the kitchen wall and a baby spits up.

The core idea behind "a love of learning" is that a child will find the challenge of a task interesting enough to persist at it until mastery. The obvious question: How do we get there from here? Can a love of learning thrive amid childish chaos, parental self-doubt, the flu, and state academic standards? Yes, it can.

At the heart of the *homeschooling* enterprise is the faith that the parent is enough—that *your* energy, resourcefulness, creativity, and passion will be sufficient for *your* children. I've had the privilege of working directly with thousands of homeschooling families for more than twenty years. I admire their courage, conscientiousness, and perseverance. I coach them to teach writing (through my company, Brave Writer) and in home education (through my coaching community, the Homeschool Alliance).

I've discovered that parents are hard on themselves. Even the ones who look competent to others, worry. A merry-go-round of "more, different, better" ensues. Homeschool parents keep worry at bay by spending *more* money, changing to *different* curricula, and applying a *better* philosophy of education. Then they evaluate the results using the same criteria as before, and wind up as worried as ever—prompting another spin through the "more, different, better" cycle.

The solution doesn't lie in materials or ideology. Rather, to experience joy, peace, and progress in home education requires a paradigm shift—a change in the criteria for how we *see* and *stage* our homeschools. I've spent the last several decades immersed in theories of learning, testing them on my kids, seeing them tested by other homeschooling families from around the world. In this book, I offer principles and practices embraced by my family and thousands of others that will help you get a little more love into that learning and a little more charity toward yourself in that effort.

The key to a kinder and gentler homeschool is attending to the details we overlook—the coziness of our homes, the principles of natural learning, and the tenderness of our intimate relationships. It takes courage to move away from traditional methods of measurement: grade level, scope and sequence, the Common Core. Our kids naturally lead the way, diving into whatever subject matter draws them, fearless in their belief that they can learn anything they *want* to learn. Yet parents waver. I did too. I wanted to know: How can I ensure that my children are learning all they *should*? You have to be brave to learn a new way to see education and to execute it, trusting that your kids will arrive on the shores of adulthood, prepared to tackle their futures.

Several years ago, at the dawn of live-stream broadcasting, I gave a little lecture I titled "The Enchanted Education." I spoke about candles and trust, eye contact and a sense of humor, predictable routines and splendid surprises, finding the school subjects hiding in a child's passions and interests, having the courage to reimagine education. I explained what the research shows: children are already engaged in learning—parents are the ones who can most effectively coax and expand a child's natural inclination to learn. The principles of enchantment—seeing the magic in the learning transaction—caught the imaginations of thousands of home educators.

I reasoned: enchantment bathes all sorts of learning—traditional subjects like math and history as well as personal passions like karate and board games—in curiosity, delight, and connection. An enchanted education makes a simple claim: learning thrives when our families thrive. That claim is complicated when what enables a parent to thrive is at odds with what allows a child to thrive. Into this quixotic mix, we thrust the responsibility to provide a college-ready education to our kids. No wonder the task feels formidable.

And yet—a few well-placed tweaks to how we view learning, relate to our children, and manifest an inviting context in our homes can utterly transform our children's educations and our experience of parenting. The reason these principles bring relief is that they are tailored to the rhythm and personality of your unique family. You are free to shed strict adherence to an ideology. Please do. Instead, sample and taste, explore and experiment, apply and discard suggestions in this book. Allow yourself the joy of discovery—how one idea will spark another and lead to a brand-new vista!

To maximize the value of the practices and attitudes I share, I invite you to be a brave learner yourself. Pay attention to your journey—to what incites your enthusiasm and provokes your skepticism. Be interested in your reactions. Journal. Jot questions in the margins. Recognize the child in *you* longing for both freedom and support. Translate those experiences into empathy for your children's learning adventure.

Families who've adopted many of these strategies in their homeschools write to me. They suddenly see their happy, eager-to-learn children who have been hiding in plain sight. Parents tap into their own natural creativity and compassion; they discover how to unlock the magic of learning no matter the subject; they build momentum in their children's educations; they stop harshly judging themselves for failure to live up to a fantasy. Children in traditional school environments whose parents embrace the principles of brave learning and family connection enrich their children's school experiences naturally too.

Most homeschooling parents would love to live in harmony with their children, sharing the wonder of this big bold universe that invites us to know it better. There's no reason that can't be your experience right now. Once you apply the properties of enchantment and connect to the hearts and minds of your kids, the world will open to you as a "write your own adventure" book. Learning will be pleasurable, and enjoyment of your children—natural. You don't have to apply these ideas and insights perfectly, either. Allow the transformation to come to you. Inhale, exhale. Be brave. Keep reading. Grab a cookie.

Let's get started.

PART ONE

The Enchanted Landscape of Learning

A lifestyle of learning begins at home—with parents who create a context that is welcoming of children as they are and that offers them happy experiences, accessible tools, and parental involvement. What is the role of enchantment (inspiration) in education? What causes learning to "catch fire"? What douses the learning impulse? How do home educators uncover the school subjects hiding in a child's interest?

CHAPTER 1

ENCHANTED LIVING

Creating the Context for Magic in Our Homes

> After all we *are* an art form . . . We produce an environment
> other people have to live in. We should be conscious of the
> fact that this environment which we produce by our very "be-
> ing" can affect the people who live with us.
>
> —EDITH SCHAEFFER, *HIDDEN ART OF HOMEMAKING*

My neighbor and coconspirator in all things homeschool, Dotty, swooped to pluck a dead branch from the sidewalk—a stroller-wheel landmine right in front of me. I stopped short: a panicked vision of my baby flung to the concrete evaporated. I sighed in relief, assuming Dotty was clearing my path, and felt grateful she had. Two hours later, I entered her apartment and there, nailed to the living room wall, was the very same scraggly branch—artfully hung, creating a je ne sais quoi feel in the room—surprise, delight. Of course. Dotty hadn't worried about my stroller. Her enchanted eye had spotted a wall hanging!

I owe my introduction to enchanted living to Dotty. She sees the world through a different lens than most of us. Dotty's hand-me-down furniture didn't match, yet it invited and warmed guests anyway. She laid a sunny kitchen rug on the back of the dull sofa smothered in plump pillows. She arranged futons into cozy nooks next to baskets brimming with puzzles, blocks, felt dolls, and a cassette player at the ready. She turned a hideous *Jetsons*-style mustard-colored armchair into that perfect accent in a room of drab gray and stocked it with fuzzy blankets, a stuffed animal, and warm lighting. Little kids, engulfed in a glow of yellow vinyl, cuddled a bear and paged through picture books.

In the center of the small living room (you know, that space into which you invite guests) stood a large sturdy table jam-packed with art supplies—paintbrushes of varying sizes in tin cans, glass baby food jars to hold water, googly eyes, pipe cleaners, glitter, all varieties of glue, colored and butcher paper, paints and modeling clay, pastels and markers, and scissors for lefties and righties. Overhead a clothesline hung art projects to drip-dry.

Her seven-hundred-square-foot home was interesting, alive—not just "cute" or "well decorated." And it was a glorious, inviting mess! Unkempt. Not unsanitary. An artist's invitation to possibilities and projects in process at all times. You knew you could take risks in Dotty's house—it had room for mistakes and flops. No one would mind.

My family lived a balcony away, and we visited Dotty's place nearly every day for five years. One afternoon, Dotty waved us in, wielding a glue gun in one hand and acorn caps in the other: "We're making fairy houses! Pull up a chair." Cookies, twigs, moss, pinecones, dried flowers, and half-empty glasses of juice littered the table. I noticed a sink full of dishes behind her. Two of her kids, heads down, didn't look up, engrossed with dangerous hot glue. Eva, Dotty's youngest, who appeared as if out of nowhere with a box of face paints, turned her cheek to her mother. Without missing a beat, Dotty drew tiger stripes as she explained to my family how to build structurally sound twig houses.

My children scattered through the tiny apartment—some making stick cabins, others disappearing to the big dress-up clothes basket in the back room. Moments later, four kids returned with a stack of hats and a book in hand: *Caps for Sale*. Brooke, Dotty's oldest, announced, "We want to perform a play for you!"

Four children lined up in a row—dressed in dad shirts usually reserved as painting smocks. Brooke read aloud as children marched into the room stacking hats and acting scenes. There were miscues and silliness, children too shy to speak up and others too free to shut up! Directing, shushing, and laughing continued until the end of the book.

The crew dispersed; several returned to the art table to join the fairy-house-making fun. Dotty vanished and magically reappeared with slices of homemade bread, jam, and lemonade on a bright blue tray. Everyone ate and drank, starved from so much creative exertion. A day in the life—with Dotty.

The first thing I did after meeting Dotty was set up my own "always open for business" art table. You can too!

Dotty's Enchanted Art Table

To bring enchantment right into your family room, amply supply a table with art materials for use at any time.

Requirements to Preserve Your Sanity, Carpet, and Walls

1. Table: Not precious, stable (card tables are rickety), and able to withstand hot glue, paint, and permanent markers. Can be covered with clear plastic. Tuck the plastic under the table and duct tape it in place so it doesn't move when kids are working. The height of the table depends on the age of the kids: low for young kids, regular height for older kids.

2. Chairs: Appropriate to the table height, back support, not easily tipped, not precious (they will be decorated in color and glue).

3. Floor: Set the table on top of an old rug or scrap of carpet/vinyl.

4. Children: Hang men's button-down short-sleeved shirts (bought at a thrift store) on a coat rack or hooks on a wall near the table. These can be donned backward (buttons down the back) as smocks to protect clothes.

5. Walls: If the table butts up against a wall, affix a long strip of butcher paper about a foot high.

A Glorious Array of Supplies

1. Painting: Tempera, watercolors, acrylics, puff paints, finger paints, fat brushes, thin brushes, foam brushes, sponges cut into stamps for printing.

2. Writing: Washable markers (Crayola makes inexpensive ones), oil pastels, Prismacolor colored pencils, charcoal, Flair black pens for outlining, highlighters, Sharpies in all colors (careful: these markers are permanent), chalk, drawing pencils, whiteboard markers (pro tip: put colored electrical tape on whiteboard markers to make it clear they are not meant for paper), regular number 2 pencils, gel pens for black paper.

3. Surfaces: Colored and white paper, stationery with pretty borders, brown paper bags, butcher paper, sticky notes, notecards, cardboard, wrapping paper, aluminum foil, poster board, cardstock, envelopes, canvas, wooden blocks, river stones, a mirror, a whiteboard, glass votive candleholders, scraps of fabric, sand paper, coloring books, felt, black paper for gel pens, small journals and notebooks.

4. Fasteners: Lots of glue sticks, Elmer's white glue, hot glue guns and crazy glue (used with supervision), fabric glue, stapler, brads, hole punch and rings, Scotch tape, double-sided tape, masking tape, clear packaging tape, duct tape, electrical tape in multiple colors.

5. Accessories: Googly eyes, pipe cleaners, glitter (careful!), confetti (careful times two!), stickers, rubber stamps, stencils, yarn, string, embroidery floss, modeling clay, Sculpey baking clay, fabric scraps, catalogs, magazines, pompoms, rickrack, Popsicle sticks.

6. Storage: Washed empty tin cans make great holders for paintbrushes and writing utensils. A shower caddy holds packages of googly eyes, pipe cleaners, glue sticks, and glitter. Hang a laundry line nearby with clothespins to display artwork and to get it *off* the table. A bulletin board mounted on a wall can serve a similar purpose (cover it in colorful wrapping paper to go with decor, if you'd like). Keep a shelf free on a bookcase to display projects that can't be hung. Use heavy-bottomed glasses (the short kind for cocktails) to hold water for cleaning paintbrushes between colors. These tip less often than tin cans. Modeling clay can be kept on small cookie sheets under the table and then lifted to the top when in use.

7. Location: Put the table in your way—underfoot and near you. Tables in basements and bedrooms are lonely.

Time to play!

The magic of the table is that it's ready to use any time. Begin with a few supplies: perhaps the paints, markers, clean white paper, glue, and googly eyes. Add fresh items (each week or every few days). Rotate old, crusted materials off the table to be replaced by fresh, new ones.

Surprise your kids! Let kids awaken to a table of twigs, bark, moss, and acorns. They might discover you already at work making fairy houses. Will they join you? Find out. Bring home smooth stones from the creek and paint them to make paperweights or stack them and glue them together to create sculptures.

Add quill pens and ink wells—write by candlelight.

A table reset is appropriate once a month. A time may come when the table becomes "wallpaper" and no one notices it anymore. Clear it up and try a different idea in this book.

Modification: For crowded homes that can't support a dedicated art table, stock a cabinet with lots of hidey-holes, drawers, and cupboards near the kitchen table.

The fairy house and *Caps for Sale* experience is one of many that Dotty and I created with ease and pleasure over the five years that we homeschooled together. Here are a few others:

* Beachside picnics with scrambled eggs over a driftwood fire
* Exploring tide pools at the beach
* Birding
* California Gold Rush–themed party
* Experiments with tubs of lard
* Borax turned to slime
* Face paint and dress-up clothes
* Moroccan tea with homemade bread, and henna painted on our hands
* Late-night solar system party with poetry about the stars and planets
* Seasonal nature tables
* Making pies from the wild blackberries picked on a hike
* Quilting
* *Farmer Boy* breakfast complete with ham, pancakes, apple pie, and hunks of cheese
* Field trips to the farmers' market and Little Saigon
* Flashlight tag

Lest you think life was perfect—it wasn't. Math facts and phonics snuck into our lives too, as did guilt, tantrums, births, doubt, boredom, bed-wetting, speech impediments, pressure, poverty, pregnancy, pinworms and lice, language impairments, loneliness, and exhaustion.

Despite the adult challenge of raising children, managing our marriages, and growing into competent grown-ups ourselves, a thread of surprise, mystery, risk, and adventure carried us too. In hindsight, we were led and nourished by the power of *enchantment*.

✳ WHAT IS ENCHANTMENT? ✳

Enchantment is about ease, not striving. Good news, right? It's the hard work of enforcing "school" or "homework" that saps your strength and bugs your kids. I discovered that being open to and using the properties of enchantment release energy—the good kind that moves learning forward naturally, effortlessly. Enchanted education and living are all about *small* surprises of happy—scattered, littered, peppered throughout garden-variety days. These *en-magicked* moments act as turbo boosts in the same way a moving sidewalk gets you through the airport more quickly.[1] You're still walking in an airport—but it's easier, faster, better somehow. The whole time, you feel competent—smooth, powerful, liberated—headed right where you need to go. In education, when we create space for enchantment, we put ourselves on a moving sidewalk of happy.

That said, enchantment is not a synonym for happiness. Enchantment is a flirt! It flatters and woos, until whoops! You're all in—lovestruck—and passion flows. Enchantment gets to happy through a surprising array of emotions and experiences too: excitement, fear, anticipation, intimacy, exhilaration, suspense, color, contentment, whimsy, flavor, cuddles, eye contact, perseverance, tenderness, romance, admiration, and comfort, to name a slew!

The thrill of Halloween is more than joy at devouring free candy. Hiding in a costume, knocking on a stranger's door, moving about the neighborhood in the dark, the possibility of ghosts, jack-o'-lanterns, and creepy music . . . These happy moments are prepared by the properties of enchantment—even deliberately choosing to be frightened!

To me, an enchanted *life* is living in my ordinary circumstances with heightened awareness—being on the lookout for "a surprise of happy." When we tune into the enchanted wavelength, it's as if we put on special goggles and now see that a dead tree branch in the middle of the sidewalk would make a lovely wall hanging. Happiness flows toward us, rather than rushing away from us.

Why is a table overstocked with art supplies and available any time of day more inviting to a child than a scripted art project in a classroom? What are the magical properties in the first and the disenchantments in the second?

✳ Everyday Magic for Learning and Life ✳

When I began this homeschooling-parenting gig, I wanted to create a warm memorable *life* for my kids and myself, not *just* an education. We're not only preparing our children to get a job someday in the future. The education of my kids had to make the present moment memorable and good. Happiness shouldn't be something to end up with; it ought to be the by-product of a whole-hearted, fully lived life.

I figured that if we liked our lives, we'd get education thrown into the bargain. I didn't believe that learning was drudgery or something to be *done* to children. I wanted my family to love learning—together—in our "feels."

I watched what happened to my kids when they were spontaneously drawn to any subject from pill bugs to the American crow, baking soda volcanoes to the Greek alphabet. I saw the power of staging a Japanese meal complete with low tables, pillows, tempura, chopsticks, tissue paper cherry blossoms, origami cranes, and kimonos. The study of Japan for a test could never leave the imprint that our humble attempt to experience Japan did.

That said: it can be taxing to throw parties and build twig fairy houses every ding-danged day! What if you don't feel creative? I didn't all the time. "Keep 'em busy, keep 'em alive" was my motto. No matter how many children you have—one to fifteen—it takes all your energy to do those two things! I imagine you now muttering under your breath: "Do I have to conjure endless parties too—in addition to teaching fractions, spelling, and using the potty?"

I hear you loud and clear. If "enchanting" an education means hours of preparation for every ten minutes of cooperation, why bother? Fortunately, an enchanted education is like kindling a fire. All you need is a book of matches.

CHAPTER 2

SPARKS FLY

Igniting a Passion for Learning

Tips, tricks and techniques are not at the heart of education—
fire is . . . Not merely the facts, not merely the theories, but a
deep knowing of what it means to kindle the gift of life in
ourselves, in others, and in the world.

—PARKER J. PALMER IN *RADICAL PRESENCE*
BY MARY ROSE O'REILLEY

On some intuitive level, I knew that learning had to be more than the
mastery of facts. I've experienced it as an adult. I become consumed
with a subject like quilting or preparing yogurt cultures, and that topic
takes over my life—fabric scraps scattered on the floor, little jars of white
sludge cuddled by blankets on my kitchen countertops. When I learned
to play guitar in my thirties, no one had to schedule my practices. My
guitar lived on a stand in the family room and I tormented our ears
multiple times a day until my fingers bled. Passion for learning has that
fiery, consuming, can't-stop quality.

Fire is a great metaphor for enchantment—I think of cauldrons and
candles, fireworks and campfires. Back before eight hundred channels
and big-screen televisions, the ancients were mesmerized by the night
sky and their own bright bonfires. As a result, human beings have been
pyromaniacs for millennia. With good reason. Fire is wonderfully warm
and glittery, unpredictable and powerful. Why else would Disney World

spend millions of dollars a year on elaborate fireworks shows every night?

The enchanted life of learning is combustible, sparkly, mesmerizing, and a little terrifying, and eventually leaves the learner with the happy glowing memory of immersion. How do we live this way? Well, little people add complexity so let's talk about that.

✳ Fire Building 101 ✳

First things first. Do you get the sequence wrong sometimes, like I did? Have you ever expected your child's enthusiasm for learning to leap into flame—without kindling? Parents tell me: "I read a chapter about Pocahontas aloud to my children, but my kids complain they have nothing to write." Of course they don't. These children have barely made Pocahontas's acquaintance in one short chapter. Worse, someone else (the author) used up all the good words (all the kindling for their own blaze). To write, each would-be author needs to go shake the bushes for brushwood—building a stockpile of words. Writing needs fuel (as do other subjects).

If we do see a random brush fire of academic enthusiasm begin, parents wonder why the flames don't stay ignited for long. Maybe the child ran out of kindling (no additional conversations or resources). When the flames ebb, it's easy to doubt the intensity of the previous burning inferno. (*Why didn't he keep writing the story? She must not like math.*) Most of us assume fire for learning doesn't expire; we aren't impressed when the flames taper to warm coals.

Is passion in learning random (like a wildfire started by a lightning strike), or can it be coaxed into being (in a hearth, carefully built from torn newspapers, a match, and dry wood)? It's this conundrum that perplexes parents and educators everywhere.

✳ Enchantment in Action ✳

Imagine your child reads a book series he loves. He watches all the movies three times until he's quoting the main characters. He discovers there's a game version of the story. He plays it. The immersive experiences act like kindling (fuel) for his imagination. All that's needed is a spark to dive deep into the topic. Your child stumbles across a fan fiction website that ignites his imagination. He wants to write! His own new scene for the characters!

Suddenly, this child is into the vision that erupted in his mind. He writes pages a day, forgetting to brush his teeth, not wanting to stop for math problems. The Word documents are filled with the unruly flames of creative passion—poor spelling, bursts of exceptional language, precise descriptions, dialogue, missing punctuation, and moments of cliffhanging suspense. He rambles and backtracks and goes right for the most exciting moments without bringing the story to a close. He expends the last bit of fuel: the motivation wanes, satisfaction replaces urgency. He leaves the computer to explore a new interest. The life cycle of an enchanted learning experience lingers as a happy memory. Our brave learners store that memory inside, where it will rekindle to life for the next adventure.

✳ Bellows or Bucket of Water? ✳

What might happen to our little fan fiction writer once a parent gets involved? You have a choice when witnessing the eruption of fiery passion in your child—to either direct a bellows at the flame, or to dump a bucket of cold water over it. Your child, the budding author, asks you to read the story. If you're a parent with the bellows, you'll notice the energy of the writing, the powerful language, the congruence between original characters and the child's depiction, the imagination, the sheer wonder that your child took the initiative to write—without it being an assignment. You may also notice rambling, run-on sentences; gaps in logic; and spelling mistakes. These you overlook in favor of the raging fire. You realize now is not the time to tamp it. It's time to blow on it! Good for you!

If you're a bucket-of-water-bearing parent, you'll miss the creativity, the narrative, the risks. You'll notice absent capital letters. You'll worry that there's no clear ending. The insider jargon will puzzle you, and you won't be able to stop yourself from saying so. Even if you see the brilliance in the story, you may worry: *How do I help his genius continue? Shouldn't he do something more with it?*

The passionate writer will either roar into an inferno at the show of support, or abandon the act when the bucket of water douses motivation.

If the fiery learner is encouraged and admired, the learning will continue for the *natural life span* of the fuel inside. It might be possible to keep the fire going through conversations, books, or imaginative play. Sometimes the fire builds, and sometimes the weather conditions shift— the wood is wet, nothing keeps it going. You may not know why the child loses interest. Occasionally the flame is short-lived because that's all the kindling that was available.

When the natural enthusiasm wanes, however, be reassured: a warm memory lingers—the experience of having been catalyzed into action from the inside by imagination. The spell cast? Enchantment! If received and honored, your child will be visited again. It's this zest for self-starting that creates a momentum in education. Children learn to trust themselves— to bravely follow their curiosity, to keep a little kindling available for the ready spark.

But you and I both know: it's easy to accidentally douse a child's flame for learning. I've done it! Let's say your cutie pie wants to learn to quilt, but you don't sew. Will you steer the emerging seamstress to gardening instead, for your convenience? Perhaps your kids are obsessed with Minecraft. What if you don't see educational value in the game? Will you ignore it, limit it, ridicule it, fight it? Worse: What if your child's curiosity seems dangerous (morally, physically, or emotionally)? What should a parent do when a child is drawn to horror films or wants to take up boxing? What if your shy child longs to go to robotics camp for a week, yet has never spent the night away from home? It's so easy to simply say no to end the discussion and adult discomfort, dousing the child's flame.

The question before us, then, is: Can parents foster conditions for that magical eruption of passion to occur, even when they are uncomfortable with the topic?

That Time When . . . the Water Bucket Sloshed, but I Blew on the Flame Instead

When Jacob (age ten) came to me with an interest in the night sky, I was all: "Hey, look over here! Can you pick poetry, please—something I know lots about?" Jacob is nothing if not tenacious. He checked out books about the solar system from the library. He asked us to buy him a telescope for his birthday. He launched a cookie-selling business to raise funds to go to Space Camp.

I acquiesced. I knew enough to value his fascination (astronomy is respectable as a subject; it wasn't *video games*, for heaven's sake—more on *that* in a later chapter), but I felt incompetent to instruct him. I had been under the impression that I was supposed to introduce my kids to subjects, not the other way around! Plus, I didn't care about astronomy. Really. I felt drained considering it. I'd made it to adulthood without knowing the constellations. How important could they be?

There's something about passion, though. It sparkles through a person's smiles; it overcomes resistance and pulls you toward it. Jacob's eagerness became irresistible. His curiosity? My first teacher. We paged through books—Jacob explaining what he read to me. We talked about the constellations. We tried to find them in the sky above our backyard. I discovered that my best gift to Jacob turned out to be my ability to research: I found people (hobbyist astronomers) for him to meet. I located our city's historic observatory (a building I hadn't even known was in our city). I purchased the tools he wanted (a telescope, constellation maps).

It was an awkward journey into unknown territory that I kept hoping would be short-lived (#truth). Working on astronomy with Jacob meant taking time away from the stuff that came easily to me and made *me* happy. His interest was inconvenient and threatened to bore me. It meant getting up in the middle of the night out of a warm, comfortable bed to head into the cold to a telescope aimed at a black night sky.

One night at 4:00 a.m., I did just that. I put my eye next to the glass lens, as instructed: squinting, eyelashes fluttering and interfering, seeing nothing . . . Jacob coaxed me to relax. A vision clarified. Into my view grew a perfectly round reddish orb with a visible flat ring circling it. Suddenly, the planet appeared real—and tears welled in my eyes. "Oh my gosh, Jake. Saturn! It's real!" All my life, Saturn had lived between the pages of a book until that early morning. What textbooks had failed to deliver to me for forty years, my ten-year-old son had given me in one charmed instant— the gift of a magical night sky. All I know about astronomy I learned from Jacob—not the other way around. How could I not be amazed? Enthralled? Transfixed? Enchanted.

CHAPTER 3

MAGIC DOORS

Lessons from Monsters and Maps

Open Sesame.

—"ALI BABA AND THE FORTY THIEVES"

It is a truth universally acknowledged that a child in possession of a good instructor must be in want of an education. Alas, kids don't care. It's impossible to demand inspiration, passion, or self-discipline without affinity for learning. Let me rephrase that: *you can't coerce caring.*

Adults try! We use grades, little statues, and ice cream sundaes to prod kids into reading, diagramming sentences, and practicing piano. Meanwhile that same child will stand in the hot sun for five hours shooting free throws to break a personal record. No reward except satisfaction. How do we get more of *that* into traditional school subjects?

Maybe learning is a big roulette wheel—some kids land on grammar, some on microbiology, and others on video games. No wonder parents simply require kids to suck it up and finish their schoolwork. It's like a mystery religion getting kids to be interested in the "right" subjects.

Learning as effortless and natural? I signed up to be a home educator for precisely that reason. I loved the notion of child-led learning, but I couldn't envision the practice. College preparation mattered too. I told myself that I wanted happy learners, but I secretly wanted cooperative learners more. In fact, I mistakenly believed that cooperative learners *were* happy learners. My kids straightened me out.

"I hate school" is a common complaint. Noah felt that way about my sincere, conscientious homeschooling efforts when he was in fourth grade. Busted my heart! Like you, when I embarked on our home education project, I did so to opt out of the tedium and requirement of traditional schooling that I associated with the classroom. But we homeschoolers often wind up in the same place—requiring, insisting, wondering how to get our little darlings to just finish the darned math page!

✳ DOORWAYS OF DISCOVERY ✳

Remember the Pixar film *Monsters, Inc.*? Each time a character opens a door in the factory, a surprising faraway place, like the snow-capped Himalayas, fills the frame. Right on the other side of the monsters' work-life lived a world to explore! Enchanted learning draws on this sort of magic, as thousands of homeschooling families have discovered. Open the door to video games and find Greek mythology and ancient history inside. Open the door to women's high fashion and catwalk into a room called "spelling and vocabulary"—*ruching*, *couture*, and *Gucci*. Open the door to back issues of *Mother Jones* magazine and discover directions to build low-tech habitats in the backyard. Fling open the door to Klingon and bump into constructed languages, linguistics, and the International Phonetic Alphabet.

I'm reminded of Robert Frost: "way leads on to way."

It's staggering to consider—literally the bathtub stopper (design, materials, production, distribution, advertisements) depends on sophisticated application of mathematics, technology, engineering, business, literature, and trucking—yet we rarely consider it. One principle of an enchanted education, then, is to see the surprising interconnections. Notice the magical doorknobs and turn the handles!

✳ Enchanted Principles ✳

To embark on this enchanted lifestyle of education, please put on these "Dotty goggles." Remember her? Dotty sees art hiding in a broken tree branch littering the street. The two key principles of an enchanted education require you to *see* differently. Got the goggles on? Wonderful. They add a pinkish hue.

Principle 1:
Everything Can Be Taught Through Anything

Let's let this unsettling idea sit on the page.

Everything can be taught through anything.

The key to a successful education is not remembering the sequence of battles in World War I or getting an A on the geometry test. A robust education is the ability to make meaningful use of *any and all* information. Honestly: History, science, music, art, literature, political theory, foreign language, the humanities, and the social sciences are naturally fascinating—but not when they are drummed into us without context. William Reinsmith—education expert, professor of English, and writer for the National Teaching and Learning Forum—states emphatically: "Real learning connotes *use*. If something isn't going to be immediately used or applied in some manner, it won't get learned."[1] Mind-blowing! We can ask ourselves each time we introduce a child to a new concept: · What is the immediate use and value of this idea or skill?

Reinsmith goes on to say that it's not enough to warn children that they'll need what is being taught someday in the future. If the item doesn't have immediate value, it becomes irrelevant and the child won't retain it. For instance, learning to handwrite becomes interesting once I care about getting a message across to a reader, not the other way around. Mastery of the mechanics does not promise inspiration *to write*.

Likewise, adults don't take regularly scheduled math tests. Math shows up in bank accounts, year-end taxes, running a business, baking, and remodeling the kitchen. Math principles are at work when training for a marathon or changing the oil in a car. Plenty of adults use math in their workplaces, whether in the form of Excel spreadsheets, engineering, or chemical formulae. Mastery of mathematics may require some rote instruction, but it's our task to help our kids see the relevance of math in their lives today, not just when they become adults.

When I introduced science to my kids, they shouted, "Let's mix chemicals!" Naturally! Who wants to read about science in a book? Much better to make slime from borax (chemistry); to cut open a dead chicken, peel back the skin, poke the muscles, and reassemble the innards (biology); to toss handmade parachutes from a second-story window to witness the properties of flight (physics).

School subjects aren't islands of learning to be visited at an institution. Charlotte Mason, early-twentieth-century British educator, liked to say that education is a "science of relations." All subjects—those that are prototypically scholastic and those that are practical skills or found in the arts—interconnect meaningfully already. In other words, any of us can *get at* the typical school subjects through a variety of magical doors. "Open Sesame" indeed!

Principle 2:
Children Already Love Learning

Ask yourself: When are human beings *not* learning? Every day, consciously or unconsciously, people learn. They learn how to get from the dry cleaners to the amusement park. People learn how to move through foot traffic in New York City. They learn the apps on a new iPhone. A sister learns how to pester her little brother. A brother learns how to retaliate! Everywhere, the world over, adults and children use the innate tool called learning to do *everything* in their lives.

HOW DO I GET MY KIDS TO LOVE LEARNING?

A noble goal!

Learning is not the chief property of that question. There's a sneaky agenda hidden behind the verb "get." The adult is asking: "How do I *make* kids feel happy about the education I'm giving them?"

Education is *done* to children by well-meaning adults every day of the year in and out of classrooms. Kids wait to be instructed by parents and teachers who say, "This will be fun!" (A coercive statement if ever there were one!) Fun, love, pleasure. These can't be dictated or required; they can't be expected as gratitude for all your hard work. Love of anything is voluntary and sourced in pleasure, no matter what you've heard from the martyrs in your life.

Love isn't duty, and it's not merely an action—it's romance, passion, liking, attraction, and joy that lead to motivation. When adults ask kids to love learning, they're asking children to find academics pleasurable so that adults will be relieved of the obligation to nag.

Is it any wonder so many educators are disheartened when their best intentions and preparations aren't experienced as pleasure-giving to children? This is where our problems begin, however. When we believe our task is to prepare education *for* our children—as something they receive *from* us and then *do* obediently—precious little space is free for enjoyment. I'll go further. Sometimes the harder we work to make a lesson "fun," the faster children resist, giggle, poke one another, and collapse into wiggly disarray. The insistence on fun drains all the mirth from the room. Kids intuitively react by having a little fun of their own—they create unappreciated mischief!

When we back off and allow our kids to show us what they love, we freak out! *World of Warcraft*? Disney movies? Stage makeup? Knitting? Skateboarding? Instagram? What about math? When will they *love* to learn the subjects they need for high school and college?

✳ Learning Naturally ✳

Brain researchers Renate and Geoffrey Caine invite us to see the true nature of learning.

Learning is the bridge between instinct and reality. Learning is what makes it possible to both consciously and unconsciously adapt and adjust to a changing world. It was going on way before schools were invented or direct instruction was thought of. It is what every child in every classroom is naturally doing every second of the day. It is the ongoing, natural process that we must understand first in order to come to grips with what education can and should be.[2]

The Caines explain in their twelve principles of brain-based learning that human beings are living systems; therefore, learning is physiological and psychological (part of our bodies as well as our minds).[3] Because people are innately social and in search of meaning, our relationships and emotions—not rote memory or the right textbooks—are key to learning. In other words, when your child feels connected and happy, your child is learning the most. Perhaps that's why parents have anxiety around video games and comic books. They see that joy, know learning is happening, and doubt the value of what's being learned! We can't create space for traditional school subjects to be loved *by* children until we help them to be meaningful *to* children.

Learning is complex; it's more than memorizing the dates of historical events or spelling lists. The Caines explain that there are conscious and unconscious processes happening simultaneously. It's possible to learn the times tables by heart, for instance, using a mnemonic trick, without understanding the mathematical action behind the numbers. When that child encounters higher math, the comprehension needed to apply multiplication isn't there. The lesson misfired.

Kids absorb complexity better when they're appropriately challenged, and when they attach meaning to what they learn. Children are inhibited from taking learning risks when they feel fearful or threatened. If an adult berates a child or gives a low grade, that student may avoid the dreaded subject for the rest of their lives.

We've all heard adult friends say "I'm terrible at math" or "I can't spell" to excuse themselves before they risk exposure again. Pressure and ridicule are turn-offs—closing the valve to a love of learning.

Let's push pause on traditional models of education. Learning is happening all the time. The questions are: What's being learned? Do our kids have the space to generate meaning, in addition to mastering facts and information? How do I, as an educator, facilitate joy in learning?

✳ MAGICAL ASSIST ✳

If we funnel these ideas through our lens of enchantment, what we're talking about is *an awakening to the need to know*. In fairy tales, princesses are put to sleep until just the right moment when they're awakened by a kiss. That kiss ushers the princess into a new identity and set of capabilities.

Children do need to learn math skills and become proficient writers. The problem with traditional instruction is that there's no patience to allow that deep sleep to be awakened by the dawning awareness of need! At its best, unschooling—the apparently magical transport to natural learning without curriculum—could be described as a patient trust that the awakening will come, at the right time, in the right subjects, for that child. A "kiss" of curiosity will draw the student out of deep sleep.

Too often traditional methods shoehorn children into programs that stifle, and even repel, curiosity and learning. Ah! I hear the echo of protests across the page: "What if my son is never interested in history?" "What if she never wants to read?" I get it. I've lived it too. None of us wants to neglect our kids. The balancing act is real: state standards for education and natural learning—together, forever, living in harmony? Feels like this marriage might need a prenup!

The solution isn't found in curriculum shopping or school funding. Rather, we've got to ask ourselves: What creates the appetite to learn anything? I wondered if it was possible for my children's curiosity to lead them into the waiting arms of fractions or punctuation. Could they be *awakened* to the value of grammar, for instance, like when Belle suddenly saw the Beast for the kind fellow he was?

The answer is yes, but like the fairy tales we love, awakening benefits from a magical assist. We fail when we expect the "aha" to occur through application of educational standards rather than through the tools of enchantment. Luckily, the properties of enchantment are far more enjoyable to bring into your learning environment than any system or schedule. Researchers tell us that the brain loves novelty. The powers of enchantment provide it in spades!

By now, it's likely your mind is thrumming: "But *my child's* passions drive me freaking cray-cray!" You're certain your kids aren't as nobly curious as mine—they only want to build Minecraft worlds all day, not examine the honorable, infinite universe like my son Jacob.

Before we go any further, let's explore your children's current interests as well as your educational objectives. As it turns out, natural learning and academic subjects live on either side of the same magical doors.

Continent of Learning

This activity helps you *see* your child's learning differently—to let go of the worry that your student is somehow not getting the *right* education. It also helps you capitalize on making connections between what your child is doing easily and happily, and how that interest relates to traditional school subjects—the ones needed for academic advancement.

Directions

Make a list of traditional school subjects. (A starter list is below.) Break it apart even further by categorizing the types of math (geometry, long division, accounting) or the eras of history (ancient, medieval, American, Far East) or the aspects of writing (grammar, spelling, formats, revision).

- Reading
- Writing
- Math

- History
- Science
- Philosophy
- Religion
- Foreign language
- Art
- Music
- Social science
- Physical education

List your child's current passions. For instance, like these:

- Piano
- Minecraft
- Disney Channel
- Fan fiction
- *Phineas and Ferb* (cartoon)
- Lemony Snicket (the novel series)
- Soccer
- Greek myths
- Board games
- Airplanes
- Zoo animals

If you believe your child doesn't have any interests, check yourself. You may be judging the interests as unworthy. Observe your child for a day. Even if the interest seems insignificant to you (watching the Disney Channel), put it on the list.

Next, tie the child's passion to subject areas as specifically as you can.

Follow These Steps

1. Look at the primary subject and examine it for all its properties—vocabulary about the subject (reading, spelling, grammar), its history (origin, location, reason), its relationship *to* history (geopolitical context, religion, conflict or war), notable persons related to the subject (creator, inventor, participant, monarch, military personnel, practitioners, scholars), controversy (conflict), its role in society or religion or politics, and so on. Books and poems, artwork and plays, movies and television series—include them all.

2. Match these properties to traditional school subjects (using your list).

3. Now draw a bubble in the middle of a sheet of paper; write the child's interest inside the shape.

4. Adjacent to the bubble, draw additional shapes.

5. Enter one of the school subject names and bullet list how it relates to the child's key interest.

6. Add additional "country shapes" in your Continent of Learning. Make an outer ring with more connections (see illustration).

Watch a Continent of Learning emerge! Save this drawing. We'll refer to it again throughout the book.

Example

Child's Central Interest: Piano

- Music: composition, theory, performance, musical styles and pieces
- History: classical composers and jazz musicians, the history of the piano
- Religion: compositions for religious services (hymns), relationship to the organ
- Science: physics of the keys and pedals; vibration and sound; writing music while deaf (Beethoven)
- Foreign language: Latin for musical language like "tempo" and "adagio"
- Sociology: various uses in society (church, bars, royal court)
- Math: scales, keys, transposing, composing, arranging, time signature, musical notation, rhythm

- Literature: *The Cat Who Loves Mozart* (Patricia Austin), *The Piano* (William Miller), musical literature (the pieces themselves)
- Film/theater: *The Piano*, *Amadeus*

See illustration: the piano is at the center and borders other subjects adjacent to it and to each other.

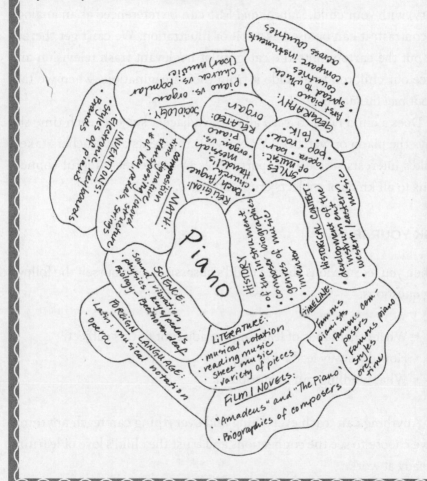

An enchanted education is one where we make use of kindling to spark interest in learning about any topic under the sun. Even a subject as apparently irrelevant to academic growth as a television cartoon series has a history, is an art form, follows a narrative arc, is created by professional writers and artists. *Phineas and Ferb* is a spinoff (what's that?); it can be examined for its script, humor, artwork, characterization, and social agenda. When discussing a work of fiction (novel or story) with your child, *Phineas and Ferb* can be referenced as an analogy or contrast; it can be used as a foil or illustration. We can't get there if we put the cartoon into the category of irrelevant trash television and force our children to exclude it from their imaginations when we talk about *real* literature.

Does a child need to *learn* all of the adjacent subjects each time she plays the piano or watches TV? No—but if parents and teachers take a child's interests seriously, opportunities to create meaningful connections to all kinds of subjects erupt into view.

ASK YOURSELF

When you feel anxious about a child's obsession, ask yourself the following questions:

* What other lands of learning are adjacent to this subject?
* How does way lead on to way?
* What kindling can I contribute?

Anything can teach everything and everything can teach anything, if we choose to see the connections and trust the child's love of learning already at work.

PART TWO

Casting the Spell
The Superpowers of Brave Learning

What is most important and valuable about the home as a
base for children's growth into the world is not that it is a
better school than the schools, but that it isn't a school at all.

—JOHN HOLT

Parents say: "I want my child to love learning." What they mean: "I want
my child to cooperate with my lesson plans sans eye roll." Children say:
"I want to have fun!" What they mean: "I want to care enough to commit video-game-level energy to this thing you expect me to do."

"I *want* to learn geometry" is what we prefer to hear. "I *have* to take
geometry to get into college" is what we settle for. How can we get a
little more want-to into their have-to?

A superior curriculum for the irksome subject is not necessarily the
solution, as tempting as it is to research products all the livelong day. A
better investment of time is to consider *how* your kids learn rather than
what to teach them. Learning is made possible not by better programs,
but by better experiences—what education reformer William Reinsmith
calls "educational intimacy."[1]

It turns out there are a bunch of principles that help kids learn—that bring about that intimate encounter with all manner of subjects, skills, and topics. I know long lists are intimidating to implement. Don't worry. I got you! I'm about to give you an easy system for eating this elephant one bite at a time.

I've happily wrangled these principles into three groups of four Superpowers for education. You don't have to apply them all to each subject every day, forever and amen. Flip through these chapters when you sink into the quicksand of tedium or resistance. Sample the Superpowers one at a time, one per month, over the course of a whole year to get started. Are you breathing easier yet? Good!

The twelve Superpowers are:

* The Four Forces of Enchantment: surprise, mystery, risk, and adventure
* The Four Capacities for Learning: curiosity, collaboration, contemplation, and celebration
* The Four Ports of Entry: mind, body, heart, and spirit

✳ How to Use Part Two ✳

Read it. Enjoy it! Then apply it. For quick studies, apply the Superpowers one per week (a twelve-week crash course). If you're the kind of person who hates a schedule (hey, friend, me too!), dip in and out of these chapters as you see fit.

The "One Thing" Principle

Go slow to go fast. As you implement any new "thing" in your homeschool, take it *one at a time*.

1. **Prepare.** Pick one item/idea/program/principle. Next, practice it, purchase related materials, make copies, organize, think about the concepts, read the instructions. Get to know "the new thing."

Take time right in the middle of your day. It's okay to hire a babysitter or to park your kids in front of the TV. Give yourself the gift of preparatory time when you're at your best.

2. **Execute.** Clear the schedule on the day of the activity (no dental appointments, no meals to prepare for your friend who just had a baby, no co-op classes). Skip other lessons—math, history, and Latin—to focus on your one thing. Turn off your phone, shut down your computer, don't answer the door.

3. **Enjoy.** Be here now. Focus on the reactions of your children. Observe them: Are they engaged? Don't think ahead to what you will do tomorrow or next week. Enjoy the experience!

4. **Reminisce.** Next week, remember with fondness what happened during your "one thing" moment. Talk about it! Solicit memories from your kids. Remembering warmly builds momentum in your homeschool and shapes your family culture.

As you invest in your homeschool one thing at a time, you create space for the next thing. You'll have energy to "feather in" additional programs or practices, giving each the "one thing" treatment. You'll provide a *quality* education to your kids, not just a *harried* one. Your children will come to believe that when you introduce a new idea, it's likely to be a good one. Those happy experiences build trust. Remember: sometimes the most sacred moments in our days with our children show no outward educational value.

CHAPTER 4

THE FOUR FORCES OF ENCHANTMENT

Surprise, Mystery, Risk, and Adventure

A lot about teaching and learning is very nuts and bolts—
pragmatic, practical, here's-how-you-do-it advice. Much of
our pedagogical knowledge is empirical, evidence-based,
and logically coherent. But neither of those explain those
magical, mysterious [learning] moments that raise hair on
necks and boost heart rates.

—MARYELLEN WEIMER,
"THOSE MAGICAL AND MYSTERIOUS LEARNING MOMENTS"

Our spinning globe is governed by four fundamental forces of physics—
forces I haven't studied, yet one of them glues my feet to the ground all
day every day, and for this, I'm grateful. Likewise, a brave learning journey is sparked into being by four fundamental Forces of Enchantment.
You may be equally unaware of how these forces enhance your life, even
now. Occasionally you'll spin right into the orbit of one of these pixie
dust–delivering potencies—and suddenly life will feel supercharged, delightful, even sexy! Then, through no fault of your own, the joy and optimism will vanish in a puff of smoke, and you'll wonder where all the
good fun went.

Every romantic comedy, fairy tale, and theme park depends on the
four Forces of Enchantment: *surprise, mystery, risk,* and *adventure.* Falling in love, giving birth, traveling to a new country, riding roller

coasters—these experiences brim with astonishment and romance. Human beings crave enchantment.

The education of our children comes with a supercharge of fantasy, whether you shop for a private school, badger the local district into giving you the right teacher for your child, or take up the daunting task of home education. When I talk with parents, they cherish visions of happy, self-motivated learners pursuing varied academics and interests. Homeschoolers expect *their* children to outperform their schooled peers and assume they're doing it wrong if any given day isn't brimming with academic conquest and optimism. Of course! Because when you have a fantasy of this scale—the better-than-gold education of one's own children—every obstacle will tower over you like the thorny thicket guarding Sleeping Beauty.

✳ A Lifestyle, Not a Program ✳

Homeschooling, as I lived and studied it for more than thirty years, is not a "thing" on its own, independent of being a family. Home education is a lifestyle in a home (whether apartment, house, or yurt)—lived 24 hours a day, 365 days a year—where the socks don't have mates, the eight-year-old wets the bed, and the math book goes missing. There are no breaks even if you choose to spend the summer studying tide pools rather than times tables. Home education continues whether you're hands-on or hands-off. Learning is natural and inevitable. What's being learned—that's up for grabs!

What I discovered is that education at home didn't look much like schooling when it was going well. My best days with my kids had a serendipitous quality—an almost "by accident" feel. Could I "count" those days as legitimate education if they weren't planned, organized by a curriculum, or tied to a school subject?

On the days we got through my schedule, I felt satisfied that I'd checked off the boxes in my plan. Yet a week might go by and I couldn't recall what was learned, exactly. Did anyone retain what I had read to them? Could I tell if dividing fractions had any meaningful use outside the workbook?

At the end of the week, no one day of box-checking stood out as a high point in learning, nor did it provide the reassurance I craved. My schedule-following self had operated under a belief that "schooling was reliable"—the notion that if I enforced a specific plan to complete grade-level work, my children would "cover" all the needed information to be well-educated.

Unfortunately, after a round of box-checking, I'd waffle. I certainly couldn't detect my high standard of self-directed learning in my kids when they'd merely obediently completed school paperwork. It wasn't that skills weren't being drilled or mastered; it's that the magical property of *learning* took a backseat to rote production of paper evidence that school had been "done." My kids led the rebellion: *Do I have to do math again today? Will I really need to know past participles when I'm your age?* It was hard to know what to say to such honest, valid questions.

When I'd reach the end of my lifeless-learning rope, I'd swing the other way. Surely the best education happened when I took my hands off. I'd been told by unschoolers (home educators who eschew the use of a traditional curriculum) that delight-directed learning led to a more robust education. I believed I had to let go and get out of the way. Yet weeks later when my wandering nomad children were bored and picking at one another, I'd find myself exasperated again. I had operated under a belief that "unschooling was magical"—that taking my hands off would automatically deliver a self-directed child-learner, equally well-educated to schooled peers.

You know what's awful? I felt bullied by home education philosophies! It seemed like whichever direction I turned, I was not doing it "right enough." If I had just managed the schedule better or had been unschooling since birth, these practices would work! I felt late to every party: *Why didn't I know about this educational practice when Noah was five? Why is it easy for others and hard for me?*

Here's the thing: even at those low points, right smack-dab in front of me was evidence of astonishingly bright learning seasons in my children's lives. I was so busy trying to shoehorn myself into an educational belief system that I was in danger of missing the rich education already happening under my nose! Researchers and experts call that experience "natural learning"; I call it magic, enchantment—*brave* learning. Because let's be honest: it takes courage to trust effortless learning. We usually require evidence of suffering to prove a child is getting an education.

✳ The Pony Express ✳

Back in the 1990s, I read a library book about the Pony Express over breakfast one morning. Inspired, Noah (age seven), asked if we could pretend to be ponies and deliver mail to one another. Johannah chimed in that if we were going to be ponies, couldn't her best friend Eva be one too? I got on the phone and called Eva's mom, Dotty; I invited her kids to be a part of our impromptu Pony Express. They ditched grammar for the day. We called two more neighborhood families who also dropped the homeschool schedule.

We met outside with bikes, strollers, backpacks, and sheets of paper and pencils. Everyone scribbled silly notes. These were stuffed into envelopes and addressed to friends. Children were assigned stations.

Anna, start on the other side of the street.

Eva, take your bike one hundred yards down from Anna. Don't forget your knapsack!

Noah, your bike goes at the bottom of the cul-de-sac.

And so on.

In moments, bikes were whizzing by with the contents of the knapsack transferred from bike rider to bike rider as quickly as possible. Nathan (age ten) used a stopwatch to time the riders. The cycle repeated! New notes were written with glee—and became sillier. Toddlers and babies screamed as the bikes zipped past. My friends and I took turns helping the Pony Express move smoothly around the circular street—comforting the child who tipped over, bandaging bloody knees. Each loop went faster. Transfers became more confident, more fluid. Express riders high-fived and laughed when they beat their times. New riders begged for turns and got them. A party broke out! Lunch wound up on the lawn as the Pony Express riders became tuckered and starved.

Accidental learning. An experience to ground all that reading from a book about a time from long ago. Bicycles and ponies—momentarily interchangeable—to showcase in a small way what it meant to rush from one place to the next with an urgent letter. Friendship. Using a stopwatch. Writing letters, addressing envelopes. Cooperation. Exercise. The 1800s in America. So much learning, so much fun. All it took was a willingness to ditch the morning lessons.

My family dropped through the rabbit hole to learning when I took a chance on Lady Inspiration. Once we found ourselves in her slipstream, the Forces of Enchantment cast their spell. Surprise, mystery, risk, *and* adventure joined us—these were the pixies that offered a magical assist, every bit as powerful as the fairy godmother in *Cinderella*. We went from a collection of neighborhood kids who practice spelling at home to a living history action performance on the stage of our cul-de-sac.

I'm not suggesting that every day be as spontaneous and creative as our Pony Express. Heck, most of my days weren't either. Before you panic and attempt to systematize the accident, let's stay with the properties of enchantment a little longer and see if we can find ways to create space for them to show up in your family.

∗ An Enchanted Education ∗

I love the word "enchantment." The word casts a spell—we expect good to follow. Or, at least I want my enchantments to be the good kind, don't you? I don't want an evil witch enchantment (aka curse!). Sometimes that's how the requirements of the school system feel—like disenchantments to learning. What we're looking for is that magical transport to focused, happy learning. When we see it, we don't want to interrupt it. We want to make more of these moments happen—we hop to our feet and get into gear: *I will enchant my child's life! I will make enchanted learning happen!*

I hate to break it to you, cupcake. You can't *make* it happen. Enchantment is sneaky. It hovers just out of view until the right moment. Then bam! Like a spell flung from a magic wand, enchantment sweeps everyone in its path into a contented, enlivened happiness. Our Pony Express was such a moment. It would have been easy to miss. I could have crushed the spell as it was being cast: a reverse curse!

The request to be a Pony Express could have been met with the governing power of the schedule: "There's no time for a Pony Express, Noah. We have a spelling test at 11:00 and Caitrin needs a nap."

It could have been met with practicality: "We can't interrupt other families during the homeschool day."

It could have been met with exasperation: "Quit derailing us! You just want to get out of finishing your grammar worksheet."

Worse, it might not have been heard at all: "What did you say? Silly you. We don't have ponies!"

Learning by accident or inspiration—you have to be alert to bring the vision to life. I trusted that ditching the schedule, interrupting other families, and investing hours into an untested experience would pay dividends. It did, that day. I chose to *see* a child's desire to play as evidence of my child's desire to learn. I *staged* a Pony Express in our neighborhood to bring that vision to life. The result? Happy engaged learning. Trust between parent and child. Educational *and* relational intimacy.

The properties of enchantment are right under our noses. Sometimes we forget to draw on these powerful allies. It's as though the notion of education itself acts as the disenchanting force—sucking the joy, life, and imagination out of learning.

Let's look at how we can make the most of these four fundamental forces. Surprise and mystery are especially powerful for young children. Risk and adventure pair well with tweens and teens. I've outlined a few kick-start practices to try at home for each one. You'll think of countless others once you get the ball rolling. Promise!

✳ FORCE 1: SURPRISE ✳

It often happens that what really gets learned is different from what the teacher had in mind—an experience both baffling and intriguing. But little can be done about it except to teach for surprise.

—WILLIAM REINSMITH,
"TEN FUNDAMENTAL TRUTHS ABOUT LEARNING"

The whole world is new to a baby, toddler, and small child. Surprises are everywhere! Scoops of powdery flour sifted with sandy sugar and salt, mixed with wet eggs, melted butter, and a cup of milk turns into a sturdy birthday cake when placed in a hot oven. Talk about magical! There isn't a child anywhere who doesn't want to get in on that action. Time to bake a magical cake of learning!

SURPRISE STARTLES A PERSON INTO DELIGHT

Surprises come out of the blue—unexpected, dazzling! Have you ever performed the math trick where you add, subtract, and divide a long list of numbers only to always wind up with seven? Startling, delightful, surprising.

Every school subject is steeped with astonishing elements. It's our task to unearth the surprise with our kids. Take learning to read. You tell your children that reading is an essential part of their education and proceed to teach them with books and pencils. You read aloud to them, hoping they'll catch a vision for reading themselves. Reading books to children *is* wonderful. But that practice may not spark a desire to put in the hard work of *learning* to read. I've had conversations with parents who've encountered this problem—they wonder what they're doing wrong. What would prompt a child to *choose* to learn to read? Harness the magic of surprise: a powerful ally. See reading and writing from a child's perspective—a newcomer to the world of written language.

MY BOOK, BY ME

Printed words carry power. They outlast spoken words and are revered by everyone. I discovered that one way to entice children to read is to start with *your child's unique, active mind-life.* Jot down the quirky, silly, interesting thoughts your children have right when they say them. For instance, when Johannah was four years old, I created a stack of little books (white paper folded in half, stapled together with construction paper covers). She liked to draw pictures of princesses and woodland animals. I asked for the story the pictures told. Johannah would narrate what she saw, and I jotted her words at the bottom of each page.

At naptime, when I'd read library books to the kids, I also read Johannah's books aloud. What a delightful moment it was when Johannah realized that the scribblings on a page preserved her story in her own words! Suddenly reading felt like a magical power, not a mere school subject.

Johannah's pride as a writer developed long before she could recognize the alphabet, let alone transcribe words herself. Her fascination with learning to read erupted—she wanted to read so that she could also write. On her fifth birthday, she declared: "Today I will learn to read!" It took several years of hard work, however, to get there. But the seed was planted. Surprise sets the foundation for learning; it doesn't necessarily do the teaching (we'll get to that).

SEE DIFFERENTLY

Brave Messengers

It's easy to adopt a "teacherly" parenting style when you want your child to learn. Remember, you're at home. Begin by seeing *yourself* differently. Your relationship with your kids is about presence, not checklists. Who you are and how you behave dictate more than you know. One way to help your kids not take *you* for granted is if *you* show up in surprising ways. Break character! Let them see the goofy, generous, inquisitive, childlike you—the active learner.

* Roust your little people from their warm beds for a backyard breakfast and read-aloud time.
* Dress up in costume to go with a history lesson.
* Admit you don't know and learn right in front of your kids.
* Do the same project alongside your children.
* Play the video game or watch the cartoon *with* your child.
* Skip the "hard" subject for the day.
* Bake brownies and eat them during the math lesson.
* Drop the schedule to play games all morning.
* Take the lessons on the road (to a coffee house or library or park).
* Agree with your frustrated child: "Latin is challenging!"
* Switch up the experience: Play-Doh letters for phonics, real money for addition and subtraction, online gaming before studies rather than after.
* Lend unexpected support (bring a snack to the gamer, clean up a mess left behind by the craft-maker, sit with a child struggling to solve a problem).
* Give unexpected independence (to work alone, to use a new tool, to have a different opinion from yours, to follow a hunch, to work at a project as long as she wants).

Surprise your kids by being honest, vulnerable, silly, free, open, generous, creative, and a little wild once in a while. They'll thank you for it.

STAGE THE HOME

Clear the Coffee Table

After your children are in bed, clear the coffee table. Place an item, art supply, game, tool, or book on the table. Say nothing about it. When the children wake in the morning, will they open the box, test the tool, use the art supply? Will they wait for permission? Give them the chance to be curious. Busy yourself elsewhere (try not to hover). Benign indifference is the idea. If they are reticent to explore the item, *wordlessly* lead the way. Walk to the table and begin—no explanation. Immerse yourself in the activity and watch them join.

A Potpourri of Possible Coffee-Table Items

* Art supplies
* Abacus
* Calculator
* Lego kit
* Blocks
* Picture books
* Puppets
* Tangrams
* A board game
* A video game
* Jacks or pick-up sticks
* A deck of cards (regular cards or art cards or Old Maid or the alphabet or numbers)
* Felt, scissors, and embroidery floss
* Brain teasers
* Potting mix, clay pot, African violets
* Baking tools with a recipe book
* Cuisenaire rods (or other math manipulatives)
* Puzzles
* Origami
* Maps
* A blank scrapbook
* Stickers
* Handheld percussion instruments, like a triangle or tambourine
* Nonfiction books
* Poetry

* A yo-yo
* Calligraphy pens with special paper
* Sock doll kit
* Rubik's Cube
* Yarn and knitting needles

There's no end to what you might leave on a coffee table occasionally. Unschoolers call a similar practice "strewing." Children are left to explore and discover what is "put in their way." No directions. Your silence acts as a faith-building partner. It's as if you're saying: "I trust you to know what to do with this." If the item is a power tool or requires use of a hot stove, naturally come alongside the child to support and supervise.

Startle your children into delight! Surprises feel like love—they tell the recipient: "I was thinking about you when we weren't together."

School Subjects

Use the "clear the coffee table" method to spark interest in a school subject. For instance, if you're studying ancient Rome, offer clippings from the front hedge to make a laurel wreath, draw a map of the region, and cook a pair of artichokes to eat.

Shop for surprise, not curriculum. Make a rule for yourself: *you will not teach what you find boring.* Explore the subject until *you're* surprised by it. For instance, to explore Latin, I might make a list of English words that have Latin roots. I'd write them on colorful notecards and stick them to objects all over the house. Would a color-in map of the Roman Empire (all the places Latin was spoken in the ancient world) make a good introduction to the language? I think it might.

Find the surprises *first* before cracking open a stiff workbook.

Back-to-Home Surprises

Surprise your children with back-to-home traditions at the start of the school year.

* Wrap textbooks in pretty paper
* Open UPS boxes of new books together
* Stock personal baskets with school supplies for each child
* Eat a big pancake breakfast

On day one, I wrote personal cards to each of my kids that I placed on their breakfast plates. I decorated the notes with stickers and described what I looked forward to learning together. I discovered after my kids went to college that these treasured notes were tucked away in sock drawers and bedside tables. Surprise your children by treating their education as a celebration—make day one as special as a birthday party, and the rest of the year as gentle and nourishing as your love.

ASK YOURSELF

When faced with resistance to learning or when drudgery has set in, ask yourself the following questions:

* How can I show up in a surprising way to deliver the message?
* What can I pair with this subject or activity that will startle my child into delight?

✳ Force 2: Mystery ✳

> Mystery is at the heart of creativity. That, and surprise.
>
> —JULIA CAMERON

Surprise takes advantage of credulity, delight, anticipation, and humor. Mystery revels in depth, awe, wonder, patience, and feeling your own size (the scale of your being) as you embrace the great, big, unknowable universe.

Right Outside the Front Door

When my mother and I took my tribe of five on a nature walk in our neighborhood, I braced myself for a slog of tired kids hanging off the back of the stroller whining for the water bottle. I wished that we lived next to a creek or in the woods. Suburban sidewalks in Los Angeles didn't offer much in the way of "nature appreciation."

Our throng had barely exited the condo when Liam (age four) detected a ladybug hovering in the air. The insect gently alighted on his arm. The other kids craned their necks to see the cheery spotted bug. Liam asked why the gauzy black wings were peeking out from under the red speckled shell. He could get the ladybug to fly, but it would boomerang back, crawling on his shirtsleeve.

Johannah noticed other ladybugs nearby. She needed to know if they were eating the plant. We looked for evidence—weren't sure we got it, but believed the edges looked a little tattered, possibly from eating. A small cluster of ladybugs, disrupted by my gang of five, rose from the bush simultaneously—sheer black wings spread—and Liam got teary-eyed watching them fly away, wondering why they would leave us.

All within two feet of my front door.

My mother observed: "Every little thing under the sun—they notice them all. They're amazed by the world."

My craving to live someplace else seemed absurd. I had overlooked the mysterious natural world just feet from my living room. Why would I be more attentive to nature just because I lived in a house with a big backyard and creek adjacent?

Mystery Sustains Our Attention

Surprise sparks interest. Mystery sustains it. Think of mystery as the kindling you add to the fire. Surprise strikes the match. Mystery (the unknowable heart of all enterprises) keeps the fire going. When my youngest daughter, Caitrin, was a toddler she only knew "chair" to mean the rocker where she sat in my lap. It was an entirely new idea to consider that there were chairs that didn't rock and chairs that were made of fabric and leather. Every new encounter with "chair" deepened her understanding of the concept and defied what was known before.

Each activity, each area of study, each school subject is shrouded in the unknowable—there's always more to know. It's why PhD students narrow their years of academic training into the tiniest topics for two-hundred-page dissertations. They're drawn to unspooling the mystery at the heart of the subject.

Children ask endless questions (sometimes to our dismay). Sustained fascination is the fruit of being taken seriously rather than waved off. To draw on this powerful potency, find the inscrutable and awe-inducing, then *draw it out*! Make it larger, more inscrutable, more awe-inducing! Resist the temptation to *solve* or *give answers*. Enjoy the unknowing and be amazed.

For instance, plodding through pages of grammar is tedious. Isn't it much more fascinating to examine a word like "table" (often seen as a noun)? It can also be a verb: "I *table* this discussion," or with slight modification, an adjective: "His *table-flat* hair stood an inch high." What other spells can we cast on language to get it to cough up its secrets?

Poke the bear, wring the fabric, toggle, tweak, and try again to uncover the mystery. When "schoolwork" becomes lackluster, it could be that it's lost its magic under a pile of rote skill development or mere compliance with the "rules."

SEE DIFFERENTLY

When the Twin Towers fell on 9/11, my first impression was that a private plane had crashed into the buildings. When the newscasters discovered that the plane was a commercial jet, the scale of the tragedy grew—how did trained pilots accidentally crash into one of the towers? When the news reported that both towers and multiple sites had been hit by commercial jets, our perceptions shifted again; this time, we dared to suspect a sinister attack.

There is no *fixed* view of any field of study. Perception follows the flow of information, what our eyes tell us, and the credibility of sources. An appreciation for mystery is the experience of a deeper and deeper recalibration of what we know to be true. Children love to alter how they see. Use these "perceptual" tools to help your kids get comfortable shifting points of view:

* Binoculars (put them near a window with a bird feeder)
* Microscope (doesn't have to be expensive; invest in premade slides)
* Telescope
* Magnifying glass
* Jeweler's loupe (for examining rocks, sedimentary layers, gemstones, human hair, fossils, arrowheads)
* Diving mask or goggles (for under water)
* Kaleidoscope
* Camera with telephoto lens
* Mirrors
* Handmade periscope
* IMAX movies
* 3-D glasses for 3-D films
* Virtual reality goggles

Try It!

* Visit an art museum and compare prints (postcards) to original paintings. What is lost in the 2-D view that is clear in the 3-D version in front of you?
* Go to the zoo and compare animals within the same category (all the snakes, or big cats, or penguins). What is similar? What is different?
* Follow a news story over several weeks (like a hurricane prediction). Notice the headlines and track how they change as information becomes more specific.
* Compare and contrast a book to its film version.

* Visit an observatory. See the night sky with the naked eye, then with increasing strengths of telescopes.

Academic prowess is built on the ability to move between viewpoints—to critically examine what is known and think about it in new ways. Tools that alter how our eyes perceive lay a foundation for flexible thinking.

STAGE THE HOME

Read, Experience, Encounter

There are three ways we deepen our relationship to a topic. First, we *read*. Reading provides background and information. To get a fuller picture, we add *experience*. For historical events, we might visit a museum or historic site. For science, we might conduct the experiment. For literature, we might throw a book club party. For math, we might sew a quilt or play a game. Experience expands our understanding—it makes theory and information practical, experiential.

The most powerful way to explore a subject, however, is through *encounter*. An encounter with a red-tailed hawk is entirely different than reading about one in a field guide or observing one in a zoo. The hawk in the book is a two-dimensional image under our control—we can leave the hawk-in-ink at any moment. The hawk in the zoo is a fuller *experience* of "hawk"—the wing span, the shriek, the odor of the droppings—yet all at a safe distance. An *encounter* with a hawk in your backyard is a whole other education—squirrels and chickadees vulnerable, flight speeds lightning quick, a heart-stopping moment of awe as the raptor screeches and soars out of view. The details of that encounter are imprinted for good! The mystery of "hawk" develops as we gain intimacy with the reality of "hawk."

Encounter puts us squarely in the heart of mystery. It provokes a pause—there's more to know that's not easily managed with our current set of skills and tools. Reading about people from another country—say, Madagascar—is a great way to start a relationship. Yet watching a film about the country and hearing citizens interviewed will add levels of experience not as easily accessed in a book. If a family from Madagascar moves in next door, however, the encounter adds depth and nuance to all that was learned before.

Reading about the solar system is one way to learn about the sun, moon, and planets in our night sky. To deepen the experience, we might take our children to a planetarium where a skilled narrator projects stars and planets onto the inside of a domed ceiling. When viewing the planets directly through a telescope, earth-bound humans are offered an encounter with the real thing—enriching all that learning.

Reading about a culture's religion is not the same as visiting their house of worship or participating in their High Holy Days. Moving to a country whose dominant religion is not your own is a whole other level of encounter. Watching a sport on television is not the same as attending a game. Attending a game is not the same level of immersion as playing it!

All three methods for learning are valid—each one deepens the learning experience, allowing us to delve into the mystery at the heart of it.

1. Read: Internet Scavenger Hunt. Read fiction and nonfiction, statistics and news stories to delve into a subject of study. Then, ask good questions. Go on an Internet scavenger hunt for topics like Shakespeare, airplanes, or racism. Create a list of questions to be answered by better and better search terms. Find as many answers as possible, then allow those answers to provoke more questions. Teens can Google on their own. Younger kids benefit from working with you. Put your computer screen on the TV, if you can.

I've written two sets of questions for you. The first batch is for young children. The second is for teens, working with a controversial topic.

Children Five to Twelve

1. What subject does the topic relate to (math, language, science, entertainment, sports)?

2. Who's good at it?

3. What country (city, state) is known for this topic? Why?

4. What historic sites are there for this topic?

5. List famous aspects of it (quotes, discoveries, breakthroughs, published works, changes in history).

6. Google images/videos for the topic. What comes up first? Which image draws your attention?

7. Click on an image or video. Where does it take you?

8. Now that you've Googled, what else do you want to know?

Teens Thirteen to Eighteen

1. Google the name of the topic plus the word "controversy." What's the conflict?

2. Who are the parties on each side?

3. What's at stake?

4. Who are the celebrity and/or expert voices in this conflict?

5. What resolutions have been attempted?

6. What hasn't been tried, but has been suggested?

7. Where else in the world is this an issue? How did that community address it?

8. What political, ethical, and religious issues are raised by this controversy?

9. What organizations are associated with each side?

10. Who catalogs reliable data for this issue?

11. After all your research, what are your thoughts?

The Internet scavenger hunt introduces the value of good questions and the power of reading widely from a variety of perspectives. It's also a chance to evaluate sources and consider which are most helpful. Take notes, if you'd like. I'd serve chocolate-chip oatmeal cookies while Googling, but that's just me.

2. Experience: Explore Places. Schedule trips to places that showcase subjects you want to study. Yes, the places you go can be wonderfully fun! When we studied the western frontier movement in America, we took trips to Disneyland and hung out in Frontier Land. Coonskin caps, muskets, stories about Davy Crockett, the "Colors of the Wind" video from *Pocahontas* on loop—these drew us in and brought our reading to life.

Look up historical sites in your city. One of the best excursions our family took (despite the 16-degree weather!) was a tour of the Underground Railroad sites in southwest Ohio. We drove along the Ohio River, toured a boat, and admired the view of Kentucky from the John Rankin House in Ripley, where escaping enslaved families were sheltered and nourished after their harrowing journey across the river in the dead of winter. We felt the chill of that winter ourselves, making the dangerous crossing even more remarkable in our imaginations.

We had read about Harriet Tubman's life, and we'd watched a documentary about the abolition movement. It was entirely another thing to stand on the ground where human beings had stood in their first moments of freedom, looking across the big pulsing river and wondering how on earth *anyone* had made it to Ohio alive.

If *going* is challenging, bring the activity into your house. *Little House in the Big Woods* by Laura Ingalls Wilder gives suggestions for making maple candy in the snow. We "churned" butter in baby food jars with heavy cream and a marble. Our family hand-dipped candles and spent an evening reading by candlelight. Bring the experience into your home whenever possible; kids love it!

3. Encounter: Getting to Know Others. Our study of Asia came to life when my family took a day trip to Little Saigon in Orange County, California. We met a Vietnamese artist who had lost his wife and children to a capsized boat when they fled to America as South Vietnam fell. In his artist's studio (sandwiched between a grocer and a bakery in a strip mall) were his gorgeous paintings of pre-war Vietnam. I'm ashamed to say that until we visited his shop, my only mental image of the country had been war-torn black-and-white photos and napalm. It hadn't occurred to me that Vietnam was a place of extraordinary beauty before the war. The encounter with this man changed all of us, our limited perspective about Vietnam overturned.

Encounter forces a shift in perspective to include these human beings, right in front of us, who are different yet reassuringly the same. Paper-and-pen ways of learning are limited. Encounter flips the switch to mystery faster than any other activity.

Try It!

* Visit a cultural center in your city.
* Locate experts in the field of interest. If your child is learning to play guitar, find a guitar shop that handcrafts guitars. If your child loves geology, visit a jeweler to see gemstones being polished. If your child plays peewee football, visit NFL team practices (they're free).
* Road-school (if you can). Move to another city or country temporarily (even a couple of weeks) to experience the deep-dive of immersive learning. Choose your vacation destinations with encounter in mind.
* Participate in a religious or cultural event different from your own.
* Meet and interview people who've survived a war, natural disaster, cancer, or a life-threatening accident.
* Make friends with people unlike you! If your family is wordy, find mathy friends. If your family is rural, go visit friends in a big city. Push out of your natural habits and into the excitement of *new*.

ASK YOURSELF

When learning goes from provocative to dull, ask yourself the following questions:

* What else is there to know?
* What can we read, experience, and encounter to deepen our relationship to this subject?

* Force 3: Risk *

Pearls don't lie on the seashore. If you want one, you must dive for it.

—CHINESE PROVERB

You're involved in a risky endeavor. The choice to homeschool is a "stick it to the man" fist pump that says, "I'm more adequate to instruct my children than the credentialed teacher down the street." Bold! The crazy thing is that you're risking your kids! You've already got your education, thankyouverymuch. Your children, however, are dependent on you. It's *your* chutzpah that led you to put *their* educations on the line. It's this conundrum that sometimes makes you the teensiest bit cranky when your children *won't finish the math page*. You have no control—you can't live inside their brains making them learn. Yet you bravely continue—giving up vacation time for homeschool conventions, so fierce is your passion for learning.

Guess what? Your kids are built the same way. They want risks that stimulate them. Just so you know—homeschool is *not* a risk for them. It's their garden-variety life inside four familiar walls with the same parental unit they've always known. They have no urgency about proving anything to anyone, unlike you—who feels you must prove everything to everyone.

If you can take stock of how well the risky nature of homeschooling motivates you to excel at it, you'll catch a glimpse of why risk is critical to your children's learning adventure. They need a vision as bold, big, and fraught with the possibility of failure as yours! In fact, that's why they want to play those danged iPad games all day long. There's risk, adventure, failure, and success baked in!

Big Hairy Audacious Goals

Jim Collins, in his bestselling book *Built to Last*, describes the difference between employees who are "bought in" to the company agenda, and those who have no driving sense of purpose. Employees won't work harder simply to see the business thrive. They need a personal stake—a compelling vision for a goal they value.

I read Collins's book thinking about the little people in my house. If it's true they don't care about my mission statement (a college-ready education), what would motivate my kids to have a stake in their own learning adventure? I was drawn to a concept Collins calls the "BHAG" (pronounced *bee-hag*)—Big Hairy Audacious Goal.

"A BHAG engages people—it reaches out and grabs them in the gut. It is tangible, energizing, highly focused. People 'get it' right away; it takes little or no explanation."[1] Collins describes the impact of President Kennedy's BHAG for the space program. JFK didn't write a verbose mission statement about the importance of exploring space. He challenged NASA to land on the moon! That BHAG provided focus—it aligned all the objectives for the space program on one measurable target that was easily understood.

My eyes widened—here was language I had been looking for! I wanted my kids to feel that their educations were under their control to an important degree.

I reached out to them and asked:

If money were no object and we had as much time as you needed, what would you love to do?

I was startled by the answers! My daughter Johannah (eleven at the time) told me she wanted to learn the vintage dances and go to a ball, like the ones at Pemberley in Jane Austen's *Pride and Prejudice.* I felt instantly overwhelmed. Couldn't we just watch YouTube videos? Alas, I knew better. I got into gear and supplied the three things parents can provide for risk-taking kiddos:

* **Research:** I found an adult vintage dance company that offered weekly lessons. They welcomed Johannah and her brother to participate.
* **Money:** We didn't have any. I asked the company if we could barter for lessons. They agreed to waive the $8-per-week fee if we'd distribute flyers each Monday. Which we did. In the snow, rain, and sleet.
* **Transportation:** I drove all six of us to dance lessons every week. I drove us in and out of neighborhoods stuffing flyers into door handles.

Our commitment to vintage dance was considerable. Weekly lessons at night with three other kids in tow, an afternoon a week distributing flyers during rush-hour traffic, practicing the dances between lessons— these activities took real time that crowded out other activities, sometimes even traditional school subjects.

The commitment paid rich dividends, however. At the end of the year, the company hosted a full-scale ball. One of the women loaned Johannah a period-accurate gown. Our family attended; we watched Noah and Johannah perform the Virginia reel, polka, waltz, and countless other dances. What a celebration of Johannah's audacious goal!

To follow a child's BHAG is a risk. Time, money, commitment of resources, faith in the project—sometimes the whole thing bottoms out! Caitrin's foray into Suzuki violin instruction fizzled, yet Noah's passion for Shakespeare led to several years of acting in a company for teens. You never know.

Money doesn't have to be an object—we can brainstorm ways to reach our children's dreams. The key is facing our mental limits and joining with our children in imagining a bold, beautiful life! Within that willingness, resources often come to our aid.

Risk invites you and your kids to dare to dream. We can't get there if we relegate our children's "far-fetched fantasies" to the leftover energy after homeschool duties and household chores are completed. It's the other way around: when we give energy to the things our kids love, they have satisfaction and happiness to draw from when they need to give hard work to what is less inspiring.

Dare to Think Differently

In addition to bold, daring activities, make space for risky thinking. New insight bubbles up. Choose to sit with ideas in conflict. For children, the way "my family does it" is the "right" way. By high school, teens notice alternatives. For instance, consider how many ways there are to eat: the way my family eats, the way my kosher-keeping neighbors eat, the way people eat in China, the way my cousin with Crohn's disease eats. These variations of what we all do form a base for difference within similarity. Twenty-first-century education values expansion and inclusion, rather than the nineteenth-century impulse to narrow and exclude. Unity through sameness has been overturned by unity through shared mutual understanding.

Risk means being willing to entertain those differences without collapsing in fear or anxiety. We can't get there if the only method of education is one that values *our* right answers arrived at by thinkers we approve.

SEE DIFFERENTLY

Our wished-for cotton-batting and rainbows-only childhood notwithstanding, our children will emerge from the safe cocoons of our families one day. The first risk we take is to *see* our children differently.

Trust Your Kids, Yourself, the Process

A child will risk telling you her desires if she believes you're a receptive audience. She'll conceal them if she doubts your support.

Give Your Kids as Much of What They Want as You Can, Then Let Go and Trust the Process

Brandon Stanton, photographer for the wildly popular blog *Humans of New York*, shared the story of a mother and her six-year-old son, Rumi, whom he met in New York City's Central Park.[2] The little boy sat on a blanket selling toys to raise funds to buy a horse. This mother knew, of course, that living in an apartment in downtown Manhattan made it impossible to own a horse, and she also knew that toy sales would not lead to a horse purchase. She supported her son's aspiration anyway. Rumi earned one dollar that day.

When Brandon came across the pair, he took their picture and shared their story on his website. His followers were so moved that they wanted to do something for Rumi. Brandon started a GoFundMe account to send the family on a weeklong vacation at a dude ranch. The money poured in: more than $32,000 in donations—enough for the vacation and $20,000 more donated to the New York Therapeutic Riding Center.

This boy's mother made all of it possible by trusting her child, supporting him, and then trusting the process (recognizing that she couldn't know the outcome of his well-intentioned fund-raising). By putting his dream in motion, aid came his way! Magic!

On a smaller scale, you'll find that when you lean into your child's dreams, resources you would have overlooked appear. A friend has an unwanted piano right when your daughter says she wants piano lessons. An upcoming birthday allows family members to contribute to the cause (acting lessons, camp, joining the lacrosse team). A neighbor offers to share a small patch of land to grow vegetables in his garden and shows your child how to compost.

Follow These Steps

* Ask your child what they'd love to do if they had all the money and time they needed.
* Find ways to support even a little of that dream.
* Trust your child.

STAGE THE HOME

Your kids take risks whether you want them to or not. Grow your capacity to tolerate risk.

1. **Bodies.** Play sports, climb trees, walk on the tops of walls, operate machines (sewing, blending, sawing, computing, filming), make concoctions, test their strength and coordination.

2. **Minds.** Read widely, solve puzzles, enjoy crosswords, play with puns, learn about other people and places, ask questions and allow your kids to find their own answers.

3. **Waste time.** Fidget, glaze over, lie around, wander, reread the same comfort book series thirteen times (hello, *Harry Potter*), and more. When they have time to go fallow, new ideas shoot up. Wasting time is not the same as being bored. Wasting time means your child doesn't look productive to you but is happily engaged with self.

4. **Friends.** Make new friends! Join teams, clubs, classes, and community volunteer programs. Get to know people unlike you and like you. Remember: online friends are real too. Count them. Naturally, ensure your child's safety and get to know who they know.

Risk implies both thrill and danger. Stay close to a child who is risking—close enough to provide kind support, far enough away that it still feels like a risk.

ASK YOURSELF

When life becomes mundane, ask yourself the following questions:

* What Big Hairy Audacious Goal might my child want to pursue?
* How can I show trust and support to my child, to myself, and to the process?

* FORCE 4: ADVENTURE *

> And at the end of the day your feet should be dirty, your hair
> messy, and your eyes sparkling.
>
> —SHANTI

Our fourth enchanted force is adventure. There are levels of adventure—from climbing a jungle gym, to indoor rock climbing on belay, to outdoor rock climbing in a gorge, to free-climbing Half Dome at Yosemite. Adventure implies an active journey. An "all-inclusive" vacation with umbrella drinks by the sea—not so much.

Adventure doesn't have to mean risking life and limb, but it does imply hazard. A learning adventure may mean that you (the parent) will feel a little uncomfortable (okay, a *lot* uncomfortable). The key difference in our enchanted use of risk and adventure is this: risk may apply to thoughts, activities, and ideas. Adventure is about location—to infinity and beyond! Or at least—somewhere not in your house.

GET OUT INTO THE BIG BLUE WORLD

Homeschooled kids are with you nearly 100 percent of the time. They don't trundle off to a building a few miles away, trying to remember to bring home their yellow sweater, flute, and lunch box. Your kids are reassuringly safe under your surveillance all the time.

Yet for their optimal growth, they need chances to test their self-sufficiency. They can only test it when you aren't there to rescue and help them. Homeschooled kids have many ways to get these experiences that don't include school. It's critical we provide them.

Academic adventures look like homeschool co-ops, dual enrollment (junior college or a local high school), online classes, and tutoring. Kids also enjoy nontraditional class experiences. For instance, Liam took night classes at the Cincinnati Zoo. Johannah and Noah took acting classes with the Cincinnati Shakespeare Company.

"Triangle in" an expert to teach your children. When teens get to the point where turning in assignments to you seems pointless, it may be *academic adventure* that is lacking. Provide it! Consider adult education, as well: art school, scuba certification, martial arts, graphic design, photography, ceramics, learning Excel, lifeguarding, CPR. Not all classes need to be "college prep" or school subjects.

Performance

Sports, dance, musical instruments, art, and theater are primary venues for kids to be out from under parental oversight. Coaches and instructors exercise a different set of expectations than parents. Kids learn to cope with these. And cope they must! It's all right if the style of instruction is radically different from what happens at home (as long as it's not abusive). Your task is to support your child in finding ways to cooperate.

Kids need a chance to "sand the edges" of their personalities. Parents are endlessly tolerant of their children's idiosyncrasies (as they should be). Other adults and children, less so. Give your kids the chance to revise, to adapt, to fit in. It matters. Believe in their ability to do so.

Travel to other cities or states for tournaments and performing on a stage—these experiences are powerful because they show a child the measure of her commitment. Not only that, the standards of performance teach kids that their hard work and investment have an impact on the entire team or company.

Away from Home

Learning to be away from home is another adventure homeschool parents ought to provide. Staying overnight with Grandma is a great first step. Sleepovers with friends, the youth group weekend away, scouting trips, and all kinds of camps (robotics, space, violin, ballet, foreign language, outward bound) provide your young people a chance to test their self-reliance. Teens, especially, benefit from these sorts of trips. Some teens go to foreign countries to do aid work; others study abroad.

SEE DIFFERENTLY

If your children seem squirrelly and cranky, it could be that they've exhausted the excitement of home. Use your parental powers to research. Don't assume that a class listed "for adults" is off-limits to kids. Lots of homeschooled kids have participated in adult programs—from yoga to working in an animal shelter to making phone calls for a political campaign.

Try It!

* Volunteering as a teen guide at the zoo
* Joining a dance company
* Participating in a Civil War reenactment
* Walking dogs at an animal shelter
* Making calls and/or canvassing for a political campaign
* Starting a chapter of Amnesty International
* Ushering at a theater
* Getting certified in scuba diving
* Joining a robotics team
* Taking art classes
* Studying cooking at the local state college
* Earning a black belt in a martial art

* Skiing with an annual pass
* Volunteering in an elementary school classroom
* Learning to decorate cakes
* Starting an Etsy shop and attending craft fairs
* Showing animals at a 4-H fair
* Backpacking
* Distance running (marathons, ultras)
* Getting a job

STAGE THE (AWAY FROM) HOME

The bigger step of sending a child away feels more daunting. Some parents worry that their children will have a bad experience, so they never permit a night away. This fear can be crippling.

It's important to take appropriate steps for the safety of your child, and then to trust that they can have experiences of their own. For little kids, there's no need to send them away. As they hit eight to twelve, they may enjoy time with a trusted relative. My mother took each of my kids away for a weekend alone when they were around eight: one went to the Anza-Borrego Desert, another to the Wild Animal Park in San Diego, and a third to the San Diego Zoo for overnight adventures. These experiences were golden! My kids still have the little photo albums she created for them from those events.

Older kids learn self-management at sleep-away camp with the Scouts or a youth group. Our local homeschool co-op organized an annual camp. More than one hundred kids attended. Even though parents were counselors, navigating a new environment was invigorating for everyone (and created lasting memories).

Sports camps, tournaments, and service trips to developing countries or natural disaster sites are all valuable for homeschooled kids. Jacob attended NASA's Space Camp in Alabama at age twelve, while both Noah and Johannah participated in Shakespeare camp here in Cincinnati. Caitrin enjoyed camps for color guard in high school.

Consider traveling as a family. We took a "trip of a lifetime" to Italy.

You can too. It took four years to save the money. International travel is life-altering for everyone.

ASK YOURSELF

When your children hit the wall and nothing entices them, ask yourself the following questions:

* Do they need to leave the house? Where can they go for new stimulation?
* What adventures can they take without you?

The Forces of Enchantment (surprise, mystery, risk, and adventure) ignite the learning journey. The next step is to consider how to sustain that energy.

CHAPTER 5

THE FOUR CAPACITIES FOR LEARNING

Curiosity, Collaboration, Contemplation, and Celebration

The brain learns by making connections between what is experienced and what that experience means to the learner.

—RENATE AND GEOFFREY CAINE,
12 BRAIN/MIND LEARNING PRINCIPLES IN ACTION

The four fundamental Forces of Enchantment spark interest. The four Capacities for Learning act like vitamin C—nourishing that interest—allowing the student to create meaningful connections to the object of their fascination. These capacities are the nutrients of brave learning.

The four capacities are *curiosity, collaboration, contemplation,* and *celebration*.

Curiosity is the capacity to wonder. The initial surprise draws learners in; then their curiosity blooms as they test the item with their hands, or share the idea with a sibling, or read more about the subject.

Curiosity fades quickly, however, when the new item or process is too challenging for the child or seems irrelevant. Sometimes in a bid to get peace and quiet, I'll give my kids a new board game. Moments later the same children are back—telling me they're bored. I find that moment intensely frustrating, don't you? I've been known to say with exasperation, "You've hardly played the game! Give it a chance!" That admonition never works. The kids were at a roadblock—their curiosity didn't get them over the hurdle of implementation. Once they hit the wall of "challenge," they gave up and declared: "I'm bored."

That's when the second capacity comes into play: *collaboration*—the capacity to partner. Collaboration busts a chief myth in homeschooling: the belief in independent learning. Children feel empowered when they have companions on the journey. There's a difference between struggle that leads to frustration, and satisfying effort that leads to success. Our task as parents is to facilitate the latter. What enables children to make progress, to problem solve, to overcome obstacles? A troubleshooting partner, that's what! When parents collaborate, kids learn.

The third capacity is *contemplation*—the capacity to sustain attention. I'm not talking about being in the lotus position at sunset, gazing at the ocean. Contemplation in this context is the capacity to *tirelessly learn*. Brain researchers Renate and Geoffrey Caine call this state "relaxed alertness." You'll notice a child patiently unwind a tangle of yarn for a knitting project, or carefully set up the dominoes yet again after accidentally knocking them over, or shoot baskets until making thirty-five in a row without missing. These are examples of contemplation in action—steady effort to achieve a desired end.

Finally, the fourth capacity is *celebration*—the capacity to honor your own achievements. Usually we move our kids rapidly from one skill to the next. "Now that you understand times tables, let's apply them to fractions." Yet a pause to mark the first achievement is essential to happy learning.

Fortunately, celebration comes naturally. When a teammate scores a goal, we cheer. When a toddler uses a big word, we laugh and write it in the baby book. When a child masters her times tables, what follows? An announcement? A high five? A banner hung over the dinner table: "Christine memorized her sevens and eights"? How do we mark the achievement in a meaningful way? Celebration is not reward, where we incentivize a child to do what she hates by promising an ice cream cone later. Celebration is the natural happy recognition of accomplishment.

These four capacities work together to create the learning-rich life you crave for your family. Once you've sparked enchantment, your task shifts to providing nutrition for the learning journey. In our family, all four of these capacities came together for Jacob when he was ten years old.

That Time When . . . Jacob Built a Cookie Empire

Jacob declared: "I want to go to NASA's Space Camp." Sticker price? $850. Our family didn't have that kind of money. I tempered his enthusiasm. "Wouldn't that be great, Jacob? Too bad it's so expensive." Jacob's dad, Jon, was undeterred by my realistic appraisal of our budget. "You know, Jake, you could pay for it yourself. What if you started a cookie business? You could make a lot of money in our neighborhood selling warm, fresh chocolate-chip cookies every week."

I couldn't imagine anyone becoming a committed customer on the strength of a Space Camp objective for someone else's kid. I kept my mouth shut. Jacob lit up! He and his dad collaborated—schemed. They figured out how much money Jacob needed to make each month for two years. They wrote a pitch, and Jacob rehearsed it until it was smooth and persuasive. Jacob made a batch of sample cookies, Jon helped him put together a spreadsheet to take orders, and the two of them set off door to door. They came home with a slew of orders.

Jacob baked the cookies and delivered them the following Sunday night. The orders continued every week for two years. He sold cookies in front of Walmart and Kroger (with permission). He pulled in over $100 on each of those days. At the end of twenty-four months, Jacob easily earned the $850 to go to Space Camp. His self-discipline in filling those orders? Sustained effort. Jacob boarded a plane at age twelve and flew away from home to stay in a new state for a week without his family. A true celebration! All because Jon took Jacob's curiosity seriously and collaborated with him to achieve his goal.

✳ CAPACITY 1: CURIOSITY ✳

Like the caffeine in coffee, the chords on a guitar, or the wet in water, genuine curiosity is not a thing, it's the thing.

—TERRY HEICK,
"5 LEARNING STRATEGIES THAT MAKE STUDENTS CURIOUS"

Curiosity is the capacity to wonder, which triggers all the learning you could ever want from anyone for a lifetime. It's incredible how curiosity rolls in like a flood, capsizing all other activities. When my curiosity is on the prowl:

* I search online.
* I scroll through Instagram.
* I ignore the person I'm with while I think.
* I test the item to see how it works.
* I scan the bookshelves at the library.
* I ask questions.
* I guess answers.
* I verify beliefs.
* I involve another person: friend, expert, my mother.
* I stir the milk in my tea contemplatively.
* I watch YouTube videos of people doing it, enjoying it, or explaining it.
* I get frustrated with my lack of talent or skill or insight.
* I get stimulated by all the options!
* I go for a run to keep thinking.
* I notice that everyone in the world is talking about my topic.

Yeah, my brain is a busy place when curiosity grabs me by the collar and drags me along. Rarely does my new interest need to be scheduled—*I'll learn about X starting Monday at 2:00 p.m.* It invariably crashes the party and undercuts some other meaningful activity.

Curious kids are no different. They will:

* Drop everything to attack the new thing
* Double down on an activity to the exclusion of eating
* Ask endless "why" questions
* Page through books, scroll through web pages
* Make up theories and explanations
* Misuse the item for a new purpose
* Touch, climb, probe, manipulate, force, taste
* Throw, clank, bang, drop, smash
* Break the rules of a game
* Ask a friend
* Declare "I want to be a _____" when I grow up
* Nag you
* Beg you to try or play or come see
* Wonder what would happen if . . .
* Ignore their playmate
* Take what isn't theirs
* Set up a scheme to test a theory

We imagine curiosity will look like a question about math, which will be followed by study. But what if "mathematic curiosity" shows up as questions about the velocity of endangered big cats in comparison to each other; or how to construct a board game or sew a crazy quilt; or in calculating how much "life" (by percentage) my character has left in an online game?

Curious Until Proven Otherwise

Let's start with what I call an "outrageous presumption of curiosity." In the court of parental oversight, follow this rule: *curious until proven otherwise.* Here's why. When you shift your perspective of a child's behavior from "in need of correction and redirection" to seeing a child as insatiably curious, you may find that problem behaviors resistant to reform suddenly cure themselves.

If your son is fighting with his brother to get a turn on the video game, the conversation looks entirely different if the focus is on how to get both kids access to this curiosity-inducing game, rather than if you focus on turn-taking and how to be kind. The issue isn't brotherly love. It's how to get total access to the thing dominating the child's imagination—a curiosity craving.

WHEN TURN-TAKING IS NOT THE SOLUTION

When do you, as an adult, share your "toys" with, say, your spouse (if you have one)? Usually both adults have their own cars, phones, laptops, even televisions in some houses. There's a reason we don't share these items. They provide direct access to our personal interests (curiosities). If we share any of these items, it takes mature reasoning to get through the conflicts.

For instance, what if you have one television in the house? If one person's Super Bowl airs at the same time as the other person's season finale of *Downton Abbey*, turn-taking is not how that problem gets solved. The goal is to help both adults watch the shows they want to watch. One solution is to invest in a digital video recorder (DVR). Another is to send the football fan to a sports bar. Maybe the *Downton Abbey* fan goes to a friend's house. No one feels better if the solution is turn-taking: "Last time you watched the show you wanted, so now I get to watch the show I want."

Adults problem-solve when interacting with each other; they lecture about character development when interacting with children. If we start with the belief that each person is driven by healthy curiosity—a hunger to know, play, explore—we can stop shaming our children for poor character and shift to meeting needs. That shift alone is priceless. When you satisfy a curiosity craving, generosity of spirit erupts.

Take children's cues of curiosity seriously. Meet those needs as readily as you would their physical hunger. Some parents worry that this disposition spoils the child. Spoiled children are given whatever they whine about to pacify them so they won't bother their parents. Parents who value a child's curiosity join them in the learning journey.

When Your Kids Are Most Curious, You May Be Most Annoyed

Pay attention to when a child's ideas irritate you. Could it be that your child is exercising an outrageous imagination? Is the idea too complicated, messy, or expensive? Are the questions bigger than what you can easily explain? Is your child's imagined activity dangerous or impossible? Then what do you do?

Drop judgment.

For example, what if your child asked: "Can I drink gasoline?" It's so easy to fly into parent-protection mode: "No, never!"

Instead, wonder: What's *behind* this question?

Stay interested. Assume that an outrageous curiosity is on display first.

Then respond by taking the question seriously (even if that "thing" is impractical or dangerous). "Gasoline! What would gasoline do for you if you were to drink it?"

Your child might respond: "I could run as fast as a car can drive."

Speed! That's the issue—the underlying curiosity hiding behind guzzling gasoline. You can work with speed. You can talk about speed. Find out what fuels a human body. Eat those foods. Get a stopwatch and record how fast your child can run a twenty-five-meter distance. Compare that speed to the same distance on skates. Compare it again on a bicycle.

Curiosity gets shut down if we say: "Silly. Gasoline is dangerous. Don't ever let me see you drinking it, okay? It will kill you."

Start with inquisitiveness, not precaution. (Then follow up with precaution, of course!)

REFINING THE QUESTION

We exercise curiosity in mundane ways too. "I'm hungry. I wonder what there is to eat?" We wander through the kitchen. Some foods require preparation, some can be eaten straight from the box, some are spicy, some are bland, some are juicy, some are dry.

We refine the question: What do I *want* to eat? It takes exploration, imagining what might taste good or what would fill the hunger. It takes handling the item (shaking the box, opening it and sniffing, reading the ingredients, picturing the flavor) before deciding. It takes tasting—a bite here or there: *Did that do the trick?*

We give ourselves permission to do all of this before determining what to eat, and then, sometimes, we pick the wrong thing anyway! I might make the sandwich only to realize I wanted an apple. I give in to the bowl of ice cream and wish I'd had a steak. The sifting and testing experience is at work with school subjects and personal interests too.

What would happen if we approached math the same way: a menu of items to sate a growing imprecise hunger? A parent could suggest to a child: "Page through this math book until you see an interesting picture." Would it be a terrible thing if she picked a process smack-dab in the middle of the book? That one math concept that drew her curiosity could be the key to making all the other pages relevant.

If we treat education like looking for the right meal or snack to satisfy hunger, our kids will feel freer to *be* curious and to tell you what leads to satisfaction rather than simply "getting through" material. If you shut off the flow of curiosity by dismissing outrageous and persistent questions (if you show contempt for their insatiable inquisitiveness), you close the tap to learning. Instead, you'll have to resort to the hard work of *doing* education *to* your child, rather than learning together.

Match.com of Curiosity

You can't make curiosity happen, but you can provide your kids with good matches. See yourself as the "dating service of education." Avoid the textbook introduction to a topic that is no more eye-catching than a blurry profile picture on a dating site. Chemistry and Latin roots need good lighting and flattering accessories so your kids will "swipe right"! Test tubes and a card game make these more interesting than workbooks. Your kids may not fall in love right away, but at least they'll be inclined to give the subject a good hearing when you serve it with root beer floats.

Remember: there are gazillions of ways to get at the core school subjects. Your primary task is to be the introduction service that makes that date happen.

SEE DIFFERENTLY

> In all affairs, it's a healthy thing now and then to hang a question mark on the things you have long taken for granted.
>
> —BERTRAND RUSSELL

By the time we reach adulthood, we're jaded. Indoor plumbing, automobiles, and air-conditioning units are the ho-hum modern miracles we rely on without a thought to their impressive power. Everything eventually becomes wallpaper in our lives.

School subjects that were drummed into us as kids are now duties to perform, not exciting voyages into the meaning of the universe. I had to ask myself: *Why should I use a curriculum that bores me so much I don't have the patience to read the instructions?* Our own curiosity fuels our homeschools. Every subject in the universe has magic in it. It's up to us to find it.

Education specialist Arthur Costa tells us that students believe the primary quest in learning is *knowing the truth*: "They have been taught

to value certainty rather than doubt, to give answers rather than to in-
quire, to know which choice is correct rather than to explore alternatives."[1]

One way to ignite interest in a subject, then, is to interrogate it—to resist the temptation to *know* the answers. If seventh grade science is nothing more than paperwork in your mind, stop assuming you understand
the scientific method. Ask science your boldest questions. Provoke it into
a response. Don't stop until you're amazed. Same thing goes for your kids.
Answers are not nearly as interesting as questions.

The Great Wall of Questions

1. Dedicate a prominent space to ask questions. A blank wall works
   best, but you could also use glass sliding doors, a whiteboard, or a
   full-length mirror.

2. Next, put stacks of colorful sticky notes (all sizes and shapes, with
   and without lines), along with writing implements (colored pencils, pens, washable markers, window markers), in a basket or
   shoe box. Put the supplies near the wall.

3. For a week, every question anyone asks or thinks goes on the wall.
   These questions can be as mundane as "Why did Josiah pick blue
   for his toothbrush?" or as complex as "What causes a black hole?"
   "Can we have Coca-Cola for breakfast?" as well as "How soon is
   Hanukah?" are welcome. No question is off limits. Add your own
   questions: "Why doesn't anyone help me clean up the living room
   when I ask?" and "What is the best way to miter a corner for a
   quilting square?"

4. Resist the temptation to answer the questions during the week
   (unless necessary). Reading the questions often is encouraged.
   Adding new questions that spring from the ones already posted is
   one of the special joys of the questions wall. Tack the sticky notes
   together in an overlapping chain.

5. At the end of the week, over a meal, take turns pulling the questions off the wall. Read them. Celebrate them. Discussion is optional (and inevitable!). Answers are not required, although some may emerge.

Good questions lead us on a scavenger hunt for explanations and more information. They also lead to, you guessed it, more questions. You may also be surprised that resentments and family conflict are more easily addressed in this neutral format too.

STAGE THE HOME

Provoking Outrageous Curiosity

The least interesting way to learn is to be told in advance what to study, how to study it, and what should be retained. What would happen if we flipped the script? How about doing violence to the structure of the curriculum first? What about play, misuse, changed setting?

The following steps should not be turned into yet another system (promise me). But randomly adopting one practice from time to time will jar you and your kids from your habits.

Steps for Introducing a New Idea/Subject/Interest

1. **Leave the thing lying around.** See the "clear the coffee table" activity in Chapter 4, page 41.

2. **Explore it.** Open it, flip through it, look at it upside down, touch it.

3. **Use it incorrectly.** Start at the end, start in the middle, test the tool before you know how to work it, imagine all the possible uses.

4. **Ask it questions.** Guess what it is, how it might be used, why it's important, what role it might play in daily life, why some people would devote their lives to dedicated study of this subject, what it would take to be good at it, what careers derive from it.

5. **Play with it.** For instance, if the math program uses Cuisenaire rods (manipulatives of length), leave the book aside. Build houses, turn the rods into magic wands, stack them, arrange them in colorful patterns, pretend they are pet food for stuffed animals. Exploration may lead to places you didn't plan, or may simply give your child a chance to get comfortable. Both are valuable.

6. **Nest the item, book, or subject in your child's existing interests.** Check your Continent of Learning from Chapter 3, page 24. How does this new book, tool, program, or process relate to what is already a pleasure in your child's life?

ASK YOURSELF

When you find yourself relying on insistence, ask yourself the following questions:

* What intrigues *me* about this topic?
* How can we explore it in unexpected ways?

✳ CAPACITY 2: COLLABORATION ✳

Follow your child, but follow your child as his leader.

—MARIA MONTESSORI

Steven Spielberg's mother bought the Oscar-winning director a camera when he was in high school. She allowed him to ditch classes and drove him to the desert to practice filming special effects. "Anything he wanted, we did," she said in an interview. "Steve really did run us. He called the shots." Steven commented: "My mom didn't parent us as much as she sort of big-sistered us. She was Peter Pan. She refused to grow up."[2]

What a great way to think about collaborating with our kids: "big-sistering" them into the learning adventure. Curiosity awakens the drive to learn. What if that drive requires lessons or special tools? Who's going to help? You are!

Collaboration is the capacity to partner. In today's environment, shared learning leads to the best outcomes. The holy grail of home education seems to be "independent learning." But the truth is, our quest for that independence is more about relieving our exhaustion than a child's mastery of material. If we want our kids to be enthusiastic, self-motivated learners, they need collaborators. This sounds counterintuitive, but what if Steven Spielberg's mom had simply told him he was on his own to be a filmmaker? Would we have *Raiders of the Lost Ark*, *Hook*, and *Schindler's List*?

Learning is not merely the accumulation of information to pull from mental mothballs for aptitude tests. The ability to work well with others; to receive ideas and input from family, friends, and colleagues; to access information from experts and put it to use—honing these collaborative skills may be the most important work we do.

Big Juicy Conversations

While many educational philosophies urge kids to write reports or narrate lessons, conversation with an interested, caring partner (you!) is the best context for learning. I call these exchanges "big juicy conversations."

A big juicy conversation has no concrete objective or goal. It's the rambling free exchange of ideas between two or more people. Parents give up the right to dictate the outcome. Children feel safe enough to risk their ideas and thoughts without fear that they'll be corrected. Sometimes parents forget to count these energetic exchanges as valid education. Yet the truth is, conversation allows everyone to make those vital interconnections between topics, themes, and experiences that lead to an education as personal as it is valuable.

Not all conversations have to be about school subjects, either. For instance, our family had countless big juicy conversations about Disney films—ranging from which ones we liked best and why (when the kids were little), to discussion about the musical scores and composers (when my children played instruments), to examining themes of racism and feminism over decades of Disney storytelling (as my kids entered their teens and twenties).

A big juicy conversation is also valuable when a family grapples with a complex parenting topic, like regulating the use of the Internet or screens. Self-awareness leads to self-regulation; we get to self-awareness when we have the chance to look inward at our experiences and then to experiment with solutions. What would happen, for instance, if when you watch your seven-year-old have a meltdown while on the iPad, you move into curiosity and collaboration rather than parental authority and regulation?

It looks like you're getting frustrated! What's going on?

I can't beat this level!

Rub your child's shoulders. *Want a break? Let's talk about some strategies for beating the level and then you can try again.*

A conversation can then take place because your child knows your goal isn't to shame her into hiding her frustration so she can keep playing, but to help her be a more peaceful, effective game player. That shift may yield surprising results if parent and child stay open to each other and an unseen solution. You facilitate a big juicy conversation when you express genuine interest in your child's mind-life, let go of a planned outcome, and show curiosity even when your child's ideas and views make you uncomfortable.

Spark or Fizzling Flame?

How should parents collaborate with a child's budding interest? We don't want to overinvest (before a child knows if this is *the thing* for them); we also don't want to treat the curiosity so lightly that we miss an opportunity to stimulate learning. And it's unfair to expect the child to learn independently (the illusion all parents cherish). Yet we're stymied by what comes next: stoking a child's flame, letting it go out due to benign neglect, or smothering it with our good intentions.

A mother shared a classic example of this conundrum in our Brave Writer Facebook group. She told us with pride that her thirteen-year-old son wanted to learn Japanese. A spark of interest! But she worried she'd invest a big chunk of change into a foreign language program, only for his interest to fizzle. This mom saw her role as the one to pay for the resource. Then it would be up to the child to sustain interest. She let us know that her son often started programs only to quit after a few short weeks. It made her wary of trusting his curiosity again. Should she provide an expensive program and leave the child on an island of independent learning? Or would it be possible to travel together on back roads, getting to know the landscape of Japanese before making a full commitment? What would you do with a child who told you: "I want to learn X language"?

That Time When . . . Caitrin Wanted to Learn Chinese

Here's what I did. When Caitrin declared she wanted to learn Chinese at age eight, I rushed online to drop $199 on the Rosetta Stone program. I assumed Caitrin meant she wanted to *learn to speak Chinese*. That seemed obvious from the words she chose, "I want to learn Chinese."

Alas, twenty years later, I found out that Caitrin meant, "I want to learn to read." She believed that the alphabet for English was too challenging. She thought Chinese characters (pictures) might be easier for her. This was the reasoning of an eight-year-old—hidden from my view—perhaps hidden from hers. She was operating by instinct, survival.

Caitrin dove into the Chinese language program with enthusiasm. After eight weeks, her energy flagged. I couldn't account for it. I didn't know how to help her. I didn't force her to continue.

A year later, I was studying Greek for my master's program. Caitrin watched me carefully copy Greek passages each day during our family copywork time. Caitrin became fascinated by the Greek alphabet. Together we made Greek place cards for Thanksgiving.

I sounded out our names and assigned Greek letters to each one. Caitrin, who had resisted sounding out English words while learning to read (she'd never seen anyone do it), had a realization: *So adults also sound out letters when learning to read.* Lightbulb moment! Caitrin trudged up to her room and forced herself to sound out an email from her grandmother. Voilà! A reader was born.

Today Caitrin has a linguistics degree from the University of Pittsburgh and speaks four languages, including Hindi. Our collaboration in Greek brought the transformation that led to a lifelong love of languages, in addition to learning to read in English. Independent learning with Rosetta Stone—not so much.

Instead of "I Want to Learn . . . ," Pretend Your Child Said, "I Want to Explore"

The language of "learning" puts us in the mind-set of curriculum. The language of "exploration" leads us into curiosity about unfamiliar territory. When a child says, "I want to learn," they're imagining what it would be like to *know*. Process is less apparent to kids. They want to *already* be soccer stars or accomplished pianists or expert readers or mathematicians. One of the ways we help them dedicate themselves to learning is to join them on the journey so that when their energy flags, they don't suffer alone.

Not only that, but your adult know-how provides the right amount of support to help them keep going—ideas they might not think of on their own. "Follow your child, but follow your child as his leader" applies here.

Big-Sister It into Being

The best way to collaborate is to see yourself as a partner with just a little more experience—a big sister, of sorts. Brave Writer mom Jennifer shared a great example about how she big-sistered her daughter into an exploration of speaking French. Jennifer explained that when she taught

French to her fourteen-year-old daughter using a curriculum, her daughter's interest tanked. Jennifer regrouped. She lowered the bar to experience success. Jennifer and her daughter went grocery shopping in Canada. To create a French-rich environment, they decorated her daughter's bedroom with maps of Paris and French train timetables.

They watched all kinds of films in French, about France, or with French subtitles. For instance, the Disney movie *Frozen* comes dubbed in French. They also enjoyed old films from the 1930s and 1940s set in France or acted by French actors. Jennifer's daughter was thrilled to discover that when you turn on French subtitles for *Star Wars*, the opening scene shows the words scrolling by in French! Together, they scoured YouTube for cat videos with French subtitles.

Mom and daughter were pleasantly surprised that the musical *Hamilton* featured a French character named Lafayette, so they took the plunge, mastering the bits of French he slipped into his songs.

Together they used the Mango app and listened to *Coffee Break French* podcasts—only writing down the words and phrases that felt important to each of them. A friendly competition bloomed between mom and daughter—who could finish the next lesson first?

The passion for all things French expanded to the point that the family switched their domestic road trip plans and decided to vacation in France instead. Jennifer's daughter's motivation to study French and master it sky-rocketed. In this way, French became more than a subject to finish by 3:00 p.m. each day. Jennifer big-sistered her daughter's interest in French into being.

SEE DIFFERENTLY

Independence and Collaboration

Schools don't teach independent learning. A teacher lectures, kids are required to show up at the same time each day, readings and homework are assigned, and progress is measured based on compliance.

Homeschool parents expect kids to work alone, independently. School doesn't.

Here's the cool part: because your kids are home, they exercise independence for hours each day—it's just that since they're independently learning, you may not notice! What they master for themselves is what they naturally care about (Pokémon cards, Wii bowling, *Harry Potter* spells in Latin, all the accessories that go with a favorite American Girl doll). Pay attention to how well your children teach themselves what they care about. Feel free to collaborate when they need it without worry that they are becoming slovenly, dependent life forms.

To help you appreciate both collaborative and independent learning, make a chart with two columns in your Scatterbook (see Chapter 8, page 184) for each child. Put "Independence" at the top of one column and "Collaboration" at the top of the other. List the subjects your child pursues without your help under "Independence." When a child shows listlessness, resistance, or a need of big-sistering support, put that topic or subject in the "Collaboration" column. Include hobbies, personal hygiene, and school subjects.

INDEPENDENCE	COLLABORATION
Chess	Grammar lessons
Baking choc. chip cookies	Rinsing hair in shower
Tying shoes	Washing clothes
Completing copywork	Math pages
Lego	Kitchen chemistry experiments
Reading Captain Underpants	Putting toys away in the right containers
Bike riding	Using a kitchen knife
Minecraft	Studying history
Telling time (digital)	Telling time (analog)
Using the TV remote	Using the DVR
Getting dressed for play	Getting dressed for formal events

(boy, age 10)

Over the course of the year, mark when an activity moves from one column to the other; add additional activities as you notice them. Pay attention to which activities bring pleasure and which require moral support. See independence and collaboration as equally valid strategies for learning, well . . . anything!

STAGE THE HOME

Collaboration requires *presence*, not help. We aren't merely providing the bare minimum of support, hoping our kids flounder into independence due to exasperation with us. We're also not taking over and doing the task on their behalf because they're ill-equipped. Rather, our job is to partner. Collaboration is an opportunity to let your kids in on the tips and tricks necessary to get "good" at a thing. Think of yourself as a coach and ally, rather than a teacher. Even LeBron James has a coach! If you establish a warm, supportive relationship, you can provide valuable insight to help them grow.

Think about baking: you naturally clue them in to tips and tricks.

* Use the backside of a knife to level a cup of flour or sugar.
* Separate a cracked egg with your fingernails so it doesn't get crushed in your hands.

We can use the same partnering strategies in math or phonics. That said, it's also important to allow freedom and space for risks. Even after giving a good baking tip, your child may *still* crush the egg. It takes practice to learn a skill.

Collaborating Strategies

1. Model the activity for your child.

2. Narrate aloud what you do as you do it so your child can follow your thought process.

3. Make the abstract concrete: "When I multiply three times two, I'm assembling two groups of three in my mind. Here—use these peanuts. Make two groups with three peanuts each. See?"

4. Turn over the activity to your child; sit with your child to provide moral support.

5. Narrate your child's process aloud so that your child can hear the steps he or she is taking.

6. Take notes for your child; hand these back to your student for the next time he or she attempts the task or process.

Follow These Steps

1. Sit with the child while she learns the task.

2. Move away (to the sink, for instance) when the child is ready to practice the task.

3. Take a quick trip to the basement when the child is ready to try alone.

4. Slowly lengthen the time and space between you and your child's efforts as competence grows.

ASK YOURSELF

When your child struggles to do a thing alone, ask yourself the following questions:

* How can I big-sister the "thing" into being?
* What else does my child need from me?

✳ Capacity 3: Contemplation ✳

Contemplation does not rest until it has found the object
which dazzles it.

—KONRAD WEISS

Your child may be curious about the snake you found in the backyard for
a day, but the kid who's into snakes for two years as a result has entered
what I call "contemplative learning." Curiosity leads children into a new
area of interest. Collaboration enables the child to take strides toward it.
It's contemplation, however, that carries the interest home and teaches
our children what they want to know.

Chess

My fourth child/third son, Liam, loves to play chess. He's been playing
since he was five years old. His older brothers and dad are excellent chess
players as well. In fact, they built a 3-D chess board. On our family vacation to Italy, the first thing the men in the family purchased was a chess
set, and they played every night.

Liam took his fascination with chess to a whole other level. He read
books about chess, he played online, and he joined the local public high
school team. By senior year, he was ranked "first board" (the top chess
player in his school).

Chess taught my boys strategy and the mathematics of gaming. Prob-
abilities and estimation, cause and effect, practice, practice, practice—
over and over chess makes players rethink their best thoughts. Think
about that! You give your best thought to the game and someone out-
thinks you. You must return and think again.

By now, you're probably wishing your kids played chess.

Stop. Reread these paragraphs. Change the word "chess" to "online
games." That's right: everything I wrote about chess was *also true* about
online gaming in my family. The boys and their dad played them to-

gether, they built a game from scratch, they read about strategy and watched YouTube gamers, they played on vacations as well as at home. Liam got so good at one game, he joined an international team whose tournaments were broadcast in South Korea.

Do you now also wish, with the same level of admiration, that your child was an accomplished online gamer? Or are you still thinking about chess?

Both chess and gaming produced similar results in Liam's life—the discipline of contemplation—tireless learning. Liam spent hours thinking about how to get better at both. He dedicated *a lot* of time practicing both. He stayed up late at night to practice so he didn't have to share the computer with his siblings.

The commitment he had to being the best at gaming and chess were similar—they were obsessions with strategy, with out-thinking his best thoughts. Seen in this light—as an investment in thinking skills—it's easier to value both.

Dedication to One Skill Transfers to Another

When Liam moved to college, he left his computer at home: "I gamed for twelve years; it's time to do something else." That something else was a Great Books program requiring him to read hundreds of pages of philosophy per semester and to write lengthy papers. How much his deep investment in gaming contributed to his ability to study at college is hard to say. Yet I make that connection.

When our children discover that all experiences are valuable to them, and that they can create a life of well-being while getting an education, they're freer to explore *every* interest—not to see some interests as legitimate and others as "mere entertainment." Not only that, skills learned in one area *do* apply to others, when they aren't seen as antagonistic to each other.

Most home educators believe traditional school subjects must be *taught*. We expect sustained attention for the least interesting parts of a child's day. We've agreed that these subjects are dreary and must be

The Fruits of Contemplative Learning

Areas of interest that began as curiosities and resulted in contemplative learning in my children's lives follow:

- Dress-up → Sewing → Fashion → Thrifting → Yearlong fashion blog
- Old English *Canterbury Tales* → Shakespeare's English → Ushering at plays → Acting in Shakespeare Company
- BBC *Pride and Prejudice* → Reading Jane Austen → Learning vintage dance → Attending a ball → Writing a novella based on *Emma*
- Animal alphabet book → Field guides → Backyard birding → Zoo classes → Pets
- Learning French by CD → French classes → French major → Study abroad in France → Teaching English in France
- Documentaries about the Holocaust → Concern for human rights → Starting an Amnesty International chapter → Interning at the UN → Luce Scholarship → Full-ride scholarship for human rights law at Columbia Law School

required of our children. We issue no invitations, no enchantment, no appetizers, no free samples. It's so easy as adults to fall into the nobility of duty—believing that not everything can be fun; therefore, some things must be learned whether we like them or not. That attitude is a setup! It leads to treating the mysteries of the universe as dull hard work that must be gotten through.

It doesn't have to be like that.

A Silent, Invisible Partner

What if you could know that your children were learning all they needed to know, right now? When my kids practiced piano or read a book, I didn't question if they were learning enough. On the flip side, if I saw one of my kids playing a game on the Wii, I filed that activity under the heading "entertainment." I didn't believe that *real* learning was under way. For instance, I attended every one of Liam's chess matches, yet had failed to watch him play his online gaming tournaments. I had to ask myself: *Why?*

A child playing an online game may, in fact, be more focused on the skills needed to beat a level than a child mindlessly completing a grammar worksheet, thinking about what's for lunch. The optimal condition for learning is what the Caines call "relaxed alertness." "This state exists in a learner who feels competent and confident and is interested or intrinsically motivated."[3] The best context to facilitate relaxed alertness is "relationship, relationship, relationship."[4] Collaborate with your child's curiosity and watch contemplation bloom.

SEE DIFFERENTLY

Value what your children value. If you've got a teen who's passionate about Quentin Tarantino films, buck up and watch together. If your young child tells you she wants to train pet rats, it's time to learn about rats (which in my family meant buying two—yikes!).

We admire kids in other families who have passions—from cello and woodworking to archery and organic gardening. Your kids will adopt passions if you value the ones that show up (fashion, horror films, redecorating a bedroom, snowboarding, building a computer, crafting purses from duct tape).

One of my friends watched stand-up comedy with her son. They stayed up past midnight watching comedians together. As Barb put it: "He was going to watch those shows with or without me. I realized the best thing I could do was to join him so that I'd get to have conversations with him." Those late nights led to talking about sex, politics, humor, scandal, literature, and the history of comedy. It also led to closeness and tireless learning.

Children's interests are often expensive, unreasonable, and impractical. It takes *seeing* differently to recognize that everything can be taught through anything—so why not give them a bit of what they want now? Start there! Notice when you want to dismiss a bubbling curiosity, and instead, say yes. Find a way to support the exploration of that idea, even if it's short-lived.

School subjects seem like they'll never rise to the level of passion that hobbies or sports do. That's because school subjects are usually taught in abstract ways. It's challenging for kids to "grab hold" of grammar, for instance, because the analysis of English has no impact on their ability to read or self-express.

See grammar differently. Examine cuss words, play with puns, notice the way nouns become verbs: I *bookmarked* the website; she *hopscotched* to the front door. Our task as parents is to *see* the subjects differently— provoking them into a meaningful relationship with our children.

Try It!

* Look at your Continent of Learning (Chapter 3, page 24) and pick one adjacent topic to the central interest.
* Explore that adjacent topic with your child for a week.
* Find as many ways as possible to see the interconnections between the central interest and adjacent topics (jot them down to help you).

STAGE THE HOME

In addition to making connections, make space for contemplative learning to occur. Remember: it might not look like learning *to you.*

* Allow kids to waste time, to have short-lived interests, to try something and give it up.
* Invest in resources for a child's passions.
* Practice, practice, practice. Don't move on until the child is ready and finds the current level of skill tedious (not challenging enough). That means if a child is ripping through times table sheets enjoy-

ably and accurately, it's okay to allow that to continue until the child's appetite is sated. Add challenge when a child gets bored.

* Dedicate an extravagant (unlimited) quantity of time to the interest occasionally. For instance, if your child is into Lego, spend a week playing Lego—no other agenda. For a child who is beating levels in an online game all evening, dispose of the bedtime. If one of your kids gets into crafting, dedicate hours to crafting every day.
* Teach your child to set personal goals. A child who plays piano might memorize a certain piece of music by a specific date. A child who knits might set the goal of knitting a scarf and matching hat. Track it on a calendar. Remove activities that are less engaging for this temporary devotion.
* Start the day with the child's interest. One mom I know taught her boys to quilt. They spent an hour each morning before school sewing. Even thirty minutes each morning dedicated to a child's favorite thing will bring energy to the rest of the day.

ASK YOURSELF

When your child shows interest in any topic, ask yourself the following questions:

* What can I contribute?
* How can I create space for tireless learning?

✳ CAPACITY 4: CELEBRATION ✳

Celebrate their achievements; be proud of their accomplishments. What is small to you may be huge to them.

—ANONYMOUS

Baby books, blogs, calendars, social media: you use these to celebrate your baby's milestones. Then, baby grows up to school age, and you shift.

Each new skill is scrutinized for grade level. Misspelled words don't make it to the baby book the way misspoken words did. We delighted in hearing "chacuzzi" but freak out reading "becuz." Yet they're the same—evidence of delightful risk and growth.

When a child values what she's learned, she celebrates. Your daughter climbs to the top of the indoor rock wall and smacks the metal bar. Bam! Proof she made it. Your son finishes the *Harry Potter* series and lies on his bed happy and satisfied: celebration. Your sweet four-year-old hands you a sheet of scribbles and declares she wrote a story. She throws herself into your arms for a celebratory hug.

Grades are not celebrations. They're the stressful measurement of what a child *should've* learned. Rewards are not celebrations. We reward kids to incentivize them to do what they don't want to do. "Clean the bathroom and I'll buy you a Coke."

The best celebrations are felt by the achiever—evidence of having achieved. You get to wear the scarf you knitted, for instance. Liam kept a book of poetry next to his bed for years. He memorized poems to recite to himself—a private celebration of poetry.

One feature of these experiences is *choice*. We've all seen kids play a sport that they hate, pushed by a parent to perform at a high level. We've also seen kids *enjoy* playing a sport, challenging themselves to get better at it. The first child resents the activity, while the second experiences pride and pleasure.

How do we get more of *that* into traditional schooling? What happens when a child masters her math facts? Should she be pushed ahead to fractions? Or is there a pause—an acknowledgment of the milestone, and a chance to use the skill for her own enjoyment?

In junior high, Noah discovered the mathematics behind computer programming. He learned that we use "base ten" for everyday mathematics, whereas computers use "base two." Noah was fascinated. He challenged himself to create a "base twelve" times table—designing two more digits and carrying them through. What a mind scramble! It never occurred to me to create an assignment like that because I didn't have a good relationship to numbers. Noah, on the other hand, took his multiplying skills and expanded them. He carried his base twelve times table in his wallet for years—a source of pride. Now *that's* a celebration of mastering multiplication.

PRETTY PLEASE?

In most educational environments, adults set academic goals for kids. I get calls from parents wanting to know how to "get" their teens to do the work they assign them. Others call to say that they have a young child who resists "the smallest request, even after being asked nicely." No matter how sugary-sweet the requirement is, most humans resist being told what to do if they don't see the value in the activity. *People must believe that their efforts lead to a personally meaningful goal.* This is what the brain research clearly demonstrates.[5]

Your kids may knuckle under to your objectives to avoid spankings (one end of the continuum), or they may comply because they want television time (the other end). Neither of these reasons has anything to do with making meaning from the material itself. There's no substitute for personal motivation, which seems like a high bar for earth science and medieval history.

There are three important factors in self-motivation:

1. The activity has value to the individual.

2. The activity can be learned by the individual at a comfortable pace (not too easy, not too challenging).

3. Recognizable milestones keep the learner on task and willing to renew efforts.

It's easier to crush motivation by:

1. Requiring the activity regardless of its importance to the learner

2. Pushing the learner too hard, moving too quickly; or conversely, repeating the same activities already mastered with no new challenge

3. Treating the activity as an endless sequence of steps toward a distant future goal, with no meaningful application along the way

Let's look at how motivation and celebration are tied together in a school subject: writing.

COPYWORK AND DICTATION

Lots of homeschools use the practices called "copywork" and "dictation" to teach the mechanics of writing. Copywork requires children to copy a passage from a book in their own hand. Dictation is the practice that follows. Later in the week, a parent dictates the same passage to the child, which he transcribes on his own sheet of paper. It's common for a parent to pick the passage and to require a child to *write the whole thing* in one sitting. Most often, a parent also selects the implement (pencil), the writing surface (wide-ruled notebook paper), and the location for writing (tabletop). Before the child even begins, copywork has been reduced to a task to please the parent. Celebration? Less likely.

What if the passage is dull? What if it's too long? What if using pencils with ruled paper raises anxiety to "do it perfectly"?

In a study about joy in learning conducted in Finnish schools, researchers determined that children are far more likely to experience happiness in their studies when they have a meaningful say in what they learn: "The students' opportunities to participate in the decision-making of their own learning and to be allowed to make choices that support their learning, strengths, and success, strengthen joy in learning."[6] When we dictate the what, how, and why a child learns, we short-circuit the chance to care on their own terms. Moreover, if they go along with your plan but give a half-effort, they develop a habit of poorly executed work to cope with the stress and tedium.

CHOICE IN LEARNING

What if we flip the script? The ability to celebrate achievement matters in learning—it means that the child has a stake in what is being learned. I discovered that when I asked my kids how many sentences they could copy with focused attention and excellent execution, they were glad to tell me. If one of my kids said they could copy a single sentence, I was okay with that. I advised them to stop, if they felt their attention flag. I offered choices for copywork (gel pens with black paper, tracing the words I wrote for them, using a clipboard while sitting on the couch, picking the passage to copy, decorating the paper).

The good news is that kids love to tell us what they can do if they believe we'll listen. The problem is that we don't like their answers. We say to a child: "How much of this passage can you copy with full attention and your best handwriting?" When the child returns, "One word," we panic. That seems insufficient to our adult sense of duty. So, we turn to bribes or punishment, and forget the value of celebration.

What would happen, though, if you took your child seriously? If she did handwrite a beautiful single word, the two of you could celebrate. "That word is gorgeous! I love the way your letter 'b' is fat and round, and how you cared so much about shaping the tail on the letter 'y.'" When kids set the goals and are honored for their efforts, they experience pleasure.

Celebration of sincere, well-executed effort leads a child to risk challenge. This is what online game designers know. They keep the challenge levels low at first to help the gamer experience the fruits of success before the next level. If we apply this idea to handwriting, the pride and accomplishment for having given dedicated attention to a single word may encourage (at some point down the road) the willingness to risk two or three words at a time. Maybe one day, your child will suddenly say: "Wow! I forgot to stop. I'm a whole sentence in."

SEE DIFFERENTLY

Foster Conditions for Celebration

Any time you misunderstand a child's lack of effort as laziness, approximate the activity for yourself (find a way to experience the challenge inherent in it). Here's an example I recommend to parents in my Brave Writer program.

> **Copywork for You.** Get on the same page as your kids. Type a few sentences into Google Translate. Select a language you don't know (Dutch, for instance).
>
> **English:** I want to create a happy life for my children. I look forward to all that we can learn together every day.
>
> **Dutch:** Ik wil een gelukkig leven creëren voor mijn kinderen. Ik kijk uit naar alles wat we elke dag samen kunnen leren.

Print the passage and copy the foreign language in your own handwriting. It's common to feel the intense need for a break and a wish for it to be over quickly. Now try the same exercise with Hindi or Russian (alphabets you don't know). How much *more* difficult did the task just get?

Remind yourself that your kids are brand-new to language, writing, reading, math, and more. They need to build stamina, as well as grow their interest in the subject. As an act of solidarity, copy a passage in a foreign language every day while they struggle with English. Each of you can set your goals on a poster board and tick them off together. High fives for all!

Our kids need choices in their educations. Create a list of incremental skills that build to a complete set that can be measured and celebrated with your child. Some examples include:

* Mastering the 1s, 2s, 3s, 4s (and so on) in addition, subtraction, multiplication

* Handwriting a complete sentence, a paragraph, a full page
* Freewriting for 2, 5, 7, 10 minutes
* Freely helping a younger sibling
* Sharing personal belongings
* Writing a thank-you note to a grandparent
* Knitting a scarf
* Reading all the books in a favorite series

STAGE THE HOME

Next, set measurable goals. The key to a good goal is that the child *wants* to do it and can measure it. A child who tells you, "Okay, I'll do *one* math problem" and then heaves a sigh and slumps over has not set a goal, but capitulated to pressure.

Instead, ask the child to set a goal for an activity the child values (not what you wish the child would do). For example, Johannah wanted to buy her own American Girl doll. We figured out how much money it would cost and broke that down by month into amounts she could earn and save. She tracked her progress on a sign on the wall.

Your child might want to learn to work a Rubik's Cube or build a Lego set without help. These are wonderful goals! If your children learn to set goals that lead to satisfying celebrations, they're more likely to set them again. Start small. Any subject will do, such as:

* Handwriting
* Addition or multiplication tables
* An online game
* Reading a book series
* An art project
* Riding a bike
* Starting a blog
* Training a pet
* Planting a garden
* Baking

Not every kid takes to goal-setting. Your task is to help your child envision a happy life. When does your child experience the pleasure of hard work and celebration? Notice! Not, *how can I trick my child into doing what I expect of him?*

Then, celebrate your child's accomplishments! Ideas include:

* Hugs
* High fives
* Handwritten cards
* Praise in front of another person
* Marking the achievement on a calendar
* Photographs
* Admiring the child's effort
* Sharing it on Instagram

ASK YOURSELF

When your children seem bored by their studies, ask yourself the following questions:

* Have I offered choices for personally meaningful goals?
* Have I celebrated with my child?

CHAPTER 6

THE FOUR PORTS OF ENTRY

Mind, Body, Heart, and Spirit

Be an opener of doors.

—RALPH WALDO EMERSON

When my five kids were under eleven, we lived in a cramped three-bedroom condo with no fenced yard in Southern California. The little rascals were underfoot one afternoon, per usual. My mother—their grandmother—had come to visit. I felt pressure to ensure the kids would behave. After several hours of rambunctiousness, the four-year-old dragged a chair to the kitchen table. He heaved his little body onto it, and then scrambled toward full glasses of milk. My already-thin patience vanished. I saw a vision of milky carpet and hours of scrubbing in my immediate future. I loaded a reprimand and opened my mouth to deliver it.

My wise mother, seeing me wind up, called out: "Look at him! Only four years on our planet. Still trying to figure things out. Imagine. Only four years." I stopped. For a split second, I saw the world through four-year-old eyes. A chair pulled up to a table to make it easier to be tall in a world of towering figures. How could I be angry? Why would I be? I exhaled, walked to his side, and supported him while he lifted his own glass of milk.

You know what I've observed? The wear and tear of parenting drains us. As a result, most adults want kids to bear the burden of discomfort—for kids to behave, to use their manners, to sit straight, to be quiet, to obey, to do what they're supposed to do all the time without mistakes or resistance, to work "independently," to make adult lives easier. Meanwhile most adults want exceptions: to be late with a payment, to forget occasionally, to be excused when angry, to be given the benefit of the doubt when they overstate, to be forgiven when they break stuff, to be helped when they need it. Of the two (children and adults), who has maturity on their side? Adults! We expect our kids to make us feel comfortable in the world, when in truth, it is our responsibility to do that for them.

Charlotte Mason famously reminds us that children are *born* persons.[1] They're not adults-in-training. Our task is to explore all the ways children learn and grow as *children* while introducing them to the world at their fingertips.

✳ Minds, Bodies, Hearts, Spirits ✳

My mother's gentle admonition to understand four-year-old Liam's table-scaling stayed with me. His mind saw a problem: *I need a glass of milk.* He solved it with his body: *I will climb onto the table to get it for myself.* His happy energy (heart) carried him confidently to attempt the task. His little spirit imagined being rewarded for this great risk—with something wet and cold to drink.

I almost missed it. I was in "parenting mode"—seeing signs of childish misbehavior where childish problem-solving was at work. Thank goodness for grandparents! My perspective—rescued.

✳ Ports of Entry to the Interior ✳

Each of us has four Ports of Entry for new information and ideas. These are the access points where education takes root and grows into a flourishing landscape. The Forces of Enchantment and the Capacities for Learning are funneled into *minds*, *bodies*, *hearts*, and *spirits*. Each port enables what is learned to become a person's own possession. Mastery is the name we give to having learned well.

The Forces of Enchantment spark the learning adventure. The Capacities for Learning deepen the learning experience. The Ports of Entry allow children to bring the meaning of their education all the way inside themselves. Beautiful to behold!

✳ PORT 1: LOOKING FOR A *MIND* AT WORK ✳

I will even go out on a limb and say that we mistakenly may have been putting all our educational eggs into one basket only, while shortchanging other truly valuable capabilities of the human brain, namely perception, intuition, imagination, and creativity. Perhaps Albert Einstein put it best: "The intuitive mind is a sacred gift, and the rational mind is a faithful servant. We have created a society that honors the servant and has forgotten the gift."

—BETTY EDWARDS,
DRAWING ON THE RIGHT SIDE OF THE BRAIN

Most of us consider the rational mind the seat of education: "the faithful servant." It's difficult to picture a "well-educated body," yet isn't that what our star athletes demonstrate to us in the Olympics or on the Wimbledon tennis court? A well-educated mind makes me think of someone who is great at test-taking, trivia, or mathematics—a straight-A student.

As a culture, we often equate the mind with the brain—the two are interchangeable in our conversations. Yet the brain/mind is more than a storage container for information. The brain is the control center for all aspects of our bodies and sense of self. It regulates the unconscious functioning of our vital organs (your brain-controlled heart is beating right now; yet it does so without your conscious participation). We learn to walk and speak due to the brain's unconscious unction to do both.

On the flip side, when we talk about the conscious activity of the brain, we use the term "mind." Our minds make millions of micro-assessments all day long, judging the space, and then risking into it. This distinction between the brain and the mind is as much syntax as anything. In education, we focus on the mind (the part we can control) and sometimes forget the brain (what happens without our conscious participation).

When six-year-old Caitrin told us she had a "cornucopia" of feelings about the movie *Mulan*, the family cracked up. Where did that big word come from? How did she know to use it metaphorically (about feelings) rather than literally (vegetables in a basket shaped like a horn)? To us, using that word in context meant Caitrin was *smart*—that she had mastered an impressive vocabulary term ahead of her peers.

This is how adults value the mind. We look for evidence of learning that is advanced or surprisingly mature for the age of the child. I get phone calls from parents telling me that they have gifted or bright children. What they usually mean is that their child is advanced compared with age-mates in some notable academic way: he's ten but reads at college level; she's seven but does algebraic equations; he's nine and already knows more about US history than I do.

I don't think a parent has ever called to tell me that their child is off-the-charts smart and follows that declaration with: she's eleven but can read people's emotions and comforts them naturally; he's seventeen and is one of the top online gamers in the world; she's so smart—she's a candidate for the US Olympics swim team. The second set of examples is an assortment of interpersonal skills, facility with strategy, and athletic talents—at least that's how most of us see them.

The mind doesn't get credit for these accomplishments—yet the brain is just as involved! Think of the artistic children you know. Usually their skill is described as "talent," which is a way of saying that their brains and bodies aren't in charge—their ability comes from some unconscious, magical place. We don't use the language of intelligence for artistic talent, even if we are willing to use the word "brilliant." What if a parent reported, "My daughter is off-the-charts smart. She can draw realistically—almost to the point of photographic accuracy"? Would you wonder what this parent drank for lunch? Had she mixed her categories? Is this "intelligence" or "mere" artistic talent she was lucky to inherit?

Betty Edwards, author of *Drawing on the Right Side of the Brain*, contends that the mind is not only rational, but also the seat of "perception, intuition, creativity, and imagination." How do we understand imaginative children whose minds wander to their well-cultivated internal world? Do we see them as "smart" or "distractible"? And what about those invisible qualities: perception and intuition? These may be at work in our children and we would never know it. The characteristic use of perception and intuition is wordless, without conscious logic, coming from some deep place that is honed through experience, not study. Intelligence and the education of a mind are not only about the digesting of information and course curricula.

MULTIPLE INTELLIGENCES

Howard Gardner is the conductor of Harvard's Project Zero—a project that revolutionized the theory of intelligence by accounting for *eight* different types of intelligence: visual/spatial, bodily/kinesthetic, logical/mathematical, naturalist, auditory, verbal/linguistic, interpersonal, and intrapersonal. Gardner explains, "Each of the intelligences is seen as a *computational capacity*—the ability to process certain kinds of information in the process of solving problems or fashioning products."[2] Gardner charged traditional measurement of intelligence as failing to account for all the ways people learn. Gardner is not prescriptive about how schools should alter their curriculum to account for these differences, but he does support the idea that an awareness of these intelligences ought to inform how we instruct our children. When I first reviewed Gardner's work and read over the list of eight, I realized right away that there are learning aptitudes I routinely forget to measure. It became important to me to help my kids develop the self-awareness they needed to know how they learn best.

Intelligence extends beyond the boundaries of traditional schooling. The active mind is engaged in thousands of ways that contribute to your children's growth. A mind at work looks like: insight into problem-solving, body coordination, self-management, organizing the physical space, cracking jokes, naming the natural world, bagging on a game or movie, artistic expression, all-nighters to master a game, comparing films to the original books, following a pattern (sewing, knitting, carpentry), training a pet, building a Lego set, decorating a doll with clothes and accessories, imagining a future, deducing "who done it," growing a garden, making plans for a backpacking trip through southeast Asia, applying a mathematical equation, writing a story, auditioning for a play, skip counting in Spanish, modifying a recipe, using a new vocabulary word, imagining solutions to Middle East conflicts or the fight with your sister . . .

In brave learning, *look for a mind at work*. Learning is not only tied to reading thick old books, writing serious academic essays, and advancing in mathematics. Today, it's just as critical to be innovative, to collaborate, and to imagine.

A Mind at Work May Not Match Your Program Expectations

When Noah was fifteen years old, he took an algebra class at the local high school. Two weeks in, he faced his first math test. I had never given him a traditional exam with a timer; he'd never been restricted from getting up to walk around. I wondered what would happen under classroom conditions.

After the test, he hopped in the car and happily announced, "Mom, I wrote two poems!" I paused: "Okay, but how did the math test go?"

"Didn't you hear me? I wrote two poems."

"I did hear you. I just wanted to hear how the test went first."

"I'm telling you. I wrote two poems during the math test!"

I blanched. "What?" I blundered forward: "What about the math problems?"

"I did them. I don't care about the test. I finished early so I wrote two poems. Let me read them to you!"

He proceeded to read two delightful poems that cracked him up. I lost focus. I wondered about the math problems: Were they difficult? Did he struggle? Did he check his answers?

These questions left him blank. His home education had not taught him how to behave in a test. He wasn't nervous. He didn't care about the outcome. He completed the problems, but became more interested in the word play happening in his mind during the quiet moments in the classroom.

Noah hadn't used the time remaining to check his answers; he did what he always did—he used his mind to grow. As a parent, however, I worried that this lackadaisical approach to serious academics would impede his chances in college. I didn't value his natural capacity to move between categories or to learn as he saw fit because I feared he wasn't living up to the expectations of the real world—of "real" study.

And so, I did what you've probably done too. I scolded him about being prepared for college. Ever the advocate for his true self, Noah famously said to me: "Mom, you raised me in an unconventional way. Now you want me to be a conventional student?"

Boom! Nailed.

I had to face my blind allegiance to traditional education, no matter how much I thought of myself as an iconoclastic homeschool rebel.

The brilliance of Noah—the mind-at-workness of Noah—did not fit traditional schooling. Study, preparation, taking the test, reexamining the test answers for mistakes, patiently sitting quietly while other students finished—these were the hallmarks of what I'd been trained to see as a mind at work, of being a serious student. Yet the genius of this home-schooled child revealed itself in two poems written during a math test at school.

Today, Noah (age thirty-one) is a self-taught, employed computer programmer. He zigzagged through various attempts at college and wound up teaching himself the programming skills he needed when he wanted them, on his own terms. We say we want educated children, but then expect them to look like "schooled" children. I had to get real with myself and admit that I secretly preferred the reassurance of "schooled" over "educated." An educated mind may not look like a "schooled" mind.

A Mind Is a Busy Place

A child's mind at work may weave and bob through materials, relationships, physical activities, and experiences—not matching the anxious homeschooler expectations of "butt in chair, pencil in hand, paperwork obediently completed."

Even the bell-bottomed, free-spirit homeschoolers struggle with what it means to see a mind at work. A friend of mine has a daughter who figured out how to cross-breed fish in their creek. I was floored! This mom explained that her daughter had successfully created two new breeds through this trial-and-error farming experiment. While I praised my friend for this incredible example of natural learning in their family, she confessed to me, "But my daughter doesn't like to read. I see your family going to Shakespeare plays, reciting poetry, and reading thick books. I worry that my daughter isn't that smart."

Can you imagine? In my mind I had been thinking, "I have earned my charter membership in HENSE (Home Educators Neglecting Science Education). My kids can hardly differentiate a fish from a walrus! All we do is lie around reading."

We tend to undervalue what comes naturally to our children and family culture. We overvalue what comes easily to others. How many of us think of education as a sturdy, steady striving that culminates in high test scores in academic subjects? Who of us is comfortable believing the mind is at work when ranting about the "lame" updated version of an online game or when telling an off-color joke? Yet both require insight and linguistic dexterity. It takes a mind!

SEE DIFFERENTLY

To the "Nth" Degree!
Look for your child's mind at work. Use the three Ns to help you!

Notice: Identify your child's aptitudes in school subjects, athletics, hobbies, friendships, and the arts.

Narrate: Comment on your child's accomplishments:

Look at you writing poetry out of the blue! I wonder how long those poems have been growing inside your mind.

Isn't it remarkable the way your brain calibrates the distance and force needed to kick the soccer ball into the goal?

You know just how to comfort your baby sister. Your mind tunes in to her needs and imagines a way to ease her distress.

Note: Record the date and activity in your journal. Track these moments over the course of a year. Treat these like entries in a baby book—short, sweet, pride-inducing. Find one "mind moment" for each child this week.

STAGE THE HOME

Create opportunities to exercise a wide variety of intelligences. Count these as part of your home education. Possible activities include:

* Playing with puns
* Taking turns
* Creative arts
* Enjoying nature
* Collaborative projects
* Sports
* Organizing
* Rearranging the home space for coziness

* Hosting a party
* Math games
* Jokes, red herrings, and logic puzzles
* Poetry writing and reciting
* Corresponding with friends (texting, social media)

ASK YOURSELF

When you worry that your child is not "smart," ask yourself the following questions:

* How can I value the "mind-at-work" in my child today?
* What evidence of intelligence have I devalued and forgotten to notice?

✳ PORT 2: LOOKING FOR A BODY ON THE MOVE ✳

There needs to be sensory engagement, physical movement, and action if a new concept is to be mastered or a new skill developed to the point of real-world competence.

—RENATE AND GEOFFREY CAINE,
12 BRAIN/MIND LEARNING PRINCIPLES IN ACTION

I bet many of you have wigglers and wrigglers. I did! Some kids never stop moving. I was such a child. In second grade, my teacher required us to put our feet on the floor. I was short. My legs couldn't reach the ground so they went numb. At some point in the day, I invariably, unconsciously, tucked my feet under my bottom on the hard, plastic chairs. The teacher would point it out to me and let me know that again, I was not eligible to be classroom monitor due to "poor" behavior. I would chide myself for not making it through one single day. As an adult, I continue to tuck my feet under me (just checked—that's where they are now!). That training had little effect, yet I suffered daily shame because my body wasn't designed to do what a teacher and classroom expected of it.

Today, the educational establishment is more aware that this need to move, bend, and fidget is natural to children. We see first-class teachers on *60 Minutes* use hand-slapping games to teach math concepts. Research shows that when little kids sit on exercise balls that roll back and forth, they stay focused more readily on the teacher than when they sit in hard plastic chairs attached to a desk.[3]

Bodies are meant to expend energy. One of the huge advantages of home education is that we can accommodate a child's need to move. Our children get to use the bathroom without a hall pass, they can grab a snack when hunger strikes (not waiting for recess or lunch). They can stretch or stand or sit under the table to work math problems, if it helps them. Let's indulge *all* that wonderful capacity in our homes and watch learning bloom.

Bodies Crave Breaks

The requirement to sit at a table persists in many homeschools, however. Parents call me to say that they can't get their children to work on writing for an hour at a time. I blanch! Writing for an hour straight is challenging even to professionals. We need moments to let our minds wander, to reread what we've written, to do a little research to escape the pressure of generating words.

Yet the hourly school schedule haunts us. The Student Coalition for Action in Literacy Education (SCALE) asserts that the average focused attention span for kids is the child's chronological age plus one minute.[4] An eight-year-old can give you nine focused minutes. N-I-N-E good minutes. Mind-blowing, right? Let's calculate the focused attention for a sophomore in high school by this algorithm. A fifteen-year-old can give you sixteen good minutes! Wait, what? Can that be possible?

The truth is, even when we require more from ourselves (to work harder and longer), our brains redirect away from focus. Think about all the ways you lose track of what someone is saying to you on the phone when it's gone on too long. Think about how you shift positions, or stop your dedicated task to answer a text or take a shower. Even if we're required to sit and listen, you'll notice your mind goes away from the lecture. When it returns, you think, "Oh no! What did I miss?"

Our kids find their own ways to take those breaks too. They listen to music, they lie on the floor or move their bodies to re-up their engagement. If attention span is so short for all of us, let's admit it and work with it. What are ways we can re-up for repeated doses of devoted energy?

One way is to involve the body—body breaks, body movements. The popular tech companies give their employees yoga mats, places to nap, standing and treadmill desks, and community work spaces where they chat with a colleague. Productivity, it turns out, is related to how well a person can rotate through the "focused attention—take a body break—re-up" cycle.

Take a Brain Break!

Joshua MacNeill, creator of the program Neurologic for trauma victims, explains that all children benefit from brain breaks interspersed throughout their lessons. He writes, "You are giving your students' brains a chance to process, while simultaneously preparing their brains for the next influx of information by calming them, waking them up, or preparing their brains to focus."[5] His book, *101 Brain Breaks and Brain Based Educational Activities*, includes breathing exercises, like blowing bubbles and humming, and energizing breaks, such as secret handshakes and walking on an imaginary balance beam of tape along the floor. Using the body in this way enables kids to concentrate for more total time, even if that time is broken into smaller segments, punctuated by breaks. Great book! Highly recommended.

Bodies Crave Activity

Our bodies also help us retain what we're learning. When my youngest children learned to count backward from ten, we used a practice we called "blast off." The two of them would stand on chairs. We'd put couch cushions all over the floor in front of them. Then I'd say: "Count backward from ten!" They would chant:

"Ten, nine, eight, seven, six, five-four-three-two-one, zero! BLAST OFF!"

Up they jumped to the sky and landed in pillow clouds below them.

This practice was so enjoyable, I quickly realized I could teach the two of them lots of rote memorization this way: months of the year, seasons, days of the week, their home address . . . Once they jumped, they scrambled back onto the chairs for the next item: "Name the months of the year!" They'd recite and then, "Blast off!" They'd leap again. The mere introduction of body activity to memorization changed everything.

Reciting times tables while tossing a Frisbee or a lacrosse ball or while jumping rope works. Writing your history lesson on a clipboard up in a tree or playing with math manipulatives to learn fractions—these are ways we recruit the body to help us learn. Using a microscope, baking a pie, origami, fingerprint kits—these are so much more appealing to children than reading information about these topics. Board games and cards have the same value—they use the body to teach.

Bodies Crave Comfort

Activity is not the only way to engage the body, though. Bodies crave comfort. Warm, gentle lighting increases receptivity to learning. Light-bulb moment (get it?)! Perhaps fluorescent lights are giving kids a headache. Perhaps the lamps are too dim. Maybe the lighting is cold and clinical.

I've become obsessed with good lighting. My mood depends on sunshine. Candles, fires, and twinkle lights help in gray Ohio winters. If this is true for me, how much truer is it for children who can't tell me why they feel cranky?

I noticed, for instance, that a corner with a blanket, basket, and a small lamp invited more reading than all the lectures on the importance of reading ever did. Children love to use a flashlight in bed because it's secretive and laser-focused on the page. Special lighting invites.

When my children got weary of handwriting for copywork, I didn't abandon what I knew to be a healthy writing practice. I sought ways to recast it. When I lit a candle in the middle of the table, they gathered instantly. I gave each one a tea light of their own. That addition of flame helped the uptight bodies relax. Striking the match, watching the flicker, running a finger quickly through the flame (yes, expect that too!), and then extinguishing it after handwriting a paragraph created just enough body comfort to support the challenge of copying. It invited. It delighted! My friend Bridgett lit fires for read-aloud time. In the middle of snowy winter, they roasted marshmallows in the hearth after reading.

There are lots of ways our bodies relax into a gentle space for learning. Not all of them are expensive or messy. In addition to friendly lighting, try some of these:

* Tasty flavors (good snacks)
* Colorful pens, tablecloths, mugs, banners, teapots, and notebooks
* Warm indoor temperatures in winter, cool temperatures in summer
* Scented candles
* Gentle music (movie soundtracks) or natural sounds (like rain, wind, or the roar of the surf)
* Back scratches
* Hand massages
* Cuddling under a blanket
* Stroking a pet's fur
* Playing with a tub of water
* Lying on the floor
* Stretching and bending, rolling the neck, rubbing shoulders

Our bodies predispose us to learn because when our bodies are happy, our minds are alert.

SEE DIFFERENTLY

Reject traditional ideas of what bodies doing schoolwork should look like. Give yourself and your kids permission to experiment. For instance, when one girl wanted to pet the cat while she wrote in her notebook on the sofa, I got a call from her mother. This mom worried that her daughter's handwriting would suffer. I told her: "What have you got to lose? Give it a try."

Later that day, I received a photo via email of a happy young lady bundled in a quilt, stroking the cat, writing. Her pleasure drove her to do the good work any parent would hope to see.

Ask your children: *What would help you concentrate right now?*

Then offer some body solutions:

* A glass of lemonade?
* Sitting in the sunshine?
* Wearing headphones to drown out the shouting toddlers?
* Eating a snack?
* Swapping out the hard, wooden chair for a padded one?
* Raising the chair or lowering the table for a better height?
* Standing at the desk rather than sitting?
* Lying on the floor with a clipboard?

STAGE THE HOME

When engaged in a learning task, keep this body-break dance in mind.

"Do, Be, Do"

Do: Warm up the body (back rubs, cuddles, eye contact, hand massage, high fives, hugs).

Be: Focus attention (apply self to the material for chronological age plus one minute).

Do: Take a break (chase the dog, run up and down the stairs, get a snack, change locations, jump on the trampoline, color a page, play a video game, use a brain break).

Repeat. Forever and amen.

ASK YOURSELF

When studies become tired, ask yourself the following questions:

* How can I enhance the atmosphere for learning?
* Have I provided breaks, comfort, or activity to my children's bodies today?

✳ PORT 3: LOOKING FOR A HEART CONNECTED ✳

> The problem—as I've said for years—is that it is hardly ever possible to separate what we think about something from how we feel about it.
>
> —JOHN HOLT, *HOW CHILDREN LEARN*

A love connection is at the heart of learning: love of the subject, tenderness toward the teacher, pride in self, the joy of discovery. Education thrives when our kids fall in love.

A child's passions, as we saw in Chapter 3, naturally lead them to topics that happen to be on our list of required school subjects. Johannah's passion for reading teen fiction led her to write her own novel. When Caitrin became interested in fashion, we subscribed to big-name magazines and made spelling lists to help her perfect her fashion vocabulary. That tailor-made copywork and dictation practice found a home in her fashion blog.

Another way love of learning grows is through a tender connection to a coach. According to research, independent practice is not enough to master a new skill. Directed practice leads to the greatest progress.[6] Think about your kids and their soccer team practices—adults giving tips, kids practicing the same skills again and again. Love in learning blossoms when a child has both a coach (someone giving meaningful input to grow a skill) and an ally (someone supportive during struggle).

Coaching allows you to be a second set of eyes with a supply of strategies. Empathize with a child's efforts, and offer supportive feedback to encourage growth. Camaraderie, a shared aim, and the triumph of progress forge the bonds of a love connection. Rely on other adult coaches in your child's life, whether in sports, theater, ballet, a science co-op, or a writing support group. The role of coach and ally in a child's life is a sacred gift.

The Homeschool Hand Grenade

Sometimes, though, we parents fumble the coaching ball. We're suspicious of too much happiness in learning. Perhaps the lesson is "rigor lite." I've watched families wreck their happily-humming-along homeschools by ditching an effective program simply because their kids found it easy. We lob what I call "the homeschool hand grenade" of a new curriculum into our happy living rooms and wonder why everyone is miserable again.

Ripping through the lesson with ease creates the opportunity for a love connection to bloom! Pleasure comes from *overcoming struggle*: relishing the newfound ability and applying it. Our kids must enjoy proficiency, sometimes for a good long while, before facing a new challenge.

Imagine teaching your son to ride a two-wheel bike. Right as he gets his balance and can finally ride down the street, you take it away and hand him a unicycle. That's the feeling here. The heart connection to learning is about mastery—ease, competence, certitude. Give plenty of time for the enjoyment of *having learned*.

Is it okay for a new reader to devour all the *Captain Underpants* books for a year before moving on to classic literature? Should a parent worry if a child is obsessed with skip counting for months and doesn't show interest in division?

Love doesn't grow through coercion. It's a response to pleasure. Patient trust allows a pleasurable relationship to evolve. There are some subjects that become favorites and others that are passing introductions. Not all subjects are pleasurable at every season of life. Yet if your children can form a close, bonded attachment to a few well-loved subjects and areas of interest, the resulting happiness spills into the rest of their education. Success and joy in one area energizes a student for more challenging tasks. A stingy attitude toward joy leads to a meltdown toward all effort. If *everything* is challenging and none of it is inspiring, the level of resistance will be profound.

Find the Right Balance of Challenge, Competence, and Meaning

To grow the lovebug in your family, keep three ideas in mind. A challenge catches our children's attention. If the first step in learning feels too big and disaster results (the attempt fails), a willingness to meet that challenge evaporates. Children are drawn to what is *appropriately challenging*—the level that helps them discover their resources.

A feeling of dawning *competence* carries children forward. That first attempt at writing a letter and seeing the clear shape emerge, the success of counting the beans to see that our mental math for two plus two really is four, beating level one in an online game, bringing right and left hand together on the piano—these are magical moments! Small encouragements at the start of a new endeavor help kids keep at it.

Freed from pressure to perform beyond their limits, children naturally create *meaning* from their work. They find ways to apply their new skills to their existing frame of reference. They may write a letter or leave a note. They might count all their collectibles or sort them by size. They may compose a piece on the piano or memorize their favorite to perform. Meaning for children can be summed up as *the ability to use a skill for a personal purpose*.

SEE DIFFERENTLY

Love of learning is supported by a loving home atmosphere—parents, programs, and living space. Remember these principles:

* Be kind and helpful.
* Admire your child's efforts.
* Use programs that appeal to your child (not the ones that appeal to you but your child hates).
* Increase difficulty when the child is rooting around for a challenge.
* Provide passionate adult coaches for subjects that don't come naturally to you.

STAGE THE HOME

Feed the Lovebug

So how do you foster a coaching relationship, rather than a teaching one? You come alongside your child as an ally. Remind yourself: kind support leads to a tender relationship. Build momentum in your child's learning experience by following these steps:

1. Model the practice to your child.

2. Do the practice with your child (sometimes for a good long while).

3. Give plenty of time and space to practice a new skill; repeat what is easy and pleasurable; use the skill in multiple contexts.

4. Notice what your child does well, and comment: "You solved five math problems correctly!" or "Look at all those capital letters."

5. Resist the temptation to say, "You missed six problems," or "You spelled most of the words right," or "You should know how to do that already."

6. Note mistakes to yourself, and address them again another day: "Let's take a look at how to find common denominators again today," or "Let's play with capitals and periods." Go back to steps 1 through 3.

7. Celebrate growth: "You found the common denominator without help!"

8. Commend your child for an academic skill applied to personal use: "Look at how nicely paragraphed your blog is!"

9. Enjoy a child's pleasure in learning (drop suspicion and worry).

ASK YOURSELF

If the learning environment is characterized by struggle, ask yourself the following questions:

* Has my child had enough time and repetition to feel the pleasure of mastery?
* How can I provide the right balance of challenge, competence, and meaning?

✳ PORT 4: LOOKING FOR A *SPIRIT* INSPIRED ✳

We must learn to regard people less in the light of what they do or omit to do, and more in the light of what they suffer.

—DIETRICH BONHOEFFER,
LETTERS AND PAPERS FROM PRISON

After the fourth People for the Ethical Treatment of Animals (PETA) video, I understood why Johannah wanted to be vegan. She wanted to matter—to make a difference in the world. I love it when teens become strident about a belief. It shows an inspired spirit—the capacity to care.

On the other hand, I had four kids and a husband who had no interest in Tofurkey for Thanksgiving dinner. Friends told me not to "cave." They said I shouldn't have to alter my family's habits for one child. But I knew the shape of the compassion Johannah had just discovered—I had lived it in college when I dedicated myself to raising awareness for world hunger. The awakening to moral responsibility is a powerful (and right) developmental milestone in a young person's life. Seeing it ignite in Johannah moved me; I wanted to fan it into flame.

My kids' dad and I both believed that the capacity to care for others was as important in our children's education as learning to read, write, and calculate. I also knew that beliefs change over a lifetime (heck, I don't believe half the stuff I thought I *knew* when I was fifteen). What mattered in that moment when Johannah declared she wanted to be vegan was the chance to live up to her ideal—to feel the full effect of aligning her personal behavior with her moral commitment. She had tapped into empathy—the capacity to imagine suffering, and the desire to relieve it.

Teach Your Children Well

Educational innovator Arthur Costa reminds adults that students are quick to pick up inconsistencies in their teachers and parents. "Children acquire much of their behavior, feelings, attitudes, and values not through direct instruction but through imitation of both adult and peer models. Students adopt new behavior patterns or modify their own behavior on the basis of *observation alone*" [emphasis mine].[7]

Your most natural behaviors ring truest to your children. If it's natural to empathize and share what you have with others, children follow suit. If your instincts are self-protecting and critical, your children may not learn empathy as young people. If your words and actions don't align, your kids will know which is the truth by what you *do* more than what you *say*. The chance to be a part of a teen's moral awakening is a privilege.

Treat Your Children Well

Are you fair? Are you kind? Do you demonstrate that your child's happiness matters to you? Do you listen? It's impossible to expect children to offer those same qualities to others if they haven't experienced them from you. If we want our kids to value the needs of others, we must value *our children's needs* first.[8] Sounds illogical. Shouldn't we model caring for others? Certainly—yet not to the exclusion of tender care for our children. If we ask children to listen and pay attention to what we believe, we need to listen and pay attention to their beliefs. If we want them to share their toys, we need to share our tools with them.

When children experience the loving care of their parents, they learn *how* to care for others. It's difficult to offer compassion to others from a poverty of resources. If you don't feel loved, you are less likely to *be* loving. If you feel unheard, you are less likely to listen. If you are manipulated, coerced, shamed, or blamed, you are likely to be self-protecting and suspicious of others.

One strain of parenting advice I heard in my early years of homeschooling ran counter to this notion. Several leaders in the movement taught parents to show children that life wasn't fair. One father boasted that he served varying amounts of ice cream to his six kids (one of them wouldn't get any), requiring each child to be thankful. This idea may *sound* innovative, but it *feels* capricious. An authority (a father) makes a choice to be unfair to several children, and no matter how philosophical the goals, the felt experience is painful and breaks trust. What child wouldn't wonder why the father picked him to go without ice cream while the others got two scoops?

Children are more likely to be generous with others when they believe they have more than enough to give away. Incidentally that's also true of adults. The moral imagination is as expansive as our resources and experiences.

What If I Don't Like Their "Cause"?

If the teen's belief appears to be dangerous (I had a student in a home-school co-op class who was overly enamored of Hitler, for instance), it's important to find out more about it—to trace back the origin of that fascination and then to address it.

That said, if the choice is simply inconvenient or not what you wanted for your child (for example, veganism), consider this idea proposed by Paul Tournier, Swiss psychologist and spiritual mentor, in his book *The Adventure of Living*. Tournier points out that one of the ways young adults individuate from parents is to *modify their parents' beliefs*. While offspring are likely to model their *values* after their parents', they tend to do so in new ways: attending a different house of worship, picking a different political cause or party, showing interest in a social issue of their own choosing.[9] Our job is to focus on the act of caring more than on the content of the cause.

Reading Aloud

One of the most powerful ways to expand the capacity to care in children and teens is through reading literature together. The so-called read aloud is a staple of homeschools. Novels give us access to points of view and ethical dilemmas, as well as a wider lens to understand the globe. In Brave Writer, we select books to study based on the following criteria I developed as a home educator:

1. Diverse authors
   - All kinds of English-speaking writers: Asian American, African American, Native American, Hispanic American, immigrant, native-born, former slave, famous historical figures, those who expanded the frontier, those with learning differences or disabilities, and those from the UK, Australia, Canada, and New Zealand.

- Both men and women, young and old, contemporary and from a bygone era.
- Writers from other countries, eras, and languages. This becomes easier as kids enter the teen years, and translations of the classics are available.

2. Diverse characters
   - Male and female protagonists
   - Older and younger main characters
   - Varieties of economic circumstances
   - Various religious backgrounds

3. Diverse experiences
   - Historical events
   - Natural disasters
   - Humanitarian crises
   - Familiar childhood
   - Humor, suspense, tragedy, fantasy

4. Diverse genres
   - Prose (fiction)
   - Poetry
   - Nonfiction
   - Graphic novels
   - Comics
   - Plays
   - Short stories
   - Fables and myths

Use this checklist as you pick books to read this year.

Moral Imagination

In most universities, students take a course called "Literature and the Moral Imagination" (or some variation). The goal of the class is to help students form values as they encounter a diverse set of perspectives, including both familiar and unfamiliar experiences. What's wonderful about homeschooling is that we can begin that formation with children's novels and continue right through high school into college. The opportunity to gain empathy via reading is the top reason I knew I wanted to homeschool.

The development of a moral imagination helps human beings become responsible, ethical, caring people in whatever career they choose. Not only that, but empathizing with the welfare of others is a fabulous point of connection when studying history, politics, and science. Yesterday's lessons from history inform today's ethical dilemmas—it's important for our young people to understand that legacy and have the tools to respond meaningfully and responsibly.

SEE DIFFERENTLY, THEN ACT

Be a Giver

The primary way we support the moral development of our children is to do for them what we wish they would do for others. So simple, yet counterintuitive.

Give Love. First, to your children. Help them, hear them, give generously to them. The rule of thumb is that it's not love if you must explain to your children that what you're doing is because you love them. Your kids know they are loved when they *feel* loved. If you regularly make love deposits into your child's life, the boundaries you occasionally set for your child's protection and well-being will be more easily tolerated and accepted. If all you offer your child are boundaries and rules, resentment is cultivated instead.

Second, show love to others in your social circle—believe the best of people in your life; resist the temptation to criticize, slander, or gossip. Read widely and then talk about those experiences with your kids. (You may cry when your child does not—that's a powerful sharing moment.)

Give Attention. Learn with your kids about a local need—a natural disaster, a civil rights issue, a shut-in, a fund-raiser for a cause. Raise your own awareness. Become curious to understand the need. Explore it with your children, if appropriate.

Give Help. Respond to a need. Volunteer, raise funds, rake leaves for an elderly neighbor, make origami cranes for a peace march, visit a friend in the hospital, walk dogs at a shelter, give up dairy and meat. Put love and giving into practice together.

STAGE THE HOME

Choose to support your child's cause in a visible way. If your child is vegan, purchase cookbooks and food items that support her choice. If you sponsor a child in another country, keep that child's picture in a prominent place—talk about that child with your children. If politics and meaty conversation are important to your family, dedicate a family dinner to discussion. Schedule time to watch documentaries together. Deliberately seek positions that differ from the ones you naturally hold. Notice the interconnections that this social cause offers—history, ethics, religion, politics, literature. Draw a new Continent of Learning with this cause at the center.

Spend time watching films and reading books with your children to foster big juicy conversations about ways of life different from your own.

Hygge: The Danish Practice of Coziness

The four Ports of Entry are best nurtured when we consider the properties of hominess and connection. In this, the Danes are experts, and their lifestyle has caught the global imagination.

In the last several years, articles and books about *hygge* (pronounced *HOO-gah*), the Danish word for "coziness," have proliferated like wildflowers in spring. The Danes, subject to eighteen to twenty hours of darkness per day in winter, have perfected the art of making the home a place of light, warmth, connection, and well-being. They believe that productivity in the workplace and restfulness at home rely not on better technology or tools, but on how well each person is nurtured and welcomed into those spaces.

The health of the mind, body, heart, and spirit depends on creating a context that relieves stress and improves concentration and relaxation. *Hygge* fits the bill! Add one *hygge* feature to your lives today. It's not always the program that's the problem; sometimes it's just the context.

- **Light and color:** Danes burn thirteen pounds of candle wax per capita per year![10] Candles, small table lamps, twinkle lights, LED or battery-operated candles, and lanterns offer warm cozy lighting. In the fall, when it gets dark early, a pot of tea simmering on a tea warmer with a bright tea light within invites children to gather.
- **Fragrance and sound:** The aroma of baking cookies, the scent of pine in a centerpiece, musical scores from favorite films, soundscapes of nature—these create an invisible mood.
- **Food:** Half-moon orange slices with cinnamon, a square of chocolate, a cup of warm tea—the simple act of dipping a hand repeatedly into a bowl of almonds and dried apricots while working on math problems can make the difference! Good protein for the mind, good action for the body, good color for the eyes, yummy flavor for the heart.
- **Cuddling:** Soft throws, fuzzy socks, a mountain of pillows, those baggy pants you only wear at home, wool for knitting, sheepskins on the floor in front of the fireplace, chairs that envelop you—cuddle up! Snuggle a puppy or kitty cat.
- **The outdoors:** In addition to making the home a cuddly, nourishing, well-lit space, *hygge* includes a love of nature at any time of year. Bring some of it inside (pinecone arrangements, roaring fires, plants) and go out to it (hikes, walks, skating, visits to parks). Look for hearts in nature. I've found puddles, snow stacked up between tree limbs, and a cactus in the shape of hearts. Getting outside in all temperatures and

seasons maintains your circadian rhythm, and keeps everyone from going stir-crazy in a long season of snow, rain, or heat.

- **Connection:** Being with loved ones is a top priority. Home-schooling allows us to spend the days with our favorite people (our kids). Connection is created when your little people see that you want their happiness—a happiness they would choose for themselves.

CHAPTER 7

APPLYING THE SUPERPOWERS

Practical Help in Core Subjects

Beautiful Language, Math and Science, Art and Nature, Becoming Global Citizens, Games, and "Party School"

It's important to remember that we all have magic inside us.

—J. K. ROWLING

Welcome to the chapter of practicality. Time to tap into our three groups of four Superpowers:

* Forces of Enchantment (Chapter 4): surprise, mystery, risk, adventure
* Capacities for Learning (Chapter 5): curiosity, collaboration, contemplation, celebration
* Ports of Entry (Chapter 6): mind, body, heart, spirit

Next, let's pair them with literature, math, science, history, poetry, video games, nature, art, and more. This chapter offers a kick-start to rethinking how you bring education to your children. It's certainly *not* an exhaustive chapter. Please use the ideas as a launchpad for your own creativity. There's a trick to this process, though, so let's start with a paradigm shift in how you understand teaching.

✳ Think Like a . . . ✳

In our urgency to educate our children, sometimes we focus on amassing information. Today's educational innovators say: "To what end?" Why are we front-loading children with information in a world where a phone in our pocket holds the answer to any question a person could ask?

The twenty-first century demands a new orientation to a quality education. Today's students need to be able to *think and interpret*, not just recite. That thinking ought to follow the pattern of the field. Take history. What is it to *think* like a historian, rather than merely to *study* and *recite* history? According to the book *Reading, Thinking, and Writing About History*:

> If students are to develop the literacy practices they need, social studies educators must embrace inquiry and interpretation. Students will not learn to consider multiple perspectives, critique what they read, or develop an argument if history lessons focus solely on memorizing names and dates or filling in bubbles on a Scantron sheet.[1]

These educational specialists go on to say that it is better to "frame history around the discipline's central goal: evidence-based interpretation."[2]

I remember reading *Little Town on the Prairie* by Laura Ingalls Wilder to my children. In the novel, Laura retells an event that impressed me. Laura ends her school year by reciting American history through 1820 in front of an adult audience. My homeschool friends and I felt like failures upon reading her impressive recitation because our kids couldn't give an overview of American history up to the current day. Yet another 150 years of information had been added—it seemed unreasonable to recite that much content from memory.

Not only that, kids today are expected to be global citizens—knowledgeable about histories all over the world. The task seems impossible because, let's face it, it is. Lucky for us, the "historical brain trust" lives digitally, freeing us to think about what to *do* with that information, rather than merely memorizing it.

Yes, it's great to be able to call up facts easily—but that's not the sum of what an education means today. A historian must know how to analyze primary documents, how to evaluate credible and noncredible sources. A historian uses linguistic skills and an appreciation for economics, religion, political theory, social customs, regional geography, and anthropology to interpret what happened when, how, and why. Each generation makes new meaning from past historical events, in fact. In other words, even the "facts" change over time.

We rob our kids of a textured education when we minimize all these elements and translate "educated" into a multiple-choice test. Is there any way to approximate the work of a historian for a young person? How can we acquaint our kids with the joy of historical discovery or insight? These are the questions to ask ourselves as educational innovators.

That Time When . . . I Dug Like an Archaeologist

In seventh grade, my social studies teacher, Mrs. Fagan, gave us a chance to *be* historians. We learned about Aztecs in the traditional way first—textbook, lecture. Then one day, she brought wet clay to class. She taught us to throw pots, following models of Aztec pottery. Muddy up to our elbows, we massaged dishes and vases into being. We allowed our creations to dry overnight, and the next day, Mrs. Fagan showed us how to paint them according to Aztec designs.

The pots were fired over the weekend. Our beautiful shiny pots were returned to our class. We marveled. Until . . . what? Hammers? Next to each pot, a hammer lay ready for action. Mrs. Fagan asked us to smash our pots into pieces! We got over the horror and enthusiastically fractured the fired clay.

Each pot was scooped into a box with our name on it. The next day, Mrs. Fagan brought us to a field behind the school. We tramped into a wide space of dirt and weeds. There, Mrs. Fagan handed out shovels and put us in excavation groups. We were now archaeologists in Malibu Canyon. This intrepid instructor had buried our pot fragments between cardboard sheets (representing sedimentary layers of civilizations past). Our task was to dig up our pots and identify which layer they were in.

The teams set to the task and cheered each time a shovel struck true. Except my team. We couldn't find anything. We dug and we dug and we dug . . . until I started crying eleven-year-old tears. *Where were our pots?* Mrs. Fagan came alongside and said gently, "You know, Julie, you're having the most authentic experience. Since I didn't remember exactly where your dig site was supposed to be, your team is now having to work like *real* archaeologists. You have to keep digging until you find the pot fragments without knowing where to look."

That pep talk rallied my spirits. I wanted to be an archaeologist right then. When our team *did* find our pots, we cheered even louder than the rest of the class. We were *real* archaeologists! The bits and pieces of vases and dishes were brought back to the classroom. Over the next several days, we reassembled them using glue and then labeled the jars for a museum display.

I don't remember a single test we took in that class. I don't remember what else we studied. I remember Mrs. Fagan's archaeological dig. In college, I majored in history.

This concept of "thinking like a . . . fill in the blank" can be applied to any subject area. How does a grammarian think? What are the tasks of a linguist? Can we look at the English language as a mystery to be unfolded first, before we tell our kids the conclusions already drawn by expert grammarians?

I created a Brave Writer grammar class built on that thinking. I ask children to collect words. Any words. Once kids spend a week collecting words and writing them on word tickets, I ask them to group those words into categories of their own choosing. Here's the catch: they determine what is alike about the words in any grouping. So perhaps several words are grouped together because they all start with the letter "b" or they all pertain to gymnastics or they are words of three syllables. By thinking about how words are similar and dissimilar, and then collecting them in groups, they've begun the work of a linguist.

Language has so many features—the abstract concepts of *noun* and *verb* are not the only ones. The experience of examining language and uncovering the relationships between words teaches a child to *think* like a grammarian. Once that transformation occurs, children can see behind the curtain to how linguists make their choices about language groupings, definitions, and relationships.

What about thinking like a journalist or social commentator? How do mathematicians and scientists think? What practices inform the development of those fields? The rest of this chapter builds from this premise. When we apply the Superpowers to learning and galvanize our kids to participate in the activity of the subject (rather than merely memorizing it), we unleash a torrent of academic power!

✳ The Subjects ✳

Beautiful Language

By age five, native speakers are so fluent in their heart language that they're the envy of all second-language speakers. The brain is hardwired for speech—it adapts, retains, and flawlessly applies the lessons it learns through community, relationship, and osmosis. We amass words with a voracious appetite in primary education and right through college. One of my professors explains that a PhD amounts to having an expert vocabulary in your chosen field. In plain English: PhDs know all the best words!

Language is innately beautiful in every tongue. Poetry and novels, religious literature and philosophy are found all over the globe at every point in history. Tapping into this rich resource is both empowering and satisfying to children. The following practices provide a deep dive into language to lay that sure foundation.

POETRY TEATIME

Once a week, my family gathered at the kitchen table to read poems to one another while munching muffins and sipping cups of tea. I like to say: poetry plus tea and treats equals magical family time and enchanted learning. Samuel Pepys in his famous diary of 1665 concurs: "Strange to see how a good dinner and feasting reconciles everybody." No wonder thousands of families worldwide consider Poetry Teatime a slam-dunk experience. Poetry Teatime is a perfect picture of the twelve Superpowers in action.

Try It!

1. **Set a lovely table.** Tablecloth or place mats; a centerpiece made from natural artifacts (like pinecones or seashells), candles, or Lego creations; teacups or mugs for each person; pretty dishes for snacks.

2. **Prepare tea and treats.** British tea is most popular but not required. The key: use a teapot to serve whatever liquid your squad enjoys. Feel free to offer hot chocolate or lemonade. Moroccan mint tea or Indian chai is also delicious. Provide snacks like scones or muffins, or apple slices spread with almond butter. Toast and jam cut into ladyfingers work well; store-bought cookies are easy.

3. **Stack poetry books.** Collect books from the library or your bookcases, or purchase through a bookseller. Include a children's anthology or two with big illustrations. I've edited a collection of poems called *Poetry Teatime Companion* if you're looking for a place to start. Pick poets known for their sense of humor and rhyme

(Marilyn Singer, Shel Silverstein, Jack Prelutsky). Try those who feature nature and animals like Jane Yolen or Amy Ludwig Van-Derwater. Knock-knock jokes, tongue twisters, and nursery rhymes are wonderful too. Spread these books all over the table (more books than children).

4. **Flip through a book, pick a poem, read it aloud.** Encourage children to thumb through the books, paging until a poem catches their fancy to share with the group. Teens like to share song lyrics too. Lines from a Shakespeare play count. If a child is too young to read, have the child pick a poem by picture. Then you, the parent, or an older sibling, can read it to the family. Parents pick poems and read them aloud too. The goal is a deep drink of language and beverage.

5. **Slurp, enjoy, laugh, marvel**. There's no need for analysis. Sometimes a natural conversation results about a poem's rhyme scheme or the humor of the limerick, or why the word "buzz" is an onomatopoeia (don't worry—you can look up that word later). The goal is to savor language, good food, and a special drink together at a lovely table.

And that's it!

Here's what's bananas: once you start this practice, it's like a runaway train. The context stirs openness—food, candles, special drinks, taking time to make the table look pretty—all that *hygge* stuff we talked about in the last chapter. The lack of academic agenda allows kids to page through books looking to arouse their curiosity. Surprise! Mystery! Both at work. It never fails. There is *always* a poem a child wants to read aloud. Risk and adventure? Sharing it. Watching the reaction. The collaboration (taking turns, helping someone read or pour the tea, setting the table), the contemplation (considering which book to page through, weighing which poem to share, wondering to oneself what the poem means or why it's funny), and the celebration of the event with laughter or tears, treats and time.

Mind, body, heart, and spirit all trained on the meaning, message, and moment.

Poetry Teatime is a slam-dunk learning experience because it maximizes all the properties of brave learning. Meanwhile, the feeling about poetry is radically altered from English class. Tens of thousands of kids have been turned on to poetry through Poetry Teatime—never knowing poetry was supposed to be a difficult, opaque school subject that nobody likes.

In my family, we invited friends from public and private schools to join us too (they loved it!); two of my kids wrote poetry for online literary magazines as adults; one launched a monthly poetry slam at his college; and another hosted Poetry Teatimes on his dorm floor when he was a resident assistant. This practice follows children right into adulthood.

For More Ideas

Visit poetryteatime.com for a free quick-start guide to Poetry Teatime and a free booklist of poetry for every age. Scroll through Instagram using the hashtag #poetryteatime to see how other families from around the world have interpreted this practice. Follow @poetryteatime on Instagram for more great ideas.

READ-ALOUD TIME

One of the purest joys I've experienced as a homeschooler was the daily ritual of reading aloud to my five children. Nothing anchored a day like the practice of gathering in the family room—me in the rocker, five children strewn across couches or on the floor, listening to a fabulous tale of adventure.

1. **Keep a read-aloud basket.** Include a variety of books—Aesop's fables, Greek myths, inspirational literature, fairy tales, nonfiction (about any topic under the sun), history, picture books, and novels. Read a little from each one.

2. **Pick a time of day to read.** Right after breakfast or lunch—when noisy toddlers or babies are napping.

3. **Busy their hands.** While you read, supply blocks, Lego bricks, knitting materials, coloring books, modeling clay, pot holder looms, puzzles, tangrams, origami, dolls to dress, watercolor paints, or any other quiet activity.

4. **Take conversation breaks.** Occasionally ask a question, note a beautiful phrase, wonder what will happen next, chat about the creations being built while you read. Expect childishness and interruption—pause to give a drink of water or take a bathroom break.

5. **Invite older children to read from one of the books.** The fable or poem, the couple of paragraphs about natural disasters in your nonfiction book, the passage in your inspirational literature—give your voice a rest.

6. **Audiobooks are great.** If you have a nursing baby who won't let you read, or you've lost your voice, or you're beyond exhausted from all your parenting, there's no reason not to listen to the book on audio! Pro tip: audiobooks pair well with lunch or breakfast and long car rides.

7. **Read everything everywhere.** Read the billboards as you fly down the highway, read graffiti, read a book at a park or the zoo, read to each other at a coffee house or ice cream shop, read the signs next to paintings at the art museum, read instruction manuals . . . Writing is everywhere waiting to be read aloud to an interested audience. When you read what you see in daily life, you alert your children to all the ways writing is used in daily life.

Reading aloud together allows you to savor story and language as a family. Your kids will get to know a wide variety of writing styles, which help them shape their own writing voices. The unexpected plot twists and interesting tidbits of information create momentum and variety. In fact, on a day gone wrong, reading a book to your children can reassure you that you did, in fact, provide a quality day of homeschooling.

READING TO SELF

I owe it all to my mother. I'm a reader because of one practice she *enforced* in our family. Ready? When we were children, she told us we could stay up as late as we wanted in our beds, if we were reading. An 8:00 p.m. bedtime—but stay up until 11:00 p.m. reading? No problem! I have countless memories of falling asleep with a book on my chest and the light on. Your kids can too! Try any of these enticements for reading to self:

1. **Flashlight reading.** Staying up late is even more fun with all the special reading lamps available today—book clip lights are wonderful. The old-fashioned flashlight works too. Supply these, put your kids to bed, and see what happens!

2. **Light a candle.** Light a candle during the day, and tell everyone that while the candle is lit, the house is quiet for reading. Read silently alone together for fifteen to thirty minutes in the morning or afternoon. Readers read, youngsters page through picture books in your lap. If everyone is of reading age, you read too. Shorten the time for success: one to five minutes to start is perfect if you have babies and toddlers who can't read yet.

3. **Establish a reading nook.** Lamp? Check. Cozy cushions? Check. Soft throw? Check. Basket of books? Check. Near the family but also a little private? Check and check! Make a gentle rule: "The reading nook is only for reading."

4. **Supply comic books or poetry.** For kids who find novels daunting, lower the bar. Put *Calvin and Hobbes* or graphic novels on the bedside table or near the reading nook. Poetry and magazines work too.

5. **Audiobooks count.** Kids can pop on headphones while they work on a craft. Some children benefit from listening while following along in the book itself to strengthen reading skills. Others listen to audiobooks to fall asleep at night.

WRITING

Ah, the big kahuna! Writing is such a Serious Subject. Parents everywhere are intimidated by writing because so few feel competent as adults. The scourge of the red pen from years in school leaves lasting damage. Time to inject enchantment and whimsy into this powerful skill. The next set of ideas are tried-and-true methods to draw the writer out of your kids. If you want more ideas, visit my website at bravewriter.com.

JOT IT DOWN

The early writing life begins before a child can wield a pencil or read. The writer lives inside. Writing is the record of a mind-life. If a person can externalize language, *someone else* can transcribe it—jot it down. Think of Stephen Hawking, the astrophysicist paralyzed by ALS. He couldn't type a word on his own for decades. No one worried about whether he could spell or punctuate. Rather, we have his brilliant mind preserved in writing through the magic of speech-to-text software. He got the byline—not the machine, not his editor. Hawking's writing is a record of his thoughts, not his spelling and punctuation skills.

Young kids can experience the power and pleasure of their own words in writing if you take the time to jot them down and then read them back.

1. **Listen.** Pay attention. One of your kids is going to assault you with a little passionate narrative today. It will come out of the blue sky—you'll be showering or stir-frying dinner. When you notice the white heat of passion erupt in the retelling (how she beat the

next level of *Super Mario*, what happened when the dog chased the squirrel), *stop* what you're doing. Tune in.

2. **Grab a sheet of paper.** Whatever is near: back of an envelope, supermarket receipt, scrap of paper, sticky note. Nab a writing implement (pencil, pen, crayon).

3. **Jot down what your child says.** No preamble. No explanation about what you're doing. Simply write the words your child says to you as best you can. If she asks what you're doing, simply respond, "This is so good, I don't want to forget it, so I'm jotting it down."

4. **Read the writing to the family.** Later that day (dinnertime, perhaps), pull the little narrative out of your pocket. Say, "Sally told me how she beat a level in *Super Mario* and it was so good! I didn't want to forget it, so I wrote it down." Read it. Discuss the content. Enjoy your child's words together.

5. **Toss the jotted piece of writing into the library book basket.** Read it again to your child during read-aloud time. You might say, "Oh, lookie here! Author Sally's writing. Let's read it!" Let your child hear you take pleasure in her words that you've preserved in writing. If you put her writing in a folder in the back of the cabinet where it dies in the "homeschool tomb," your child never understands the purpose of writing. Reading to an audience shows your child that you mean for their writing to be enjoyed and reread.

6. **Lather, rinse, repeat.** As often as inspired. And yes, you can use this practice with sixteen-year-olds. It's incredible to see how valuing your children's spoken thoughts in writing transforms how a child *sees* writing. What they didn't know is that the words *inside* are the ones you hope to see on the outside in their own writing. This practice demonstrates it without explanation.

That Time When . . . Johannah Jotted a Story

We arrived home after Caitrin's bedtime. Jon and I were greeted at the door by Johannah—waving a clipboard, shouting, "Mom, Dad! Caitrin wrote a story. Her first one!" Caitrin? She was five years old and couldn't read. Johannah, twelve, continued: "I helped Caitrin get ready for bed and asked her to tell me a story. Once she got started, I realized I should write it down for her. So I did! Want to hear it?"

I glanced at the clipboard. The white paper had no lines and Johannah's handwriting sloped in an arc down the page. Spelling errors and missing punctuation abounded. She must have had to write fast to keep up with Caitrin! Yet what stood out? Caitrin's sparkling prose!

What I had done for Johannah (jotting down her stories), she now did for her sister. She knew that Caitrin was already a writer—even before Caitrin could pencil the alphabet, because that's how I'd always seen Johannah, before she could read.

The "jot it down" practice capitalizes on surprise (your children don't expect their oral language to be taken so seriously that you'd write it down and read it to others). It provokes celebration (the pride of sharing). It promotes collaboration—parent and child working as a team to get the child's thoughts to the page. It engages the heart and spirit—love and meaning all bound up in this shared experience of valuing a child's thoughts.

FREEWRITING

Once a child can wield his own pencil, putting those original thoughts into his own hand is the next step in the writing life. Peter Elbow, writing expert and professor emeritus from the University of Massachusetts

Amherst, popularized the practice of freewriting in colleges across America in his book *Writing with Power*. He borrowed from the habit of professional writers who give themselves permission to make a mess on paper or screen when they begin a writing project. He discovered that when students are provided space to transcribe their thoughts as they occur (no matter what those thoughts are—even words like "I'm stuck!"), they become competent, comfortable, fluent writers. Freewriting unlocks the words and gets them out where they can be seen, revised, and edited. "Freewriting helps you learn to just say it. Regular freewriting helps make the writing process transparent."[3]

Freewriting is best done with children who can read and already know how to handwrite a bit—usually eight or nine years old. That said, younger children can dictate their freewrites to you and you can jot them down, or they can be encouraged to draw or doodle during freewriting time. I recommend that *you* freewrite with your kids as well. Your participation creates a collaborative environment and a supportive structure for writing risks.

1. **Make a list.** On the day before your first freewrite, have your children list all of the things they love and know well. The list can include academic subjects like the war in Sparta as well as their favorite stuff like ballroom dancing, Wii bowling, baking cookies, and abalone. On the day your family freewrites, ask your children to pick an item from the list as their topic. Or they are free to ignore the topic and simply write what comes to mind. Some children need the clarification of a topic (helps them focus). Others need liberation from a topic (helps them relax). All words are welcome, even if the child deviates from the chosen topic.

2. **Rub shoulders; crack knuckles.** Relax bodies. Roll the head around on the neck, flex fingers. For active children, recommend they take a lap around the backyard first.

3. **Use scratch paper.** Freewriting means you're free to write your exact thoughts, even if you can't spell or punctuate them accu-

rately. Some kids worry about perfect spelling and handwriting. To set the right tone, use real scratch paper: the back of a flyer or a sheet of paper you ball up into wrinkles and then smooth out for writing. Kids immediately see that this writing can't be the finished product—all those wrinkles! That's when many of them relax.

4. **Set the timer for five minutes.** Start with one to three minutes if freewriting is new or intimidating.

5. **Write the entire time, no self-editing.** The only rule in freewriting: keep the pencil moving. Yes, freewriting can be done on a keyboard too. Don't pause to think: "How shall I say this?" Go ahead and write, "How shall I say this?" if the thought occurs.

6. **When stuck, write, "I'm stuck."** Or whatever comes to mind. Some kids need to hear that it's okay if they write: "This is stupid. I can't believe my mother is making me write." The only way to get to the deeper thoughts inside is if we permit the ones cluttering the surface to come out in the writing. So, encourage your children and teens to write whatever comes up.

7. **Allow for fragments and spelling mistakes.** A child who obsesses about spelling may pause to ask how to spell a word. Soothe your child: "We'll fix the spellings right away afterward. For now, I want all those thoughts as fast as you can put them down."

8. **Keep writing until the bell dings. Stop.** Phew! Everyone should be a little tuckered out. Freewriting feels like a race against the wind. It's fast-moving, it's risky, it's free. Freewriting once a week promotes writing growth. As your children get comfortable, gradually increase the length of time.

Caveat: some kids don't like the timer. That's okay! Freewrite without it until they feel finished.

For more fun with freewriting, visit the Brave Writer blog. It features thousands of Friday freewriting prompts, and the website offers tools to help launch a healthy writing life for your kids.

Add *Hygge*

To increase a sense of freedom with writing, use an array of writing implements such as gel pens on black paper, quill and ink, markers, sidewalk chalk, pastels, finger paints, colored pencils, squirt bottles of colored water, and fountain pens. All sorts of surfaces can be used for writing too: windows (with window markers), sticky notes, butcher paper rolled out on the floor or taped to the wall, whiteboards and chalkboards, a basement wall, the underside of a table, clipboards. Write on fingers and toes (skin-safe markers). Lastly, when writing grows dull, try a new venue: treehouse, coffee shop, library, on a blanket in the backyard, under the table, at the zoo . . .

Freedom in writing means freeing the writer to write—whatever it takes!

FORMS AND FORMATS

Before we adopt formats for writing, it's essential that children and teens learn to be comfortable with writing (hence the two practices offered above). But what do we do about academic writing forms and formats? Can these be accessed by the Superpowers? I believe they can!

Principles at Play

* **Read the form.** Don't ask a child to write in a format they've never read. The reason fan fiction is popular among teens is, in part, because children have read fiction from the time they were wee babes. They *know* dialogue, cliff-hangers, and description. Likewise, any child can write an advertising jingle—the form is (unfortunately) embedded in all of us from hours of uninvited saturation. If you want your kids to write description, read lots of powerful descriptions. How many teens have read an essay, let alone ana-

lyzed one, before being asked to write one? Read, read, read first. Then . . .

* **Talk about the format conversationally.** Use the readings as grist for a big juicy conversation. Sometimes teens are more inclined to discuss an essay or article if you share it via computer or phone. Note the features, ask what grabbed their attention, identify the persuasive elements or the weak arguments.

* **Interrogate the format.** Ask it your toughest questions. Find out why this form is powerful and worthwhile. Notice its limits.

* **Play with the format.** Treat it like a toy. Can you snip the essay into sections? How do you determine the length of a section? Highlight a repeated term. Ask why it keeps coming up. Triple space and print—clip the sentences and rearrange them to make no sense. Now go back and arrange again—is there a better arrangement than the original? Are there unimportant ideas that can be eliminated? Reimagine the format to match today's writing opportunities. Instead of a book report, consider writing a Facebook review or a book's dust jacket or creating a PowerPoint presentation.

* **Practice, practice, practice.** What are the key ingredients in the format? How might you use them? Test the theory and write a little bit in the style of the original.

Math and Science

Let's tackle the big two. Everyone knows that mathematical and scientific aptitude is the true measure of intelligence, right? At least, that's what anyone in the STEM field wants us to believe. Unfortunately, if rote instruction is the primary model for teaching STEM, only students with natural aptitude will find it interesting. The rest of us will think math and science are difficult, boring, and irrelevant.

Understanding is the fruit of *learning*, not rote *training*. Back when I was in the third grade, I memorized some of the times tables incorrectly. When I scored low on the test, I panicked! I didn't understand what I did wrong. In fact, I didn't understand the essential meaning of multiplication until I taught it to Noah—by then I was thirty-five years old.

Kids who bake, woodwork, and quilt have a better grasp of what fractions are about than a child who encounters them on worksheets. The worksheets can be meaningful once a connection to the real world is made. But typically, it's more challenging to get to that same understanding in reverse. Children who game online, join robotics teams, and play chess are open to mathematical principles.

To think like a mathematician or a scientist, curiosity is the way in. Remember the Great Wall of Questions (Chapter 5, page 73)? Use that practice to stimulate mathematical and scientific inquiry for a week. Stir up a raging curiosity. An engineer friend of mine used to pose mathematical questions to his children while driving in the car. He'd spot a semitruck and ask: How many whole frozen chickens do you think would fit in that trailor? Together, they'd build a strategy to make a good guess.

He used to play a game with his kids where each one guessed whether the next traffic light would be red, green, or yellow. If they were correct, a red light earned two points, a green light earned one point, but a yellow light earned ten. Naturally, the person with the yellow light took the biggest risk, but also experienced the greatest reward if they happened upon a yellow light.

When I first heard these two stories, I marveled. It had never occurred to me, even once, to play games in the car that related to math. Our driving games always centered on language.

Starter Questions

What percentage of "life" do I still have after getting blasted by my opponent in this game?

How many gallons of water fill our backyard pool? How can I figure that out?

What is the right ratio of chlorine to water to ensure that it's safe to drink? How do we know this?

How do TV shows get to our television?

Why does the nuthatch hop upside down on our tree?

How many miles is it on the freeway to downtown? How many exits are there? How many exits per mile?

Why do lightbulbs burn out?

What causes my computer screen to show animated characters that move? How do they move?

Is there a difference between vitamins injected into my food (cereal, for instance) versus vitamins that are naturally a part of the original food item (an apple)? Which are healthier?

What is calculus? When do people use it? Does everyone think it's "hard"?

What temperature does water boil and freeze at in Celsius and Fahrenheit? Why are they different numbers? Who decided that? Which is easier to use?

How far away from Earth is Saturn? How cold is it? What makes up its rings?

Principles for Understanding in Math and Science

* **Ask questions.** All of them, lots of them, even ones you can't answer. Before you teach a process or lesson, have your child guess. "We have these three groups of two marshmallows. What's a quick way to figure out how many there are total?" "How can we make fingerprints?" "Why do leaves change color?"
* **Make the connection tactile first.** Games, manipulatives, tools (like microscopes, rulers, and beakers), puzzles, tricks, and experiments speak to children. Look at online videos of the thing in action if possible. Board games are wonderful tools for practicing a variety of math skills naturally.
* **Rote learning should follow understanding.** Before a child can be expected to memorize math tables, repeat the experience of sorting and combining using a wide variety of items—whether 4 + 4 buttons or 15 − 8 apples.

* **Use math textbooks in new ways.** Let your child page through a math book the same way she paged through the poetry book, looking for what piques her interest. Dive in, see if the problem is too difficult, look backward in the book for skills to solve the problem. Learn just enough to work the problem. Is something still missing? Treat math like a journey of discovery. Challenge your children to create tests for you. Ask them to consider any other way to get the same answers—ways not present in the book. Expand their thinking to that of "problem-solver" not "right-answer-getter."

* **Study by topic.** Take a break from linear sequential learning from time to time. Pick a topic and go deep. For instance, if it's time to learn algebra, stop doing the problems and take time to explore the history of algebra. What is the "story" of algebra? Then return to the lessons and application. Science can be approached similarly— solar system, hurricanes, kitchen chemistry. Visit the nonfiction section of the children's library. Check out a cluster of books on one topic and read them for a month. Find experiments online (or in a book) that relate to the topic.

* **Collaborate!** Too often, math becomes a solo activity without friendship, camaraderie, or conversation. One mother, Melissa, discovered that doing math problems at the same time with her son during his online math lesson transformed his experience: "My nine-year-old has had an aversion to his math lessons ever since we started, and thus, this part of our day tends to take verr-rrry long. . . . Then the other day I had the idea to grab a pen, some paper, and sit down next to him while he did his lesson. When the practice problem came up on the screen I wrote the problem down on my own sheet, as he copied his. Before I knew it, we were both racing to get the answer before the other person. There were smiles and laughter, and a look in his eyes that showed interest. We breezed through *two* whole lessons that day and every day thereafter. The change in him is remarkable."

Tea Times Two

Nadine, a Canadian mom of two, shared that her son found it difficult to sustain concentration while working on math problems. One morning, he asked his mother if she'd make him a pot of tea: Nadine made two pots—a blue one for her son and a yellow one for her daughter. They lit a candle and sipped tea as they worked the problems. It transformed how everyone felt about math—they remained engaged longer and dropped their natural resistance. Creating a gentle, welcoming space transformed the math book; no new curriculum needed.

Math and science do have characteristic challenges. They appeal to a certain kind of thinking that is not natural to everyone. Barbara Oakley, author of *A Mind for Numbers*, reminds us that some people need more time to master math and science, and that's okay. "You may be surprised to discover that learning slowly can mean you learn more deeply than your fast-thinking classmates. One of the most important tricks that helped me retool my brain was learning to avoid the temptation to take too many math and science classes at once."[4]

Concentration for long periods of time can wear out children who "just want to get done." Remember: when all else fails—sweeten the deal! Add brownies, add yourself, take more time. Kids need to be reminded that you're on their team when they struggle.

ART AND NATURE

Kids get fidgety, bored, and distracted when they spend too much time at a desk. Children love the change of pace that art represents. Visiting a museum is like time travel to eras past. The abstract world of history springs to life! Nature offers a similar escape. Recent studies in Scandinavia confirm what we all believe to be true: time outdoors, gazing at trees, enhances a child's attention span for the rest of the week.[5] Fresh air, the embrace of nature, feeling the scale of your being—all good for learning.

Art appreciation doesn't have to mean studying art history necessarily. When my family made trips to the Cincinnati Art Museum, we didn't wander aimlessly. We picked our favorites and visited them every time. We drew ancient Egyptian artifacts in little notebooks, like the old, curly-maned lion. We counted cherubs in medieval paintings, and we purchased famous painting postcards from the gift shop, using them for a treasure hunt to all the best artwork in the museum. There's nothing like seeing a painting in print first and then meeting it a second time in person. That second meeting is powerful! Like a real date after meeting someone promising on a dating app.

At home, I hung prints and kept large anthologies of art in a basket. We enjoyed a video series called *The Story of Painting* (by Sister Wendy, now available on YouTube). Watching this enthusiastic British bucktoothed nun effuse about art turned us into passionate fans.

Sometimes my children would describe a painting and I'd jot the description for them; other times they'd write their own response. I kept these in a notebook to page through. I hung several of the drawings and narratives on the wall (they're still there).

We approached nature study similarly. Our family spent copious hours peering at the sidewalk in our suburban condo unit looking for pill bugs and snails in Southern California. Lucky for us, we moved to the Midwest mid-homeschooling and were introduced to chipmunks, squirrels, raccoons, and backyard birds.

To make nature connections powerful, we liked these ideas:

* **Bird feeders:** We hung bird feeders on our trees, and a big backyard bird poster on our wall next to the window. We kept count twice a week for the Cornell Lab of Ornithology (a nationwide backyard bird count that collects data from backyard birders). We

learned to make our own suet and tested a variety of birdseeds. Liam studied bird biology for high school.

* **Field guides:** I supplied field guides for birds, insects, wildflowers, trees, and more to help us name the natural world.

* **Journaling:** The art of nature journaling was introduced to us through the Charlotte Mason method of home education. In our house, that meant taking clipboards outdoors, drawing the scene, recording the temperature, and adding details (like the raccoon we spotted). We kept these entries in clear page protectors in a three-ring binder.

* **Hiking:** Most states have state parks with hiking trails. In California, we found trails to hike *down* to the ocean and tide pools, which we examined, naming all the tiny shelled creatures and urchins. The English are big believers in getting outside every day no matter the weather, so we adopted that attitude as well. We fulfilled that goal with snow skiing in winter and puddle stomping in fall and spring.

Quick Tips for Outdoor Trips

* Bring water, sunscreen, and snacks.
* Give each child a small backpack or ziplock bag for collecting natural items (so you don't have to carry *all* the rocks).
* Provide one or two field guides.
* Keep clipboards and sketchbooks in the car. Take photos to use for drawing later. After the hike, find a place to draw near the parking lot (so you don't have to lug supplies around).
* Hike for under an hour. "Leave while they're happy."
* Encourage water play—bring a change of clothes and towels.
* Carry a plastic bag to collect trash you create or find. "Pack it in? Pack it out."

There are so many ways to enjoy nature: caring for pets, planting bulbs in the fall and a garden in the spring, counting the leaves on a tree branch and graphing the rate at which they fall, and keeping a seasonal table to display natural artifacts (pinecones, bird's nests, acorns, river stones, lavender, feathers, seashells, igneous rock, fossils). For a more permanent nature collection, dedicate shelves of a glassed-in cabinet. Create museum cards to name the item, where it was found, and an interesting feature.

Art appreciation and nature study expand a child's vocabulary. The sense of scale that nature provides (we are small, the universe is big) and the sense of epoch that art reveals (paintings are snapshots of life from another era) *show* children more about history and time than lectures. Not only that, literature, poetry, metaphor, and song draw deeply from these two fields. Strong connections help kids tap into the "cultural cache."

Global Citizens

Voting, participation in community life, being a neighbor—these matter! One homeschooling friend named Barb said to me once, "My kids may not go to an Ivy League college, but we're raising them to be good citizens—solid members of society." That objective struck a nerve with me. How do we shape a child's self-understanding so that the result is, "I want to be a neighborly neighbor; I want to care about my community"? We do it through the social sciences.

That said, textbook teaching in these fields has deadened the study of history and political science for millions of students. Who cares about a war from thousands of years ago? Why should it matter who figured out farming before everyone else? And if our country's government is a democracy, how important is it to understand monarchy or communism? The social sciences help our kids become global citizens.

History

Home educators are gaga over the study of history. When homeschool moms gather, they can be heard passionately discussing the mummification practices of ancient Egypt or the appalling child labor laws of nineteenth-century England. It's as though once you get two to three decades under your belt, history springs to life as essential and thoroughly absorbing. The classical education four-year history cycle, historical-fiction unit studies, the fond gaze given to Charlotte Mason's dusty old reading lists of a century ago . . . Parents pursue history with passion!

Kids? Some jump in, but many glaze over. Yesterday, two years ago, and two centuries BCE are hidden behind the same veil of "unreal time." What they care about is happening now!

Thinking like a historian means being in touch with the *effects* of the passage of time. In concentric circles, establish your children *in time*, then expand to include family, community, state, country, continent, globe—reaching backward to connect to other eras and stories. History is the collection of reports about the past that we examine and evaluate over and over again. There is no "fixed" history. Each era understands what went before in new ways.

Because history is story-centered, we can access the past through the power of adventure tale. The narratives provide a basis for the day when "time" clicks into place. That said, focusing exclusively on history as "story" misses an opportunity to *think* like a historian, even at a young age. The following guide can be used to explore how a historian examines and interprets events. Each layer asks you and your children to consider two experiences: familiar and not familiar yet. The study of history depends on a capacity to stand in the shoes of the community at the center of the historical moment—and to do so without immediate judgment. It's a challenging skill, even for adults!

LEARN TO THINK LIKE A HISTORIAN, IN CONCENTRIC CIRCLES

All About Me

Begin with your child and do the following:

* Create a timeline for today. Snap photographs of a day's activities. Print them.
* Working with your child, sequence them in the right order. Discuss why one photo comes before another and what clues help you to make that determination.
* Do it again with photos from a full week. Same process: print, sequence, discuss.
* Now take photos over the course of a month. Sequencing at the end of the month should be more difficult.
* Include all kinds of events (toothbrushing, trips to the store, playing with toys, watching TV, skinning a knee, eating a snack, taking a bath). The sequencing gets trickier the longer the wait between taking the photos and then revisiting to sequence them.
* Talk about all the clues you use to help remember what happened when (including a calendar). Evidence of seasons or holidays or birthdays? Notice that a sibling was present in one photo and not the next because he had gone to soccer practice. This kind of detective work establishes sequence, time, place. Discussion about correlating information establishes historical fact. Interview family members with photos in hand to see how they remember the event.
* Post a timeline of photos on the wall with dates and times in colored pencil.
* Retell the story of the day, week, or month using the pictures. Then ask: What isn't shown? What memories do you have of the day/week/month that aren't in the photos? Do those memories matter? Can they be recorded and added to the timeline? What happens if we preserve some memories and not others? What did

we learn about the main individual in the photos? What did we learn about the "supporting cast"—other members of the family or friends who are in the photos? What else stands out?

All About the Family

Reach back a little further and look at your extended family. Share photographs from your own childhood with your children. Find pictures of your children's grandparents as kids. Aunts, uncles, cousins—compare photos of their younger selves to how they look today. Are there photographs of your childhood house or car? Where do these sit on the timeline of your family history? Make one! Draw a long line in the middle of a sheet of butcher paper and post the pictures along it with dates.

Ask questions of the photo, such as:

* Who are the people in it and what are their names?
* What year is it? What month? Can you identify which day of the week?
* What story does the photo tell? What might have happened right before it? What might happen right after it?
* Who took the photo? Is there a way to know or guess?
* Name all the items in the photo. Can you? Do you know what they are and who they belong to?
* Are there any obvious symbols to establish the year or date (for example, visiting a cemetery for a fallen soldier, birthday candles, a high school performance)?
* Add any other questions that occur to you as you look.

Now, pair the photos with memorable events that occurred during the time of the photo. Wars, natural disasters, technological breakthroughs, presidents (or leaders of your country), notable births or deaths. Use the top of the timeline for your family's experiences and the bottom of the timeline to include national/global events. This project can take several weeks or months (one family I know used an entire year). Add detail as you gather information. Feel free to contact relatives for interviews and conduct online research.

Expand Your Work as a Historian

What important events are occurring in your children's childhood that will be remembered? Correlate well-known events with members of your family and their story to demonstrate that history impacts real people, just like your family.

All About Your Home Culture

Your community, city, country, continent—the places and people that make you, you—shape history! Does your family celebrate religious holidays? Are you in a country where your spiritual beliefs are the majority or the minority? What is the story of your country's ideas about education, government, religion, and natural resources?

Explore how habits are interpreted in different ways in other cultures. For instance, research breakfast foods around the world. Try eating other breakfasts—soup and fish? That's how they do it in Japan. As you include cultural variety in your understanding of history, you open the door to *past* cultures as unique and bound by time and location too.

All About the World

The first three categories (self, family, culture) focus on modern life (within the last century). Your children are now ready to imagine other centuries and parts of the world. Let's do it!

* **Read stories—myths, legends, histories.** Read a variety of viewpoints (avoid the temptation to get all your information from the same source).
* **Act out scenes and activities.** When we studied the Puritans, we made up our own list of infractions and created a set of cardboard stocks. When someone forgot to clear their plate or said a taboo word, they went into the stocks for a minute (by egg timer). We

also dipped candles, we dyed muslin fabric by boiling onions and beets, and we lived by firelight for an evening.

* **Visit sites.** Field trips to historical locations are ideal. Make use of YouTube and documentaries when travel is not possible.
* **Learn about the culture, not just the events.** Why would Egyptians enslave people to build pyramids? What drove western Europeans to colonize the world? Why didn't China venture to North America to set up colonies? Cultural perspectives were at work in these decisions.
* **Use a timeline.** I love the book *The Timetables of History* by Bernard Grun. It's designed to show history and politics, literature and theater, religion and philosophy, visual arts, music, science and technology, and daily life throughout time from 5000 BCE to the end of the twentieth century. It's somewhat Western-centric, yet it is still a useful tool to see the events and categories side by side.
* **Watch documentaries.** Films that include footage of ancient sites and archaeological digs, and locations for current events, wars, and human rights struggles, are powerful tools of education.
* **Watch the Olympics.** Use the parade of nations to identify countries (with a globe or Google Maps as the countries enter). Look up their languages (so much fun!) and capital cities. Choose a country that is not your own to follow in the games. Learn about the host country.

Cross-Cultural Study

If possible, travel! Go *there*. Lots of homeschoolers find a way to get to other places and countries as part of their home education project. If you can't, find communities that have come to you. Los Angeles has many that our family visited: Olvera Street (Mexican), Chinatown, and Little Saigon, for instance. Going to cultural festivals (Oktoberfest, the Italian or Greek festivals, the tulip festival) provide kids with a chance to learn about other foods and customs, dances and songs.

Political Science

Use election season (if your country has one) to learn about the system of government in your country. Watch debates, read about candidates, campaign, and compare and contrast the parties. Hold a mock election in your own family. Give speeches.

Teach young children about their nation's flag, the Pledge of Allegiance (in America), and a basic framework of state versus country, or city versus province. For teens, comparing government systems and state versus federal rights is appropriate. Look at the monarchy system of the medieval era and compare it to the modern era: democracy and communism as two solutions to royal rule.

The social sciences give you and your kids a chance to find their footing in a complex world of diverse people and ideas.

Play Games, All Sorts

Shall we tackle technology and game playing?

Every parent I know considers tabletop games *good for kids*. Online and computer games? Not so much. Computer-generated games are seen as a threat to a child's intelligence, are described as "addictive," and are considered to be "enemies of the state" of learning. Let's back away from the edge of despair and begin with games universally approved by parents.

TABLETOP GAMES

Board games teach without nagging. Counting, dispensing money, reading, turn-taking, applying strategy, marshaling vocabulary, winning and losing while staying friends, sustained attention, repetition, reading dice . . . the list goes on! Cards offer a similar experience, plus they show kids how a single set can be transformed into countless games. Tabletop games provide a wide array of opportunities to learn academic skills as well as to think strategically. They come in collaborative versions now too, where the players compete with the game itself, rather than each other.

ONLINE GAMES

Online games have similar properties, even if the structure is different. You play against the machine or yourself or online opponents. Strategy, following rules, reading, calculating, sustained focus, learning to win and lose gracefully, immersive narrative . . . online gaming appeals to children in part because the child is building their own action story. It feels like entering the movie, not just passively viewing it. Computer games bring the board game to life.

Seen in this light, games of all kinds lead to a plethora of skills and aptitudes that benefit kids. They also naturally draw on our twelve Superpowers. The main difference between board and online games is that tabletop games tend to be out in the middle of the room for everyone to see. Computer games are hidden behind a screen and occupy the imagination of the game player and no one else. If you want to have a better experience of your gaming child, ask to watch your child play. Pull up a chair and watch what your child does for an hour. You may have a change of heart.

Purchase Games and Play Them with Your Kids

1. Witness gaming in action. Play tabletop games, watch your child play online games (sit next to them).

2. Best advice I ever got in homeschooling: whenever a child asks to play a game with you, drop the agenda and play.

3. If you want to attract more interest to a subject, find a game that features it. There are games for math, language, geography, history, nature, science, and strategy. Spend a whole morning playing with no hurry to finish.

4. Card games count—all kinds. Go Fish and rummy, as well as Yu-Gi-Oh! and Pokémon.

5. Use the "clear the coffee table" strategy and leave the game out to be discovered (tabletop, card, and video games).

6. Make your own game patterned after an existing game. My kids created Clue using our house as the model, and Trivial Pursuit for *Seinfeld*.

7. Outdoor or backyard games are great for engaging the body.

8. Learn to play your children's favorite online game. (They'll love you forever.)

Take a Cue from the Digital World

Last week, I strapped on my Apple Watch and skipped down the stairs—two flights—to the basement with a loaded laundry basket. I looked down. My watch was dark. It had not been charged. Disaster! I resented that I couldn't "count" the stairs toward my ten thousand steps. There are days when I need five hundred more steps to make my count and I hustle out the door at 11:30 p.m. to squeeze them in under the midnight wire. My watch is the best exercise partner I've ever had.

Digital designers have tapped into the secret to self-motivation: quantify and celebrate. From badges to bells to "like" buttons, human beings love the chance to measure and mark achievements. Traditional instruction relies on carrot-and-stick techniques—reward the student with stickers or punish with low grades. Today's children expect something else. They're accustomed to bells and whistles when they beat a level in a game. They want to unlock new tools and powers to attack the next challenge.

There's an entire field of study called "gamification theory" dedicated to identifying the sweet spot between effort and celebration. Kids rely on celebratory music, lights, chimes, and unlocked tools to grow motivation to tackle the next challenge. Every kid wants that! Heck, every adult wants that—which is why wearing a Fitbit is not just a fashion accessory, but an adult's chief way to stay motivated to exercise.

Why are adults more interested in taking the stairs at work because a watch keeps track of the steps than simply because it helps us avoid heart attacks? The right reason is too abstract for the daily commitment— death seems far away, but a bright completed circle on my wrist is immediately satisfying. If rational adults *know* they should exercise for health but prefer working for the daily badge, how much truer is it for children who can't be made to feel that "college admission" is a reason to write an essay in seventh grade?

How might we use some of these "gaming elements" to help our home-schools?[6]

Gaming Elements

* Narrative (story—with heroes and antagonists, places to go, and mistakes to avoid)
* Immediate feedback (you click, something happens that you understand and need)
* Fun (music, lights, bells, delightful images, magical results from risks)
* "Scaffolded learning" with challenges that increase (not too easy, not too challenging)
* Mastery (for example, in the form of leveling up, or joining a team, or repeating the joy of accomplishment)
* Progress indicators (points, badges, leaderboards, also called PBLs)
* Social connection (chat while playing, comparing your skills to others')
* Player control (player determines when to play, how long, which character, what weapons or tools, what risks to take, what risks to avoid, and more)

I find this list instantly inspiring. For instance, what's the "story" that informs math instruction? I remember when my second-grade teacher taught my class about counting. She told the story of how ancient people kept track of herded animals. Before human beings had invented symbols for numbers, people kept track of their herds by collecting sticks to represent each sheep on the hill. One stick equaled one sheep. A big bundle of sticks would represent a big herd of sheep.

Of course, as the herd grew, matching each stick to each sheep became tedious. The first step in managing the count was to group the sticks into smaller, similar-sized bundles. The teacher then did a magical thing. She drew hash marks on the blackboard to represent sticks. She drew one diagonal line through four vertical lines to show us a bundle of five. Suddenly we could count bundles. A thrill ran through me. I *got* it! The miracle of the story of counting was riveting (I still remember it today more than forty years later).

Applying that one idea—narrative—to any subject is a fantastic way to draw your kids into a subject. Consider the others: What forms of PBL can you create for your child in any area of study? Coupons for treats? Brand-new colored pens to use once they "beat a level" in copywork (writing a complete paragraph in one sitting)? What about mastery of times tables? Using the idea of a leaderboard, create a multiplication chart in

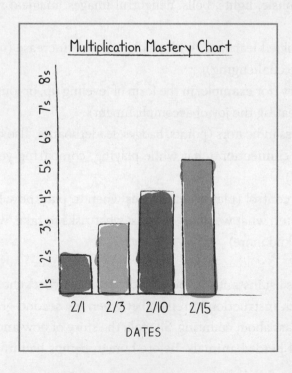

bar graph style. After mastering a set, the child can color a bar that measures the achievement, showing progress as the bars get taller and taller.

(Alternatively, if you're artistic, create an imaginary planetary system or a magical tree to color in one leaf set at a time. Sky's the limit here for creatives!)

How might you encourage social connection for a subject? A book club party? What kind of control can you give your child? For instance, goal setting or creating a cozy context or deciding what time of day to work on the subject?

Gaming need not be the enemy of learning. Let's adopt some of its strategies and see our children's pleasure in learning surge.

PARTY SCHOOL

I went to a progressive public middle school in Malibu Canyon in the 1970s. Each year, the entire seventh grade enacted a Renaissance Faire for a full school day. Students had to ply a trade or skill to barter to enjoy the booths and offerings. We used class time to make costumes, do research, and learn about medieval life. The fated day arrived each spring. Every seventh grader got to miss all their classes to participate in candle-dipping, leather-working, and court-jesting.

Perhaps that's why it occurred to me decades later to throw a party when I studied California history with my kids. Noah (fourth grade) and I hosted a Gold Rush party for other homeschool families. Our party included a Pin the Gold Nugget on Sutter's Creek game with a hand-drawn map by Noah. We built a sluice and stocked a sandbox with fool's gold, a garden hose, and punctured pie tins to pan for gold. Noah researched historical figures of the time. He put each one on an index card and assigned the characters to party attendees. We sewed small bags to hold the panned gold and then used a set of scales to measure the weight against licorice or a glass of sarsaparilla so that miners could purchase refreshments. The party ended with franks and beans cooked over a fire and a sing-along to "Oh! Susanna."

Any subject can benefit from a party mind-set. Since we're home, why wouldn't we throw a party? Even one party a year is enough to add texture and delight to a child's experience of learning. Parties include guests, foods, games, activities, party favors, decorations, and music. Here are a few ideas to try:

* **Book club parties:** Invite friends to read the same book your child is reading. Meet at the end of the month for a themed party. My kids held a book club party for the *Harry Potter* series. They decorated cookies to look like each of the characters, they played Trivial Pursuit, they sorted themselves into houses, and they argued good-naturedly about what they expected to happen next.
* **Math party:** Set up table stations with manipulatives and problems to solve. Include paper or whiteboards. Check off a score card that keeps track of your answers and attempts.
* **Solar system tea party:** Hold it at night! Look through a telescope, binoculars, or black construction paper tubes. Read poetry about the stars and planets. Make apple slice moons and star-shaped cheese cutouts. Memorize the planets in order.
* **The report:** Pick a topic (for instance, a foreign country) and do research for the report. Invite friends over to experience what you've learned. Make posters with facts and illustrations for decoration. Prepare food, learn to wear traditional dress, draw a map and play Pin the Star on the Capital complete with blindfold and spinning. Write the report after the party is complete.
* **Birds:** Examine a raw whole chicken to identify wings, legs, neck, breast, innards. Test different types of "beaks" (chopsticks, tweezers, turkey baster, toothpicks, ladle) to eat different types of foods (gummy worms, sunflower seeds, Swedish fish, raisins). Make a pinecone bird feeder with suet or peanut butter rolled in birdseed. Examine feathers of different types (contour, flight, down). Listen to bird calls and name the bird.

You'll think of many more. Preparing a party changes the mission of learning and makes it communal, celebratory, and special. Children gain a slew of additional skills: working to a real deadline, writing invitations, hosting, preparation and cleanup, and being experts.

Try It!

When learning becomes stiff and lifeless, apply a Superpower to the subject. The next questions invariably become: How do you keep a semblance of order with all this inspiration afoot? Can you measure your progress and know that your family is on track for the broader goals of education (completing high school or mastering grade-level math)? The next section helps you sustain the magic.

PART THREE

Sustaining the Magic

When I think of home, I think of a place where there is love overflowing.

—"HOME" FROM *THE WIZ*

You've cast the spell for learning. What do you do on the days when home is anything but magical? Tantrums, siblings picking at each other, fights over cookies—yes, even cookies could cause a meltdown in my house! How do we sustain the magic—the optimism and joy that we wish to see in our children's education? How can we manage the inevitable ups and downs of energy, interest, and vision? What's the plan, Sam?

CHAPTER 8

LIBERATION FROM SCHOOL

To Schedule or Not to Schedule,
That Is the Question (Answers Inside!)

School's out for summer. School's out forever.

—ALICE COOPER

Some parents are gaga over their decorative planners and Bullet Journals. Can't live without them! I'd been seduced into believing that a well-ordered calendar was the magic wand for homeschool success. I successfully implemented a daily schedule for my two oldest kids for three whole months. Right at the zenith of my gratification, ten-year-old Noah declared: "I hate my life." Shattered, I realized that my idea of success and his didn't match. I returned to essential questions: What is learning? How do I measure it? What is the relationship between inspiration and discipline, joy and steady effort?

Unschoolers treat an ordered schedule like a taboo, replicating the school system and undermining their children's natural ability to self-instruct. Eager to try a better approach, I ditched the schedule. I adopted the unschool doctrine wholeheartedly. We burst into new energy: *This is the way to a happy, free homeschool!* Until it wasn't. The helium escaped our balloon of happy learning; I couldn't figure out how to sustain that level of natural curiosity every day—and neither could my kids. I caught them drifting aimlessly through the house. Paralyzed: I didn't want to overly direct them, but I also couldn't bear their sudden listlessness and apathy. I knew that *real* unschoolers weren't having such a flat experience, but I didn't know what to do.

Over the next several years, I experimented (like you do) with as many philosophies of education as I could. Each one felt fraught with both amazing power and tedium, until one day, I reconsidered everything. I turned my attention away from homeschool philosophies and toward our daily lived experience. In other words, I dropped my *school* focus and, instead, paid attention to my *home* life.

✳ HOME, NOT SCHOOL ✳

Homeschoolers: we're at home—that place we return to where we kick off our shoes, rip off our bras, and flop onto the couch. We *yearn* for home after too much time away. Home is where I get to *be myself* without the pressure to be some other version of me.

When I began homeschooling, the temptation to transform the house into a school (it's baked right into the word "homeschool") was profound. Yet home and school combine about as well as oil and water. In school, you need a hall pass just to pee! In school, you can't flop on a couch—you're trapped in chairs attached to tiny desks. Class starts with a bell. Snacks are scheduled. Behavior is monitored and evaluated.

What happens at home when you impose the structure of school? Irritation. Children instinctively rebel against turning the place they love into a place with pressure and guidelines. They also know that the imposition of "the homeschool schedule" is false. They watch you take a text message in the middle of the math lesson. They see you dart to the refrigerator to grab a glass of juice for the toddler while you were supposed to be reading aloud.

In your bones, *you* know that you're not required to live up to the schedule you set. Everyone knows it! You make exceptions for yourself freely—which makes sense. You're at home. Home is all about accommodation of each person's needs and wants. People come first—not the schedule.

To have a more effective home *education*, I realized I needed to abandon the trappings of school and harness the energy of home. I dropped my allegiance to the sacred "school schedule." Instead, I adopted the more forgiving "home routine."

✳ Routine, Not Schedule ✳

Have you ever planned a week of meals for your family? On Sunday, you head to the store to purchase a list of ingredients. Breakfast, lunch, and dinner—times seven days.

Monday comes: oatmeal for breakfast, grilled cheese for lunch, and stir-fry for dinner. So far, so good. Everyone eats; everyone is satisfied.

Tuesday arrives: a breakfast of scrambled eggs and toast. You all eat it with pleasure, using the designated ingredients. Out of the blue, a text message arrives from your best friend: *Can you meet us for lunch at the park? Don't worry*, she writes. *I've got tacos and chips for everyone!*

Oh no—what about the eating schedule? What will you do with the lunch you have already purchased and planned? You reason: *I wonder if I can get the kids to promise to eat the tuna sandwiches with dinner so we don't get behind.* Of course, they agree to do just that, because picnics are fun! But when dinner arrives, tuna sandwiches plus baked chicken and mashed potatoes is too much food. Your children swing their feet under the table, whine that they're full, and promise to finish the leftovers at breakfast.

The pressure of the eating schedule mounts. What must be consumed the next morning? Cheerios, half-eaten sandwiches, and cold mashed potatoes. Just to catch up. Lectures ensue: "You promised to eat it all and now you won't. That's it. No more picnic outings for you!" Your children, stuffed, exasperated, and confused, wonder what they've done wrong.

Theater of the absurd. What parent would stuff a child with food to keep up with a meal schedule? Yet many parents run their homeschools just like this. Scheduled learning based on numbers of pages, days of the week, sometimes even times of the day, leads to performance anxiety. I had a friend who didn't take a single Monday holiday ever because her curriculum had scheduled pages for every Monday of the year. She hated to "get behind." Schedule feels like this judgmental, critical aunt with the hair growing out of her mole, who looks down on you for not keeping up with her exacting expectations.

The truth is, we don't eat by schedule. We eat by routine. We purchase foods that can be prepared for any of the three meals so that we'll be able to eat when we're hungry. If we get a better offer—someone invites us to lunch—of course we're going to scrap our tuna sandwiches. When we return home, we simply eat the next meal—we don't also stuff ourselves with leftover tuna sandwiches. In fact, sometimes we realize we had a *better* eating experience by *not* eating the planned meal.

Fun Aunt "Lady Inspiration"

Education benefits from a similar strategy: embracing a routine over adhering to a schedule. If you homeschool according to a schedule, it's tough to allow inspiration to lead. Inspiration is your fun aunt—the one who brings cans of Silly String to class. Lady Inspiration wreaks havoc on a schedule. She comes in the form of an invitation to abandon the plan—that's her chief mode of transport. Alas, inspiration is not a lengthy visitor. Once the can of Silly String is empty, she departs without so much as a goodbye! What do you do now?

Parents who temporarily abandon the school schedule worry that their children will get behind in academics; they wonder if the detour to inspired learning was worthwhile; they double down. But what if we treated learning the way we treat meal planning? Sure, we can plan a week's worth of lessons, but we gladly follow inspiration to a better learning experience. After inspiration leaves, we simply pick up where we left off.

Does this work? Can our children *learn by routine* rather than schedule? The routine is sturdy: it's there when we need it, ready for us to resume. Not only that, when Lady Inspiration moves on to her next family, we aren't left wondering how to fill the empty hours. My unschooling dilemma was quieted. I had a plan for how to spend our days when our inspiration ran dry.

In my family, our routine looked like this most years:

* Wake up whenever (once rested).
* Eat breakfast and play for about thirty minutes. I usually spent some time on the computer and listening to the radio before the day got going. The kids played with blocks, clay, dolls, arts and crafts, or video games.
* Gather in the family room for an hour of read-aloud time, which included a chapter from a novel, an Aesop's fable, a poem, a paragraph from the current nonfiction read, our history text, and a couple picture books for the littlest ones.
* Head to the kitchen table for copywork/dictation or handwriting pages, phonics and vocabulary, grammar or logic—our "language arts" portion of the day.
* Use our bodies to learn—math facts, prepositions, our home address, letter sounds.
* Take a break (jump on the trampoline, get a snack, run in the yard with the dog).
* Tackle math (game, worksheet, manipulatives).
* Eat lunch.
* Work on a project (history, writing, science).
* Have free time or take a trip to the library or a movie.

This routine could be adapted if we had a dentist appointment or when my friend called to offer free passes to the petting zoo. I ditched the day's plan to feed the goats. Goat feeding is almost *always* a better exchange on learning than filling out a worksheet. The next day, we returned to the routine—the predictable pattern to our days together.

Most people agree that *eating* by routine is obvious. If you miss lunch, you really *aren't* behind in eating. What about subjects like math or grammar, though, that depend on a series of steps? Isn't it possible to get behind in those? Shouldn't these be scheduled?

"Getting behind" implies that you believe the program designers know the pace at which *your* child *should* learn. Because you *are* at home, you have a front-row seat to whether your child is, in fact, learning the material. If it is true that you have become so cavalier about your child's education that you're traipsing around town every day and not dedicating time to mastering phonics or skip counting or exploring the solar system, you have the complete freedom and prerogative to turn down the "better" offers. Stay home. Focus on your routine until you feel that your homeschool has stabilized.

That said: most people do not lead from inspiration every day. Having a learning routine and a predictable pattern to eating and sleeping help you stay sane. Not everything can depend on a child's outsized curiosity or a parent's inspired initiative. Establishing habits brings calm rather than anxiety.

Interval Training

There's no magic number of minutes, hours, days, or workbook pages that will reassure you that your child is educated well enough. Once you capitulate to measuring a child's academics by external standards, you'll never rest because those standards shift year to year and subject to subject. Instead, focus on growing stamina and competence.

To learn anything means to apply your current set of skills to the new challenge without losing heart. Some lessons require greater concentration or sitting with the discomfort of not being good at the "thing" yet. That's why stamina is so important in learning. The axis of learning goes like this: the newer the concept, the greater the effort required to master it. If the concept is familiar or built from an existing framework, and the next step is not too big, a child can make an earnest attempt with her current set of skills and energy to learn.

One model helped me enormously in building stamina to learn. Consider the structure of athletic training. I'm a marathon runner. When we prepare for a marathon, each day of the week we run different distances as we lengthen our mileage week by week. A typical week is structured like this:

Monday: Rest

Tuesday: Run 3 miles

Wednesday: Run 5 miles

Thursday: Run 3 miles

Friday: Rest

Saturday: Run 8 miles

Sunday: Cross-train

Notice that there are rest days before the longest run (each week Saturday goes up by one mile). Sunday is a "cross-train" day, which allows for aerobic activity of a different kind.

If we apply this model to homeschool, what would happen if you talked with your child about goals for math, for example?

The goal is to learn the multiplication tables by the end of February. It's January now. What if we set up a training schedule to help you grow into your times tables?

That routine might look like fewer practice problems on some days and one day per week that mixes up all that's been learned up to that point, with more problems than any other day. Why wouldn't there be rest days or a day where you play Yahtzee as your cross-training day? Example:

Monday: Do 3 problems

Tuesday: Do 5 problems

Wednesday: Do 3 problems

Thursday: Take the day off

Friday: Do 8 problems

Weekend: Play Yahtzee for fun!

What would it look like to work on phonics and reading? Could you "read" a wordless book first, then try a book that has only words your child knows how to sound out, then read a book to your child, then try a book with the most recently acquired phonics? Do just a page and then have a big snack and hug for all that effort?

My running partners and I looked forward to snacks on our long runs. Like, we *totally* obsessed about them. Mile 6, mile 12, and the end of the run at mile 18 held magic—cherry Life Savers, blue Gatorade, orange slices. Manna from heaven! All that effort rewarded.

What if your child reads a paragraph with you, sounding out with all her little heart? What if she pauses to take a big swig of her favorite juice before the next effort? We forget that our kids are working their mind-muscles—concentrating, making sense of abstraction. They can get there if they know they aren't required every single day to push *just that much more* because you said so. It helps if they can see the pause coming, marked by a deliberate break. Use the interval-training mind-set to grow stamina. Competence will follow as your child becomes more and more fluent in the skill.

Seasonal Schooling

I have a saying: classical education in the fall, unit studies in winter, and unschooling in the spring. There's a tendency to be ship-shape schoolish in the fall when all the books are easy to locate and every pencil is sharp. By winter, home educators gravitate to unit studies and projects. But once the first waves of spring arrive, everyone wants to head outdoors! It's natural that big projects, sports, and nature hikes dominate. Everyone's tired from all that "scholastic" effort. Plan your homeschool with these seasonal shifts in mind and you'll feel so much better when your homeschool dribbles to an unceremonious end in mid-May. Use the fall for the dedicated book study, plan projects for winter, and schedule field trips in the spring, for instance.

If you use the ideas of routine, interval training, and seasons to help you create reasonable expectations, your kids will feel so much more able to cooperate with your academic goals for them.

✳ Meaning-Rich Materials ✳

The predictable pattern of a lovingly created routine will fall flat, however, if the materials you choose are tedious. Unschooling parents know this. They're allergic to traditional curricula. Mention on an online discussion forum that you're teaching reading with a phonics program and prepare yourself for a sound digital flogging! There's a reason they're so staunchly against schoolish materials. Most programs written for education are mind-numbingly dull. They take the adventure of learning and turn it into a system of rote paper production.

I remember my first encounter with a writing program for homeschoolers. I read the sample paragraph in the first chapter. I turned to my friend who owned the curriculum: "Did you like this paragraph?" She looked puzzled. I pressed: "Do you wish there were a second one?" Her eyes widened. She did not. I wished there hadn't been a first!

I told my friend, "If the sample paragraph in a writing program is this unmemorable, why would you want your children to learn to write based on this model?" And that's the problem with most curricula of every kind. If the program doesn't inspire *you* to use it, to enjoy it, to learn from it, why would it work for your children?

We can do better! When I researched math programs, for instance, I looked for materials that made math concepts concrete and approachable, because my background in math was poor. I also knew how dangerous it would be to my children's love of math if all they ever did was fill out worksheets at a certain dogged pace each day.

Math games, picture books and novels about the story of math, hobbies that use math (like knitting, origami, woodworking, Lego, computer programming, online gaming), and running a cookie business were all ways we made math more meaningful in our family. Toggling between skill work and math used in context helped us ground all that learning in real life. It kept us from merely completing abstract objectives for some future date of certification (like college admission).

Homeschoolers are brilliant at bringing meaning to learning when it comes to literature and the study of history. Historical fiction, for instance, brings the two together, delivering beautiful writing about a remote time period and empathy for the people living through those events.

Science instruction lends itself to hands-on activities at home. We can provide enough tools for everyone. We don't have to worry about liability or safety in the same ways schools do. There's time and space to let an experiment evolve over weeks.

To ensure that you select great tools, read programs before you buy them. Ask yourself: *Am I drawn in?* If you're not (if the grammar

Checklist for Meaning-Rich Materials

- You like it!
- The information is presented in a way that you can understand.
- You can comfortably explain it to your kids.
- The materials are attractive. (It matters!)
- The learning experience provokes curiosity, not only rote skill development.
- The lessons are multifaceted (incorporating mind and body, heart and spirit).
- Your children also like the program and buy into it.
- Materials apply to multiple subjects (across the curriculum).

book is so tedious, you resent it before you begin), set it aside. Look for a program or book that invites *you* to think more deeply about the subject. Try some of the problems or exercises yourself and see how they feel to you. Make sure you aren't asking a child to do what you find dull and lifeless.

When all else fails, triangle in help. Find another adult who is passionate about the subject and let that person teach your children. I swapped writing instruction for math tutoring with a dear homeschooling friend. I brought passion for writing to her kids and she brought a dish of candy and mathematical aptitude to mine.

☀ Invitation, Not Insistence ☀

Once you've got a vision for your routine, you may wonder how to enforce it. What if your kids fight you? That moment is excruciating! Every so often I read a Facebook plea from an exasperated mother: "I'm ready to give up! My kids hate learning and I don't know what else to do." How can these little people topple your big efforts of love on their behalf so easily—with an eye roll or a shrug?

When I got exasperated with silliness or the lack of attention to the lessons I had prepared, I whipped out the parental power tool: insistence. I'd simply get bigger, louder, and angrier. I'd *insist* that the work had to be done, whether they liked it or not, and if they didn't get with my program, dire consequences would follow. I prophesied doom, when dealing with teens: "You'll never get into college" and "No one will hire you." Insistence, coercion, shaming—these power tools sever the parent-child connection. Suddenly your kid is cooperating to get relief from accusations and punishments. Gone is the love of learning and nurtured bonds of homeschool.

Instead of *insistence*, try *invitation*. At the moment of your greatest frustration, pause. Ask yourself: *How can I invite my child to participate in today's plan?* Here are some examples of how to invite your children and teens to the table of effort:

* **Notice what's missing.** Surprise, mystery, risk, or adventure? Adapt the experience to provoke one of these enchanted forces— move the lesson to a new location, introduce new tools (like gel pens and black paper for copywork), add treats, create a cozy environment, introduce an element of danger (like a drill or sewing machine or candles), help your child set a personally meaningful goal.

* **Become curious about the topic yourself.** Find the edge of *unknowing* so that you approach the subject with your own interest on display. *Lead* by doing the activity yourself, without preamble or explanation. You might complete a page of the workbook after breakfast, in front of your child, without saying a word. You might mix chemicals for a science experiment. Perhaps you set up the board game or copy a passage from your own book. Lead by doing.

* **Collaborate!** Do the page, project, or process *with* your child or teen, side by side.

* **Give time to explore.** Save the hard work for another day. Begin by handling, contemplating. Try a little, take a break, discuss.

* **Suggest micro-lessons.** Ask for a single effort (one word, one sentence, one thought, one problem, one chapter, one conversation). Celebrate the concentrated effort.

* **Appeal to the mind, body, heart, or spirit connection.** Introduce surprising facts, add movement, pair the lesson with a subject your child loves, find the angle that tugs on a child's natural compassion.

Insistence establishes hierarchy and resentment. Invitation creates connection and responsiveness. Choose which one you want to characterize your home life.

Measuring Progress

Even if you get the plates spinning and establish connection with your children, how do you know you're making *measurable progress* in their educations? The biggest challenge most parents face is the anxiety that they can't know their child is learning what ought to be learned at the appropriate pace.

Schedulers are tempted to rely on *plans in the future* to reassure them that they'll get a certain quantity of information "covered." Schedulers like to plan tasks and then mark them complete. The quickest way to kill joy in learning, however, is to put too much trust in planning ahead. How can we quantify inspiration's contribution to homeschooling?

Planning from Behind

Many parents feel guilty when they follow inspiration. I remember when my family became immersed in World War II. We watched endless videos while I recovered from childbirth. I read the book *Number the Stars* to my children from my king-size bed, while breastfeeding the newborn. The older kids drew pictures to go with their descriptions of the book. Noah built a rudimentary website with his dad to showcase tanks. We checked out books of WWII weapons and my kids traced them onto tracing paper.

Each day over dinner, our family conversation organically turned to aspects of WWII—sometimes in-depth, other times flippantly. My children played with dress-up clothes, pretending to be war orphans in need of medical care from the Red Cross. It dawned on me at the end of the six-week period that I hadn't planned any of it.

Did I feel elated and pleased with this excursion into a worthy topic? I didn't! I felt guilty. I worried that I was cheating in some way. In my imagination, dedicated home educators made lesson plans, thought ahead, and studied history chronologically. They organized reading, math, and spelling units. Why couldn't I plan a quality unit study like those superior mothers? I wondered if I could "count" the postpartum period as "real" education since, in truth, I was scrambling to fill time.

I can't say when it happened, but one day it dawned on me that *this inspiration-led learning* was the core of homeschooling. I realized that I *had* spent hours reading books; discussing learning online; attending homeschool support groups, conferences, and seminars learning about learning. I kept notes of movies, books, math games, and poetry that I hoped to share with my kids one day.

All those ideas and recommendations worked invisibly inside me, influencing how I spent time with my children. In the moment when I needed an activity or course of study, I drew from the swirl of ideas that had secretly rearranged themselves into practical action. Inspiration rarely appeared when I stared at a blank planner page, begging my mind to create an integrated course. Rather, inspiration caught me off guard when I moved with the currents of enthusiasm, my energy level, my children's curiosity, and available materials. In those moments, our fun aunt Lady Inspiration led the way, and she did so beautifully.

I learned to *count* these educational excursions by recording them on my calendar *after* they occurred. I call this practice "planning from behind." It turned out that many of my best homeschool plans grew inside me without my conscious awareness, only to flower into a wonderful learning experience serendipitously. I noted these learning moments confident that we had been on task—deliberate, thoughtful—even if spontaneous. I had a record of how all that reflection and study had led me to some of our best homeschooling experiences. I also could see what was missing—which subjects had not risen to the level of importance that month. My mind would then deep-dive again into more reading and conversations that would help lay the groundwork to explore those subjects.

The framework of our days (the routine) remained, but I allowed the role of inspiration-led learning to grow. I trusted it more over time and became amazed to see how powerful it was to both pay attention and lose focus, to research and ponder followed by concrete action and practice.

In addition to keeping a calendar record of activities and learning experiences, I offer you two tools that will revolutionize how you track your children's academic progress. These tools work well with both the routine you establish for your garden-variety days, and those weeks when your fun aunt Lady Inspiration shows up.

Sketch a Narrative

The learning you care about *is* likely happening in your home right now. It's especially likely if you've been applying the Superpowers of brave learning. Let's shift our gaze from measurement by rubric, to *sketch by narrative*.

When a child writes a paper for a school assignment, a teacher reads the paper, marks the mistakes, and evaluates the content. She then assigns a letter grade. The grade tells a parent that the child is performing well, average, or poorly compared with age-mates. The letter grade offers no description of the process the child went through to write the paper. A grade can't tell a parent whether or not the student enjoyed or hated the assignment. The teacher's grade doesn't account for a child's illness that caused a poor performance, nor does it highlight the interconnections between subjects that show up in the writing. Grades are a stingy system of evaluation.

In homeschooling, we get to dump summary judgment of school work. But with what do we replace it? Too often, parents joyously give up grading, but then succumb to pressure to do year-end testing or to get an evaluation by a teacher, or they call me and ask if their child is "writing at grade level."

You can reassure yourself that your children are learning, and you can pay better attention to their struggles and strengths, if you shift how you assess. I recommend writing a *narrative sketch* of a single twenty-four-hour day in your homeschool each month. Because homeschool is not confined to six hours of instruction, it's important to jot down the events and conversations that occur even when "school" is not in session. That means that the great conversation about how cavities are formed on the way to the dentist counts. It means the bathtub recitation of "The Three Little Pigs" by your first grader matters.

If you include all the activity from Lego building to Minecraft playing to the questions about why dogs sleep so much and how to make suet from scratch, as well as soccer and ballet practice, you'll discover that your children are learning all the time—and from more sources than you realized. Not only that, you'll also pay better attention to struggle and find new ways to address it. You may also note what you haven't featured in your children's educations for a while—*It's been two months since we did a science experiment.*

Your narrative may include a child's tears when he can't sound out the words quite yet, or the eleven-year-old's complaints because she finds handwriting painful. Writing a narrative sketch once a month allows you to gently face the truth of what's happening in your home, rather than reacting with shame due to low test scores. By writing a sketch once a month (rather than daily), you also resist the temptation to micro-assess (focusing on day-to-day fluctuations). Some parents enjoy doing

Written Narrative Evaluations in College

Until 2001, the University of California, Santa Cruz, issued written narratives of student performance crafted by professors (the university has since succumbed to the pressure to issue grades for the sake of graduate school applications). My sister, who majored in Spanish at UCSC in the 1980s, received written evaluations from her professors describing her progress.

St. John's College (Annapolis, MD, and Santa Fe, NM) uses oral narratives to evaluate student progress instead of grades. At the end of each term, students attend a meeting called a "Don Rag" with their "tutors" (what most colleges call professors). These tutors describe the student's participation in class, their strengths and weaknesses, and their overall performance in front of that student.

Written and oral narratives require the instructor to pay close attention to the student, not just the student's output. The information in the narrative is meant to help students improve for the next term. Attention to the whole student is what makes these evaluations so valuable.

them weekly. Pick the frequency that frees you to celebrate your children's learning adventure.

In my Homeschool Alliance coaching community, the monthly written narrative sketch has transformed member homeschools. The discipline of a page-long description of activities and conversations on a single day gives parents reassurance that they are, in fact, leading a lifestyle of learning, and that their children are making meaningful progress in subject areas and personal development. Parents can compare the September narrative to the one in March and May and note the growth. They also have a place to put their worry. They can wonder in October if a child's struggle in handwriting is temporary or a sign of a larger issue. By March, they'll have more information to compare. These narratives can then be compiled to submit to a state assessor, if your state requires end-of-the-year certification to continue homeschooling.

When I began this practice in my family, I kept my Monthly Narrative Sketches on a private blog. I liked being able to pair photographs with my descriptions. Some parents prefer Word docs, and others still journal in a notebook. Use the tool that motivates you to keep the practice going.

WHAT TO INCLUDE IN A MONTHLY NARRATIVE SKETCH

* **Conversations:** Direct quotes from your kids; big juicy family conversations about any topic, including nontraditional school subjects like film, puns, sports, and gaming
* **Reading:** Books, websites, game manuals, song lyrics, inspirational literature, and poetry your children read to themselves; your reading to your kids—books, poems, instructions, websites, placards at the zoo . . .
* **Activities:** Dance, quilting, archery, tying shoes, telling time, making a smoothie, dumping all the pots and pans on the floor and banging them like drums, reading spontaneously to a sibling, texting a friend, painting, bathing self, training a pet, arts and crafts,

gardening, bird-watching, attending Shakespeare camp, martial arts, making stop-action videos

* **School subjects:** completing X number of problems or pages in math; grammar, spelling, and vocabulary in copywork or dictation; French; applying a subject to a real-life activity; mastery of a rote skill; co-op or online classes
* **Games:** Tabletop, video, cards, online
* **On the way:** Meals, bath time, lying in bed, trips to the library or orthodontist—all the conversations and tiny learning moments tucked into the ordinary routines of life
* **Household tasks:** Cleaning, laundry, organizing, meal prep, yard work
* **Spontaneous learning:** Moments when inspiration grabs hold and won't let go!
* **Challenges:** The stuff that feels hard, upsetting, or puzzles you or your kids
* **Field trips:** The zoo, library, museums, historic sites, travel to new places
* **Parenting:** Questions about how to reach a specific child; how well you give attention to each child individually and as a group; sibling rivalry

Write your narrative in your natural voice. Don't treat it like a checklist assessment. Tell the story of a single day. Take notes throughout that day to remember the conversations and topics. Don't worry about picking *the best day* or *the right day*. Any day will do because you'll continue this practice once a month. Eventually, you'll have a full portrait of your homeschool and how it functions. In fact, sometimes it's worth writing about a day gone wrong. You may notice characteristics of how that day went when writing about it that help you adjust for the future.

Below is one example of a narrative sketch from Homeschool Alliance member, Christina. To read others, join the Homeschool Alliance (bravewriter.com/homeschool-alliance).

Christina's Blackberry Fool

We started the day today with a trip to the library. I always look forward to seeing what my children wish to learn about every week. They find so much delight in searching the shelves for the perfect book (or, to be a little more realistic, thirty to fifty books) on whatever strikes their fancy at the moment. This week, the theme seems to be insects and amphibians. This is no surprise, as we have spent the first few evenings of summer waiting for the sun to set so we can chase and catch lightning bugs and toads. The kids aren't the only ones who look forward to this every day. I think I get more pleasure out of seeing them run through the yard with their arms up, squealing, trying to catch lightning bugs. My heart warms when I hear, "I found one!" from the darkness, only to see one of my kids appearing from up the street, toad in hand.

So, we schlepped home with our three totes of library books and decided that next on our agenda was whipping up some Blackberry Fool. Today is Tuesday, and that means Teatime. We are going to read *A Fine Dessert* by Emily Jenkins. It is about four families, over four centuries, who make and eat the same dessert. We thought it would be fun to make some and eat it while we read. We usually read poetry or do an artist study during Teatime, but we thought we would change it up a little today.

While the Blackberry Fool cooled in the fridge, my daughter sat down to do her French-style dictation taken from a passage from *Secret of the Andes*. She then decided that she would draw and label a butterfly's parts and lifecycle for her science journal.

The Fool is still cooling, and all three kids are in the family room collaborating on a robot motorcycle, patiently waiting for Teatime. I love moments like these.

We did not do a math lesson today in favor of using a cooking lesson with lots of measurements. The afternoon will be relaxing, with some quiet independent reading time and perhaps a movie

> night. Not every day is as relaxing and laid back as this one. That's
> what we love about homeschooling. We take days as they come,
> go with our moods and interests, get excited about what to do
> next.
>
>   Time to check the Blackberry Fool . . .

Try It!

The purpose of the Monthly Narrative Sketch is to reassure you that
learning is the ongoing, continuous state of affairs in your household.
These portraits also offer you a gentle, nonjudgmental glimpse into
struggle. Writing a narrative alerts you to fatigue; braces that were recently adjusted, making a mouth so painful it was difficult to concentrate; and more. Most importantly, your family's unique story of learning
becomes apparent—how subjects interlace and relate to one another,
how your family grows together. No two families will have the same
story. It's exciting to discover what yours is.

THE SCATTERBOOK

The second tool I recommend is what I call a "Scatterbook." You're probably
familiar with scrapbooks and journals. The Scatterbook is the name I gave
to my assorted collection of notes in a notebook. I didn't have neatly organized sections or even clearly delineated categories (though feel free to
create them if that works for you). What this book included, however, was
a wide array of notes that helped me be a better home educator, such as:

* I jotted thoughts from books I read about education or a specific
  school subject.
* I drew bright, abstract shapes and colors, overlaid with keywords
  that put motivating concepts in a place where I would see them
  regularly.

* I copied important quotes about learning and parenting.
* I made endless lists—books, birds, parks, plays to see, family-friendly films, websites, businesses that let us take field trips, artists, musicians, materials to introduce Shakespeare, meaningful poems, etc.
* I taught myself to appreciate art; I also learned to draw.
* I made notes about individual children; I kept track of who needed extra attention.
* I journaled about what *I* was learning (history, math, science) while teaching my children.

HOW TO KEEP A SCATTERBOOK

1. Pick a notebook. Functional or pretty, you choose. Or download an app like Evernote.

2. Begin. Don't wait for a special day to start. Start now. I began by copying quotes from books I was reading while my kids did their copywork. My copywork practice helped sustain my children's practice as well.

3. Freewrite. Kick-start your Scatterbook by freewriting about education and your learning adventure.
   * My happiest memory in school was _____.
   * If a genie could grant me one skill, aptitude, or awareness, I'd ask for _____.
   * If I didn't have children, what would I study for my own enjoyment?
   * What do I wish I understood better right now?
   * Who told me I wasn't good at _____? (Did I believe them? Do I still believe them? Why or why not?)
   * If I could add one thing to my life to make me happier, what would it be?
   * How do I know I've made progress (in anything)?

4. Collect memorabilia. Glue a few envelopes into your Scatterbook to hold brochures, ticket stubs, receipts, and flyers. Or if your Scatterbook is digital, photograph these and put them in a folder.

5. Label a page for each subject. Keep track of ways your kids express learning in those areas. When you notice a page staying blank for a long time, plan a day of deep diving into that topic. Give it an all-out daylong treatment. See how that goes.

These two tools, the Monthly Narrative Sketch and the Scatterbook, will ground your homeschool. They enable you to track your journey, to store your worries in a safe place for further reflection, and to keep all your homeschool aspirations and ideals together.

APPLICATION

1. Begin. Keep your Scatterbook with you.

2. Title and dedicate a single page to each of the Forces of Enchantment, Capacities for Learning, and Ports of Entry. List ideas to help you on days when inspiration flags.

3. Make a monthly date with yourself to review notes and narratives.

4. Community helps! Meet with a group of friends who also keep Scatterbooks and write Monthly Narrative Sketches. Read to each other, discuss ideas for applying the Superpowers, brainstorm solutions to your most pernicious struggles, and *definitely* order mimosas with brunch.

CHAPTER 9

HOUSE-SCHOOLING

Recruit Your Home to Help You Educate
(and That Pernicious Topic: Chores)

An enchanting home is not an ideal home but is made for the
people who live in it. We have small children, and our home
has to allow noise, breakage, chaos, and much physical use.

—THOMAS MOORE,
THE RE-ENCHANTMENT OF EVERYDAY LIFE

We talked about how to create a lovely space for family life and home education in Chapter 6. We discussed how to create a soothing routine that alternates with flashes of inspiration in Chapter 8. These principles will fall apart, however, if the place where all this good stuff happens is not conducive to a messy, creative, open-hearted learning environment. I'm talking about your house! We're all stuffed into this box together— how can we inhabit it harmoniously without tripping over cast-off shoes and running out of clean dishes? How can the house itself contribute to a thriving home education?

✳ THE MESS ✳

Let's get one thing straight. Homeschooling is messy. The more kids you have, the messier it is. When a family lives in the same square footage all day every day, without a break, it's impossible to maintain showroom-worthy housekeeping. In fact, a homeschool house more likely resembles the "before" picture in a home-remodel TV show. I know mine did.

Additionally, the incentive to replace ancient linoleum, for instance, should be low. There's a difference between creating a home that is cozy and inviting, and one that is immaculate, gorgeous, and up-to-date. Is there an ideal "house" for homeschooling? Yes! It's yours—the one you have right now. The key to a great homeschooling house is to *use* the house you have to its fullest. That means your priority cannot be protecting its resale value. Your priority is to make your house safe and inviting for learning risks.

In fact, your home doesn't have to be a house. It can be an apartment or condo or townhome. The "house" can be big or small, with or without a yard. The less you care about the furniture and the floors, the freer you'll be to have the homeschool of your dreams. Tell yourself you can remodel the kitchen after your kids graduate and move away (that's what I did).

Unfortunately, today there's a glut of online images showcasing other homeschooling families living an idyllic, rustic, Pottery Barn semirural life. One scroll through Instagram can dash your best intentions to let go of *House Beautiful*. Should you also have creeks and blackberry brambles right outside your French doors? Are gray-taupe walls, unfinished bookcases, and high ceilings with exposed wood beams necessary for the most natural learning experience? Are you doing it wrong if you don't keep chickens or haven't started an organic garden? Drop those images now. Your real home is adequate—even in the middle of a city, in an apartment on the eighth floor. The house you have and its unique location are brimming with learning opportunities. See them, use them, relish them.

✳ Farmschool, Cityschool ✳

Because we associate the term "natural" with nature, it's easy to be misled, thinking that to promote natural learning, the best homeschools are also mini-farms. There was a movement back in the 1990s called "Urban Homesteading," where homeschoolers were grinding their own grain for homemade bread, making their own soap, and hanging laundry on a line—while living in the suburbs. I remember a big discussion about how to overturn a home association prohibition against laundry lines in backyards. Abstaining from dryer use felt essential to homeschooling effectively, for some reason. I suppose if we were bringing school back to the one-room schoolhouse model, it felt logical that we ought to re-create frontier life.

I got depressed. I lived in a condo in Southern California. We studied sparrows and juniper bushes for nature journaling. My kitchen was far too small to keep a grain mill or can tomatoes. I had no fenced yard—which meant my kids couldn't play outside without supervision or they'd be hit by cars.

You know what, though? We made the most of every inch of our condo and our neighborhood. Five of my best years of homeschooling happened right there. I didn't care about a formal living room. I decided that someone else had solved the soap "problem" and I could just buy it (not make it). I turned all my attention to providing a great educational experience to my kids. We found a dry riverbed for hikes, we went to the ocean as often as we could, I kept an art table in the living room, and we did bake bread together every Friday night. I bought my flour at the supermarket.

We visited art museums and I hung prints on the walls. I suspended my children's artwork, not their clothes, on a laundry line strung through the kitchen. Because we were renting, I didn't care about carpet stains the way I did when we bought a house. What a gift it was *not* to care! We used our garage sale furniture to the max. When Johannah painted the couch, I thought, "Oh well. There's fifty bucks down the drain." I tossed a blanket over it and we moved on.

Dotty, my neighbor during those years, was a savant in maximizing a house's spaces for learning. Her son wanted to build a fort (with hammers, nails, and boards of wood). Since our condos didn't have yards, she set him up in their parking space. He built his fort in space D, next to parking space C, which held a minivan. That's how it's done.

Being in a densely populated town had huge advantages. All the places we wanted to go were within five miles of us: post office, rock climbing gym, library, youth group, park, nature center, ballet, soccer, speech therapy, and farmers' market. When we moved to our house in Ohio, everything was fifteen to twenty minutes away. I was stunned to watch my easy, at-home life turn into car-schooling.

All this is to say: your house right now is brimming with unique learning opportunities. There isn't a better one somewhere else. Is it worth moving out to the country? If you don't mind driving to activities. Is it worth it to stay in the city? If you don't mind driving to nature. The point is, put your attention on learning, not on the house. Use the one you've got to its fullest potential and supplement with driving.

✳ Design Your House ✳ to Play to Your Strengths

One homeschooling family I know lives in downtown Toronto. In their tiny apartment, this mother placed a table for schoolwork right under the window that overlooks the busy city streets. As the kids work on grammar, they watch traffic roll by or see snowflakes light up under streetlamps. Bins on wheels store materials they need so that homeschool supplies can be rolled out of sight when company comes. A comfortable couch and a pair of chairs invite kids to flop and read. Bookcases decorate the walls. This family has easy access to all the downtown action from museums to theaters. City life brims with educational opportunity.

I met a family in Boise, Idaho, who made the opposite choice. They moved to acreage just outside the city. Their precocious children adore animals and have a dad who's an expert woodworker. They kept pet dogs, egg-laying chickens, and ranging goats. They needed space for ongoing carpentry projects, rabbit hutches, and archery. A house downtown didn't cut it.

Identify the kind of family you are. If you're inclined to Shakespeare, film, and ballet, perhaps your basement needs to be transformed into a media center. If your family is great at gardening, get a home with a big yard or sign up for a community garden (like they have in New York City, Portland, Vancouver, and other big cities). Gardening with your kids will allow you to live your best homeschooling life because that's what you love. Whatever your family's personality and culture, pass it on to your kids, using your home to do it. If your house can't support it, find a place in your town that does and plug in.

Too often, a family idealizes *some other family's strengths* and assumes that they should adopt those behaviors to "be good homeschoolers." Let that go. Ask yourself: *What are we good at? What are we into? What do we want to feature in our homeschool?* Use the house you have as best you can, and supplement with excursions for whatever else you need.

* Or Move . . . ! *

There's nothing wrong with moving, if you get to the point where you *know* in your bones that the move will allow you to live your best life. My sister moved from a big house in a farming town to a tiny rental on the coast so that her family of surfers could surf every day. They needed the beach more than they needed square footage. Another friend of mine moved her family to Hawaii from Minnesota because of their passion for water sports. Another family I know uses the father's five weeks of vacation to "world-school"—traveling to other countries. They rent! Why own a house? They want maximum flexibility for travel.

Figure out who you are and find a place to live that helps you be *that* to its fullest. It may take time to drill down to what you need to live your best life. While you think about it, use the current place you have—completely, joyfully, proudly. It's good enough.

✳ House-School Essentials ✳

The next step in house-schooling is to ensure that the space where you live supports the 24/7 activity of home education. Rather than tackling endless decorating projects, focus on making the space where you reside conducive to learning. Painting the walls bright, happy colors is a great idea, particularly if your kids pick them and paint their bedrooms. It's not required, however. It's an even better idea to leave the old carpeting in the family room where your children are likely to use the glue gun and sprinkle glitter. You can't make space for creativity if you're worried about stains. The attractiveness of your house is not the priority when you homeschool. Your children and their education are. Maintain a home designed for that.

For a happy homeschool house, try these:

* Furniture that can take a beating
* Bedroom walls for writing (I mean it! You can paint over the walls when your kids leave for college.)
* Space to create and leave a project in process
* Bins for materials that are easy to find and store (with wheels!)
* Tables of varying heights for various ages of children
* A wall or dining room table painted with blackboard paint
* Floors that can withstand spills, scuffs, and stains
* Play items in the room adjacent to the kitchen
* Enough technology that everyone can have turns (more than one computer, tablet, television, game system, cell phone)
* The mainframe computer in the family room
* Sets of wireless headphones for television so those who want to can watch TV while others play cards or read
* Wall space dedicated to art prints, posters, and signs

* A big whiteboard—use it!
* Comfy chairs
* Stepstools in the kitchen (cooking, baking, preparing your own meal)
* Laundry basket for quick pickups; sort items at the end of the day
* Low bookcases with picture books for small children
* Tall bookcases organized by fiction, nonfiction, poetry, and graphic novels for older kids
* Basket for library books and daily read-alouds
* Empty floor space for puzzles, blocks, Lego bricks, dominoes
* Art table (Chapter 1, see page 5)
* Good lighting!

Invest in quality art supplies and inexpensive sofas. Hang van Gogh prints. Dent your new kitchen table right away so you don't worry about the future dents your children make. Fill a box with bird-watching supplies (field guides, binoculars, birding notebook) next to the window view of the bird feeders. Store all math tools in the same rolling bin (compass, egg timer, calculators, graph paper, sharpened pencils, Cuisenaire rods, coins, flash cards). Pro tip: put all school texts back in the same cubby every single day so that the books never go missing.

Keep a pencil sharpener with the pencils. Stock batteries to go with it. Toss dress-up clothes into a basket in the corner of the family room. Place a globe on a tabletop as a knickknack or purchase a rug that features a map of the continents. Use placemats with the table of elements or the alphabet or fifty states or anything else you want your kids to learn. Stick poetry magnets on the refrigerator and build sentences. Dedicate an entry table or glassed-in bookcase to display finds from nature walks.

The key to a house oriented to learning is easy access to what a child wants to know or what you want a child to know. There's nothing worse than the spark of an idea and not having the tools to do it. If your house is so nitpicky neat that children need permission or adult help to get the right tools, their enthusiasm will wilt before they start. *Accessibility is critical to exploration.* Being allowed to make a mess, even more important.

What is this mess you must accept? Lego bricks where your poor bare feet may tread, spilled water and paint, glue stuck to the coffee table, shoes cast off in the middle of the room, plates with scraps of food ignored while children are absorbed in an activity, a suddenly unprogrammed remote control, clothes left in a heap next to the dress-up bin, markers without their caps, artwork on the couch, pieces of the game gone missing, muddy shoe prints, broken chair legs from tipping backward one too many times . . . You'll think of others.

The point is that you can't expect learning to magically occur if your energy is directed at maintaining a tidy, attractive house. Our need for a perfect learning moment and a perfectly neat environment are in conflict. You must pick one. Famed writing instructor Anne Lamott puts it this way: "Perfectionism means that you try desperately not to leave so much mess to clean up. But clutter and mess show us that life is being lived."[1] Celebrate the messes that show you life is being lived!

✳ Helping Around the House (aka Chores) ✳

I'm reading your mind: "So when can we clean up the mess?" you ask. We've come to the awful subject of "chores." My friend Carol hates the word so much, it's banned from her family's vocabulary. She's never called "washing the dishes" a chore. I admire that! When I think of the word "chore," I freely associate the terms: labor, work, tedium, and obedience. There's nothing about the word "chore" that inspires me to act. Yet for some reason, parents love using it. They're all about duty and chore charts and responsibility and maturity and a hundred other irritating coercions associated with basic home maintenance.

The word "chore" describes the daily required activities on a farm. If you don't milk the cow at the same time every day, your cow will not produce enough milk. Today? Most of us don't own cows. Vacuuming the living room is hardly a make-or-break activity for a household. Let's scale back our urgency around teaching our kids to be responsible house-keepers, and focus instead on what it takes to function in a house twenty-four hours a day, seven days a week, together, cramped into these usually too-small quarters.

You've Got the Power!

Kids don't get to pick where they live. They don't decide on square footage, the size of the backyard, the scale and scope of the kitchen, or how many children to stuff into a bedroom. They have no say in furniture: beat-up garage sale couches or a new off-white Ethan Allen sectional. They don't select the cherry wood floor that must be protected from scratches for resale value.

Parents make these decisions. Then they impose the maintenance requirements on kids under the banner of "chores." Who doesn't assume that children ought to keep house because "they live here too"?

Meanwhile, the requirement to do chores drains energy from learning. If you spend your relationship equity on requiring Marcus to do the dishes, how eager will he be to do his two pages of math? If you nag Penelope about making the bed, is it any wonder you get resistance to working hard at phonics? In fact, some families start their days with chores and then wonder why their children drag when asked to come to the table for lessons.

Let's start over. For the smooth functioning of the family, laundry, dishes, meal preparation, dusting and vacuuming, bathroom cleaning, and yard work are necessary. The question is, who does them? I offer you solutions to consider. Let's start with the most expensive, most effective solutions, and work our way down to what you do when you have no money and a slew of kids, shall we? Here we go!

HIRE IT OUT!

If you can afford it, by all means: *hire it out!* Get a housekeeper, a lawn-mowing service, and a meal-making subscription. Why not? You're a full-time career educator with a gaggle of children.

I know, you're worried about spoiling your kids. Will they learn responsibility if they don't vacuum or swish a toilet? Let me help you with this. My parents hired help for housekeeping and gardening. I never had to mow a lawn, wash a dish, or clean a bathroom. Guess what? I can do all of these as an adult, and I'm a responsible person. So are my siblings. My parents provided these services to our family, which allowed us to be active people with deep interests. Learning to clean a house? Not rocket science, easily learned as an adult. I didn't miss out on some set of skills as a child. I just got to live a full, rich life. I look back on living in a home that was tidy, ready for activity, and felt calm and peaceful. I'm grateful!

So: guilt-free! If you've got the money, give your family the gift of a well-maintained house and yard. Focus on the stuff you love. Learn with your kids; enjoy your house.

QUARTERLY DEEP CLEANS

Maybe you can't afford weekly housekeeping. Maybe you aren't ready to hire out all the yard work. What about a quarterly deep clean of your house, or someone to tackle the mulching twice a year? When the windows are spotted, the carpet is dingy, and you're too short to dust the tall-people places (above the refrigerator, the ceiling fans, the tops of the cabinets), hiring someone for a deep clean two to four times a year is a great relief. It acts as a reset button on your home experience. Getting your carpets steamed or your windows washed before the holidays can give you a lift right when you need it most.

It's possible to maintain the basics as a family team (more on that next). But knowing that there is a thorough deep clean and yard reset on the horizon will help you stay out of the pit of messy-house despair. Hiring professionals to handle these big areas of responsibility is a wise investment to support your homeschooling efforts. Hold off on the new math program and use the money to plant flowers or wash the baseboards. Remember: sometimes what transforms your homeschool the most is creating a peaceful, clean context—making the place you live a place you want to be.

THE "DO-IT-YOURSELF" MODEL

Alas, as an adult, I didn't have a disposable income—even for the occasional deep clean. I remember asking my dad for the gift of carpet cleaning as a birthday present one year. That's how underfunded we were.

To add insult to home injury, I went ahead and had a slew of children—five, to be exact. We lived first in a too-small condo without a yard in California with three boys packed into one bedroom and the two girls in another. Then we moved to a *huge* property in Ohio with a larger house and more bedrooms. Suddenly there was so much yard and house to take care of! My kids became interested in pets so we added two rats, a bunny, two ferrets, and a dog.

The temptation to nag children into performing household chores was powerful. We succumbed. My kids' dad and I set up a weekly housekeeping routine. Every Saturday morning, we all had "jobs" (reluctant to use the word "chore," we called these tasks "jobs," which was not much of an improvement). Each able-bodied child and both adults were assigned one aspect of house maintenance: bathrooms, downstairs vacuuming, kitchen, bedroom vacuuming, and dusting. These rotated weekly. We all cleaned together on Saturday mornings, and everyone got to play music or an audiobook while they did their job.

Not everyone liked doing their jobs. There were complaints and half-efforts. Yes, we resorted to shaming, blaming, and lecturing—guilty as charged. I didn't like any of that and felt powerless for a long time to find an alternative. The one part I did like: we only had to put in effort once a week, and we all did our tasks at the same time. I didn't believe in daily housekeeping during the homeschool week. I was unwilling to spend relationship capital enforcing chores on the days I wanted my children's goodwill for learning.

Homeschooling families address the need to maintain a semblance of order and cleanliness in lots of ways, but the universal experience is that no one solution works for all ages, for all time. One principle that has meant a lot to me over the years was to make sure that the task I asked a child to do was challenging and interesting. Squirt bottles for a seven-year-old are exciting. They're less interesting to a fifteen-year-old. A snowblower is more stimulating than a shovel.

In fact, remember that machines help maintain a house. One family I knew had nine children. This family washed their dishes by hand because their dishwasher couldn't accommodate all the dishes eleven people generated for each meal. One day it dawned on her: they needed two dishwashers. So, they bought a second one, secondhand, and it changed everything for them. If you have a large family, you might need more than one washing machine and dryer. Two vacuums may be essential to a large house. Our family used two lawn mowers for our large yard.

Doing a task as a family and celebrating at the end works well for big projects. When raking leaves, provide enough rakes so several people can rake at once. Blast music, invite kids to jump in the piles of leaves before you bag them, and serve hot apple cider when you finish. Other tasks benefit from swarming. If Mom makes dinner, Dad and kids clean it up. Housekeeping as a group is preferable to solitary tasks. Home-schooling also means *a lot* of meal prep. Consider taking Sundays off every week. Let the clan fend for themselves so the parents can have one day away from the kitchen.

Another principle that helped us: pass the home maintenance tasks *down* to younger children. Teens need to experience work out in the world, not in the kitchen. Younger siblings can take over until they are teens. Admit that housework is tedious—brainstorm ways as a family to live in harmony while providing a baseline for order and cleanliness. Everyone's standards count. Compromise is necessary. Changing the routine occasionally, essential.

In our family, the weekly requirement to do a job became more and more irksome as my kids got older—and particularly after some of them left for college. Dividing up the tasks among fewer people felt unfair. Not only that, my teens' standards and mine didn't match. They were okay with a messy bathroom or an unmade bed or clothes on the floor of their bedrooms. Their differences of opinion grew in volume. I was torn between my need for help (I couldn't do it all myself) and their legitimate different standards around what constituted a clean enough, neat enough house.

HELP! I NEED SOMEBODY

What I needed was help. I realized: Why not just ask for it? Go belly-up, admit my need, and invite my family to pitch in. If my standards and my children's didn't match, what would happen if I asked them to help me meet mine occasionally without shaming them into agreeing that my ideas about *House Beautiful* were more legitimate than theirs?

Before I could ask, however, I needed to take responsibility for my own standards. I had sometimes blamed my kids when the truth was, I didn't have a good system for house management. So, I signed up for emails from a housekeeping guru who sent daily messages that taught me how to take charge of my living space. I learned tricks and tips that relieved me of some of my biggest frustrations. I shined my sink at bedtime; I did five-minute purges of my drawers while on the phone.

I began doing what mattered to me without expecting anyone else to pitch in. For instance, if I saw that one of my boys had a stack of empty pretzel bags and an assortment of dirty drinking glasses at the computer, I simply picked them up. I stopped nagging. I only did what I felt compelled to do in the house, and I let a lot go.

When the mess got to the point where I could not function well, I asked for help: "The kitchen is piling up with dishes. Would anyone have time to help me load the dishwasher? I would really appreciate it." I knew, of course, that I couldn't require yes if my question was genuine. My kids said no many times. I persisted in picking up after them and maintaining a basic level of order that mattered to me. Then I'd ask for help again. I still remember the first time Liam said yes. He looked up from the computer and said, "Let me finish beating this level and then I'll help you." And he did.

Knock me over with a feather!

A few months later, while I was washing dishes late at night, Liam called out: "Hey, why don't you go to bed? I stay up late and can wash the dishes for you later." I was floored! I woke to a clean kitchen.

The pivot to admitting my need and asking for help was transformational for all of us. I discovered that my kids liked helping more than they liked doing chores. I also realized that my standards were malleable. Sometimes my need for order was a cry for someone to care about me. I had to be honest about that. I'd say: "I'm stressed today! Seeing the family room filled with books, shoes, coats, and video games is adding to it. Would you mind helping me do a quick pickup to reset my mood?" There were days when I might explain, "I can't wait to read aloud to everyone! I can start as soon as we straighten up the living space. Who wants to help? Now would be a great time!"

The shift to *owning* my need made it possible for my children to *give* to me. Giving feels different than obeying. It feels like love and reciprocity. I sincerely thanked them when they did help me. It changed our dynamic to one of mutual care, rather than character evisceration about their laziness.

I also lowered my standards. *House Beautiful* could wait. Interestingly, I now live alone and my home is most always tidy. I enjoy the tidiness. But I also miss the people who make the mess. I smile during the messy holidays when my house becomes a home of people loving and living together again.

Try It!

* When you ask for help, if the child says yes, let your child determine *when* they will help you.
* Lower your standards for how they help (accept their effort and thank them).

* Add a little *hygge* to the task (candlelight for dishwashing, audio-book for bathroom scrubbing, smoothie to the lawn mower).
* Do the task together.
* Set the timer for five-minute bursts (a quick pickup, a quick dust-ing, a quick vacuuming). Get some of it done in five minutes.
* Keep one room or space in the house immaculate that is *just* for you. Retreat to it when the rest of the house overwhelms.
* Get rid of stuff. Bag it up and give it away.
* Keep self-serving snacks in easy reach.
* Use paper plates on busy days.
* Give everyone their own water bottle to fill and use (no glasses).
* Teach your kids to do their own laundry in fourth grade. Spend that year doing laundry with your child, then leave the responsi-bility to that child. Let that son or daughter determine how often to wash clothes. (Make peace with your children wearing dirty clothes.)
* Keep the guest bathroom pristine (your task). Leave the kids' bath-room to them. Clean it once a quarter if they won't.
* Give your teens powerful tools for house maintenance (riding mowers, snowblowers, kitchen appliances, power sprayers, leaf blowers). Make household tasks cool.
* Be generous: offer to pick up after your children from time to time, bring them food, laugh at a spilled drink, forgive a hole punched in the wall due to frustration . . .

Admit your need, ask for help, receive what's offered, drop resent-ment, lower your standards.

A happy house for homeschool is one where every inch is used for learning, messes are welcomed, people are more precious than furnish-ings, and household maintenance is a varying standard with fluctuating amounts of help, and we're all okay with it most of the time.

CHAPTER 10

THE PIXIE DUST OF REASONABLE EXPECTATIONS

Embracing Our Limits

Only connect.

—E. M. FORSTER

A mother called to complain about her four children. She went into detail about their flaws, calling them "strong-willed," covering the mouthpiece to yell at them for being noisy. She told me life would be easier if her kids would follow the plan. But no! They refused. She was at her wit's end.

I paused and said, "Four kids. All strong-willed. That's unusual."

"Oh?" she replied.

As gently as I could muster, I asked, "Is it possible they have a strong-willed mother?"

The phone went cold; her quick-paced description of her children's war on homeschool was over. "I hadn't thought of it that way . . . What do you mean?"

I explained—if all the kids resisted her plan, perhaps her plan was the issue. Was she willing to adapt her expectations to meet their needs? In other words, was she the strong-willed, inflexible person in this equation?

If the plan she had crafted would make her children's lives happier and better, they would've jumped at the chance to carry it out. The only person who was likely to be happier if the plan was adopted was this mother. She simply hadn't seen it that way.

✳ Principles for Homeschool Sanity ✳

It takes courage to spend all day every day with your children. Whenever I attended a soccer game with other moms, one of them would say to me, "I could never homeschool my kids. We'd drive each other crazy!" You know what? My kids drove me a little nuts sometimes too. I felt guilty about that. I wanted to spend 24/7 with my kiddos, but negotiating living and learning *all the time* took a toll. I couldn't just "be Mom." I also felt responsible to (serious voice) *provide their education.* Sometimes those two roles came into conflict.

Five Principles Helped Me Keep Going

1. **No two years of homeschooling are ever the same.** Your children get older and change grades. Each child has a unique personality. What worked with one won't necessarily work with the next.

2. **You get bored.** Just because a curriculum is effective doesn't mean you must keep using it. If you're "sick to death" of the reading program, find a new one for the next child. Years pile up—what you loved doing in year three may feel like overkill in year seven.

3. **You can't solve homeschooling.** There's no philosophy or practice you can adopt perfectly enough to end your quest to get it right. You'll reexamine and adapt every year.

4. **Real life intrudes.** Cancer, pregnancy, foreclosure, hurricanes and fires, elderly parents, death, special needs, divorce, job transfers, military deployments . . . There's no escape. The years when

crisis hits, homeschool takes a backseat. (Don't worry—it's flexible enough to accommodate.)

5. **A pretty good homeschool is good enough.** No matter which philosophy you adopt (as structured as classical education or as unstructured as unschooling), you're human. Your ability to put that philosophy into action is limited. You'll have great stretches of imagination and flow, and others where you wonder if anyone is learning anything. Your aim is not perfection, but peace and progress. That's good enough!

I read once that expectations are resentments on layaway. The cure? A wholehearted commitment to reasonable expectations for your homeschool, yourself, and your kids.

✳ REASONABLE EXPECTATIONS ✳ FOR YOUR HOMESCHOOL

EMBRACE LIMITS

One of our Homeschool Alliance coaches, Stephanie Elms, shares this principle regularly: "There are no educational emergencies." The pressure I felt to ensure that my child would be college-ready by sixteen, seventeen, or eighteen caused me to unfairly push my child and resulted in tears, hurt feelings, and low performance.

Instead, I discovered that school standards are arbitrary—designed to herd groups of children through a system. Home is homier. I could allow my child to learn to read at her own pace. One of my kids read at age six and one read at nearly ten. Both are fluent, devoted adult readers today. The date on the calendar they each became independent readers was as unimportant as the date they each took their first steps.

High school math could be spread out over six years or delayed and condensed to three years depending on my child's aptitude. Another child might need four years for junior high. We could postpone college until age twenty. I learned that it was never too late to enlist tutoring for a special need like dysgraphia or dyslexia. Taking a gap year between high school and college became not only feasible but desirable. Learning lasts a lifetime—we don't have to cram it all in by age eighteen.

A second principle follows the first: lower the bar to experience success. If your child is unable to read a chapter book, focus on what she can read. Point out single words she knows on signs or menus. Enjoy sentences or paragraphs together. If your son is struggling to keep up with the math schedule, reduce the quantity of problems per day until he finds his stride. Measure him against what he *can* do, not what you wish he *would* do. Encourage him to set personal goals: How many problems can he give full-hearted energy to today? Accept his answer. Allow for variations through the week. Support him in meeting his goal and celebrate when he attains it.

If we believe that education is unique for each child, we can relax into whatever time it takes to learn rather than flipping out when our kids don't line up with what Becky's children are doing down the street.

THE POWER OF PLAY

Noted education critic and theorist William Reinsmith reminds us: "The more learning is like play, the more absorbing it will be—unless the student has been so corrupted by institutional education that only dull serious work is equated with learning."[1] Institutional learning threatens to rob children not only of the power of play, but even the ability to *imagine* learning as playful. What a blow to our deepest educational goals: the delighted aspiration to know.

When I write about play and learning, I'm not only talking about toys and board games. Play is also an attitude of exploration and freedom. Play implies fun, joy, whole-body participation, and positive energy. When children play, they're absorbed. It's amazing to witness. Somehow their absorption worries us, though. Play is "not serious" enough, or something. Exertion and struggle demonstrate learning, right? Ease and flow must mean our kids aren't challenged. What if we flip our view of education? Play does all the work, if we let it.

David Elkind, expert on childhood and the value of play, reminds us that young children "see this new world as artist, naturalist, writer, scientist, and much more. That is why young children are so satisfying to watch. One moment the child is a naturalist busily examining a grasshopper, the next a writer describing an experience in highly original language, and always the sociologist exploring the potential of social interaction. These many roles are fulfilled with joyous excitement."[2] As children get older, parents lose confidence in joyful exploration as the key to educational growth. We set school schedules and require obedient study. What would happen, though, if we expanded our ideas of learning to include playful engagement at every age and stage?

Fun + Subject = Learning

In the 1990s, I relied on an unconventional source for my primary homeschool program: *Family Fun* magazine. It acted as a terrific "uncurriculum." *Family Fun* put me on a firm path toward that sweet spot: the combination of play and learning. The creators shared my values—hang out with your people, do cool stuff, grow. In hindsight, I can see that these were the seeds of the natural life of love and learning I advocate today.

This early foundation set an expectation inside me—playful engagement demonstrated children hard at work. While parents think about the word "fun" as something to do *after* the work is done, I discovered that children used the word "fun" to mean they had been fully invested. "Fun" for children and teens means "caring," which leads to exertion. Why is there a dichotomy between what we consider "play" and "work"?

I have watched children "play hard," putting in extraordinary effort to achieve the goal they have in mind (whether it's building a fort with blankets, preparing a play to perform with friends, or beating a level in a video game). I've observed their frustration set in followed by tenacity to overcome whatever obstacle is preventing their vision from being realized. If you've watched a child doggedly fold origami, you know that play can look like work.

Conversely, there are times when school lessons, like copywork or a page of math problems, are sheer joy—easy, satisfying, and effortless (the way most of us think of play). Johannah approached copywork like an absolute treat! She made her own paper using a kit, selected a pen that was a pleasure to hold, and copied her favorite passages first in pencil, and then painstakingly traced them in ink. She decorated each page with colored pencil drawings.

As your kids age, it's easy to get more and more serious about schoolwork, forgetting that there are ways to invoke the power of play for teens too. A high schooler who drives can be sent to Starbucks to work math problems, listen to music, and sip coffee. The excursion turns "studying algebra" into an experience of play. Hosting a book club party to discuss literature transforms the lonely isolation of "reading for English 10."

I've often advised that if your teenager is resistant to writing, for instance, make a rule: "You may only write at midnight by candlelight." Some kids like participating in the National Novel Writing Month Young Writers Program as a challenge.[3] They commit to a daily word count in the company of thousands of other would-be novelists. Inject the Forces of Enchantment into a teen's world and watch their appetite to learn grow. Homeschool values play.

The Re-upping Moment

No matter how well you homeschool young children, a day of doubt will come. Homeschooling requires you to commit to a vision—that you are adequate to educate your children. Most parents make this commitment twice. They commit the first time when their children are young. Parents can imagine teaching addition, phonics, and ancient history— they're skilled enough to do that. The re-upping moment arrives as their kids prepare for high school. It's intimidating to consider teaching biology, advanced math, foreign language, and AP classes.

Some parents come to the re-upping crisis sooner than others—they see fourth grade as the "it all counts" moment. Or they see junior high as critical to high school preparation, so they borrow worry from high school requirements right into sixth, seventh, and eighth grades.

No matter what year you're in, get comfortable with re-upping your commitment. The same way you gathered courage for kindergarten is how you face the more daunting upper grades. Each season of homeschool requires a blend of your competence to instruct and guide while triangling in help—adding people to your children's lives who can bring richness and skill to their education. That's how everyone does it.

✳ Reasonable Expectations of Yourself ✳

A Peaceful, Easy Feeling

Peace, ease, progress—I wanted these—and I'm sure you do too. Homeschooling families experience well-being when (1) children are happy, and (2) parents can measure academic growth. In other words, happy kids who learn and grow produce relaxed parents. Miserable kids who are above grade level or happy children who are behind academically produce anxious parents. It goes without saying that miserable kids who resist every educational overture produce alarmed and despondent parents!

The problem with homeschooling as your big bold adult adventure is that homeschool success rests on the cooperation of little maturing people. Homeschooling is not like knitting, where you decide which patterns to learn and how to execute them according to your own standards and timetable. Home education requires participation *from children*. Your sense of pride and accomplishment is locked up in how well they receive the education you want them to have.

If your kids fight your program plans, your ego is on the line. The temptation to put pressure on children to live up to adult objectives is huge. Accountability shows up every Thanksgiving when Aunt Betty pop quizzes your kids with math equations over baked yams, and Uncle Bob brags about the cousins who are honor students at their junior high. If our sense of accomplishment as adults rests on the variable attitudes and behaviors of our children, we're doomed. That can't be healthy.

Powerless and Loving It

Repeat after me: we are powerless to produce academic results in our kids.

Let that thought sit here for a moment on the page. Powerless.

We can provide the resources and conditions for learning to take place, but we don't live in our children's heads. They do the work of learning and growing—we're their witnesses, not their control panels. Their receptivity to learning is directly related to how they feel about their relationship with you and the presenting school subject. Not only that, but because homeschooling and hormones, personalities and passions collide (your kids' and yours), relational peace is variable.

The beginning of sanity, then, is admitting that we can't "do it right." Homeschool is an imperfect work in progress over time with little people. We revise it each year, sometimes each month, and sometimes in a single day. Once you accept your inability to get your kids to be who you want them to be, you can stop striving. Put up your feet, pour a Diet Coke over ice, and focus on connecting to your children and teens. It turns out—that's the key to a great homeschool experience. The good news: you can work on yourself to grow that connection.

Tone of Voice

Years ago in an online homeschool community, the leader said, "Everything we teach can be ruined by a single tone of voice." I've never forgotten it. When a parent tells me that they've "tried everything" and nothing works with their kids, I wonder about tone of voice. Did the parent insist and disapprove right out of the gate? Did the parent's tone of voice reveal desperation or pressure? Did the children feel manipulated and tricked into cooperation?

If you find that principles and practices commonly enjoyed by other families are falling flat in yours, ask yourself: "How have I presented them?" Is your tone stern, urgent, harsh? Do you convey doubt or cynicism? If it's difficult for you to hear yourself, ask a spouse or good friend how you come across around your children. Sometimes we reserve our sweet voices for friends and revert to a dour, insistent tone when alone with our kids.

I've also noticed that home educators who were once classroom teachers struggle. They know how to plan a lesson. They expect their children to jump in and participate with gusto. They feel disappointed when their kids don't notice and affirm their efforts. I remember one teacher-mom telling me she wanted to be back in the classroom because her schooled students knew how to appreciate her hard work.

Fundamentally, however, your kids don't care. They get to take everything you do for granted. That's one of the rights and privileges of being family. Your children don't care about your efforts—they care about your cuddles. They feel no need to affirm your self-worth or your talents. They resist the pressure to help you feel better about yourself as an educator, even while they'll lavish you with love and kisses if you scrape your knee or get bad news. If you use your schoolteacher voice at home, you violate the properties of home—and your children know it intuitively. That's why it's important to learn collaboratively—along the way, together. A democracy of learning.

We are important to our kids. *We* are important—not our lesson plans. We create the conditions for learning when we come alongside and value our children as people, not as our students. All the teaching gets tossed into the bargain when we've gained their goodwill and trust.

Bring your friendship voice to the table—the one who is also curious, who doesn't know all the answers, who wonders aloud, who's inspired by a child's idea, who gets a kick out of her children's antics. Let go of your need to be obeyed, thanked, and appreciated.

SMILE, AND THE WORLD SMILES BACK

One surefire way to foster cooperation in the home is to smile. Smile more. Smile when you speak, and your tone gets sweeter. Smile when you ask for help. Smile when you introduce a new book. Smile when you tackle a challenging project. Relate to your children with kindness, gentleness, and warmth. A smile conveys these readily.

Ron Gutman, founder and CEO of HealthTap, shared in an article adapted from a TED Talk that smiling not only has a positive effect on those around you, but may also alter the course of your own destiny. In a thirty-year UC Berkeley longitudinal study, students who smiled the widest in their senior photos in their high school yearbooks were found to be the most satisfied in their marriages, scored highest on standardized tests, and were most inspiring to others.[4] While correlation does not equal causation, the link Gutman wants to make seems reasonable. Smiling goes hand in hand with optimism and ease in our lives. Your sense of confidence and brighter outlook may grow if you face your challenges with a smile; likewise, you may be more likely to inspire your little people to have a positive outlook if you greet them with a grin.

Smiling also builds stamina. Distance runners know that when the going gets toughest, smiling releases energy to push harder. On those days when it's all going wrong, what if you paused to find one reason to smile? Watch your children until one of them delights you. Toddlers are fabulous for pulling us out of the doldrums, but you may find that if you raise your gaze to your teenager, you'll be moved by the child-nearly-adult flashing in and out of view.

Go first. Please don't require a child to smile at you (that action breeds pretense). However, you may provoke a smile through your own cheerful face. Perhaps smiling feels forced or fake. When that feeling comes, look inside. Remember a moment when you felt genuinely happy with the child in front of you—tap into a memory that brings warmth and fondness—then smile.

One time a child told me that he wished his mother smiled as much as I did. Perhaps his mom was unaware of her serious countenance. With such responsibility on our shoulders, it's easy to hold tension in our jaws. Release it. Next time you load up a request or announce the activity on tap, move your jaw around. Practice smiling to yourself first, then smile at your children. See what happens! It can't hurt.

CONNECTION, CONNECTION, CONNECTION

Jeanne Faulconer, another fabulous coach in the Brave Writer Homeschool Alliance community, reminds parents: "Connection, connection, connection is to homeschool what location, location, location is to real estate." Connection is the most important feature of a harmonious homeschool family. Our relationship to our children can't be built on performance. Enjoying each other lays the foundation for learning. It's *the* essential ingredient, in fact. Makes sense, right? We're together all the time. It helps if children and parents genuinely like and enjoy each other. We get worked up when we don't see academic growth that reassures *us* that *we* are doing a good job. If we project that anxiety onto our children, we short-circuit their receptivity to learning by damaging our connection.

What can we do? We're human. We worry. There's a delicate balance between care to urge our children forward into an education, and pressure that saps their joy and willingness to participate. One of my homeschooling veteran friends told me that whenever she wondered if one of her kids was "on track" (you know, after hearing about *someone else's brilliant kid*), she'd take that child out for lunch. An hour of talking together always reassured her. A child's interests, thoughts, vocabulary, hungers, and imagination reveal themselves when we sit patiently, open-hearted, listening to our children. We perceive the complexity and richness of their learning journey rather than our laser focus on the one thing they aren't doing well enough yet.

Sometimes conversations will be the key to a new path or direction for your child too. What if your daughter is worried that she's not getting the level of help she needs in a subject? Can she ask for a change and will it be heard? Connect to your children. The academics matter, but they follow. Your children's happiness and safe, supportive relationship with you come first. Believe it or not, your children are happiest when they believe you are delighted by them.

✳ REASONABLE EXPECTATIONS OF YOUR KIDS ✳

MINDS BUILT FOR LEARNING

One deliciously freeing insight to support you as you build your parent-child connection is to tap into the findings of the biological basis for learning. In other words: understand how your children's minds work so you don't expect more of them than they can deliver.

Today's top educational researchers challenge the typical curriculum strategy used in most traditional school environments. The complex thinking required to be a well-educated person grows incrementally, over time, with both bursts of new awareness followed by plateaus of integrating what was learned. Schools don't allow for this kind of burst-pause-burst cycle. Students are measured against the phantom "average" student and expected to move at a steady, orchestrated pace through prearranged materials.

Lawrence Lowery, educational specialist and professor emeritus at the University of California, Berkeley, asserts, "For thinking to develop properly, people need a long childhood—one in which children are free from having to carry out survival activities until all the stages (of development) are in place."[5] A long childhood without attention to survival—the kind of childhood homeschool so easily accommodates! The temptation to burden our kids with forecasting their eventual responsibilities once they leave home undermines the free and slow-paced childhood they are meant to have to grow the most developed minds. By keeping them home and attending to their natural development, we create space for the burst-pause-burst cycle to occur naturally and effectively.

Schools, on the other hand, push students to more and more advanced types of thinking earlier and earlier. A friend of mine shared through tears that her son, a passionate student of classical music, had failed three of his academic classes in the local high school. The blow to his self-esteem was acute. He didn't yet see the need for history or psychology. He wanted to devote himself to the baritone saxophone. A long childhood for this student would mean allowing him to dive deeply into his love of music while making the academics less taxing for a season.

Home education provides the ideal context to move at each child's individual pace in traditional subjects while affording ample time for that child's passions and pursuits. Lowery continues: "Educators act as if the distance from childhood to intellectual adulthood is measured only in terms of quantity—that is, as students get older, they acquire more experience, greater information, and broader knowledge."[6] Lowery warns that this is "an incomplete view of intellectual growth."[7] Each increasingly complex view of the world is built on a previous organizational structure. Our task is to remember that a learning plateau is not the absence of learning, but the critical stage of skill consolidation.

When we focus on what a child *ought to be studying* rather than on how our children are *processing what they study*, we skip a critical developmental milestone that leads to fluency. The foundation of a secure education at home, then, is connection—seeing the truth about your child's interests and aptitudes, and then providing the space for those to flourish, all while scaling the study of academic subjects to an appropriate pace for that child.

COMPANIONS AND CHAMPIONS

Our kids know we are for them when we're their companions and champions. Remember the second Capacity for Learning—collaboration? That's the companion piece—coming alongside, supporting, providing guidance and resources. We can take companionship a step further. To be a child's champion means you believe deeply in the abilities of your child, even if your kids don't yet. Your child may think she'll never learn to read. A champion goes further than vague reassurance ("Don't worry, honey. Everyone learns to read eventually"). A champion takes on the challenge with the child, believing the best the whole way, identifying strengths and skills that will aid the journey and pointing them out: "You've mastered your phonics, which is the first step to reading. Sounding out will come to you when you're ready. We'll keep practicing together." Reasonable expectations of your child enable you to be a supporter, rather than an evaluator.

That Time When . . . My Bapa Was My Champion

When I was thirteen years old, I spent two weeks with my grandparents in Chicago. As grandparents do, they bought me an art kit on a whim, just because I showed interest in it. The kit included several copies of the same colorful image, a small picture frame, adhesive, an X-acto knife, and a box of wooden matches. The goal was to cut various layers of the picture, and then build a 3-D image using cut-up matchsticks and a special kind of glue.

Two nights before I flew home to Los Angeles, I couldn't sleep. I felt so guilty! My grandparents had bought the kit, and I already knew I would *never* make it. I felt entirely intimidated by the instructions, the glue, the matchsticks, the X-acto knife. My grandmother overheard me crying in bed. She asked me what was the matter. I confessed—I wasted their money, I was never going to make the project, I should give it back.

My grandmother called my grandfather into the room and told him my predicament. They exchanged glances and then said: "Get up! We're going to do the project now." It was eleven o'clock p.m.!

We trekked down to the kitchen table in the dark. We climbed into the breakfast nook and turned on a lamp. My grandma made tea and cookies. My grandfather cut matchsticks and showed me how to hold the knife so I could cut them too. We made mistakes, we got confused, we worked at this project for well over an hour. My grandparents complimented my efforts, they delighted in the emerging 3-D image, and they celebrated when we finished.

Companionship. My champions. They believed in me. But they didn't believe in me from afar or through a lecture. They "helped my unbelief" by taking the journey with me, treating my anxiety and worry with care and kindness.

I placed the little framed art project on my bookcase in my bedroom. It reminded me for years that my grandparents loved me and believed in me. It also reminded me that I could do hard things with support.

Schools provide teachers and coaches, the next best thing. You get to be the best thing: companion and champion.

Countless times as a homeschooling parent, I thought of the compassionate, gentle way my grandparents supported me out of my crisis of confidence. When handwriting was too challenging for one of my kids, I looked for ways to make it more inviting and less intimidating. We drew on walls, we used gel pens and black paper, we wrote on tiny sticky notes. When sounding out words became such a struggle that my daughter collapsed into tears, I put away the workbook and read a story aloud instead. Naturally, I learned these lessons the hard way—after insisting, shaming, and lecturing about hard work—none of which worked.

My motto became *When the tears come, the lesson's done.* I also learned that when the tears come, it's time for love. Love feels like offering support or relieving pressure. Sometimes a child simply needs that extra ballast of parental backing and new ideas as they struggle to get through challenge. Other times, they need a break—allow them to step away from what causes pain, knowing that the child can return another day to try again. It's not always apparent which is the right choice each time, but since there are only two options, try one. If it's the wrong one, try the other. It's okay to double back!

What matters: being open to the varying abilities of our kids and standing with them as they grow. All we have are love and trying.

Connecting to your kids comes easily when you maintain reasonable expectations of your homeschool, yourself, and your kids. When you align with reality (the way things are rather than how you prefer them to be), you release pixie-dust-level energy into your life. If you slather your family, self, and homeschool with a big yummy layer of love, warmth, forgiveness, and cookies, while attending to the academics, you'll realize your dream of peace and progress. We've tried grades, stern voices, and punishment. Let's give connection and love a try; then we can meet back in twenty years to see how it turned out. Are you game?

CHAPTER 11

AWESOME ADULTING

Expanding Our Horizons

What is the point of being alive if you don't at least try to do something remarkable?

—JOHN GREEN

I spoke as the keynote for our local homeschool graduation. I explained to the gathered graduates what they may not have known about their strict, conservative parents: these parents were badasses. I knew better than to use that language in a church, so I described their parents this way: "They're the hippies of the twenty-first century. They're 'sticking it to the man' and fist-pumping against institutional education. They may not look like rebels and radicals, but trust me: they are! Even in denim jumpers, even when they set curfews, even when they monitor which movies you watch—your parents are brave, risk-taking revolutionaries. They expect nothing less from you."

Adults throughout the room beamed at me and chuckled. They felt seen, known, understood. I did understand. I had undertaken the same courageous journey—daring to imagine that I could provide an adequate education for my kids without any training whatsoever, defending my right to do so if pressed by the state or local school board.

This ambitious adult adventure, however, was largely invisible to the kids in that room. Homeschooling and life were one and the same. It

hadn't occurred to many of them that their parents had made an audacious adult choice in the face of governmental oversight and neighborly
skepticism.

One of my friend's daughters declared to her mother: "I never want
to homeschool my kids. You seemed so unhappy all the time—and
stressed. You never got to do anything fun. I want to be a happy adult!"
Crestfallen, Jill asked me, "Did I seem unhappy to you?" It was a moment. I thought about her question. I do remember Jill being anxious
about her daughter's refusal to go along with the high school program Jill
had planned. I also remember Jill worrying frequently about whether
she was qualified to teach her kids (she hadn't gone to college herself).
Her insecurity led her to impose stringent requirements.

It dawned on me as we chatted: Jill wanted her children to get a
better education than she had had. She pushed her girls to academic
success as schools defined it, which made her cranky when they fell
short or didn't care as much as she did.

Sara, Jill's creative daughter (today a graphic designer), felt stifled by
the pressure to live up to her mother's expectations. Worse, the only vision of adulthood her mother offered was that of a martyr—the put-
upon, home education enforcer. Jill wondered: had she failed to give her
daughters a positive vision of homeschooling and adulthood?

✳ THE PERKS OF BEING AN ADULT ✳

Children know the day will come when it's up to them to live alone and
pay the bills. What they also know is that their independence can mean
all kinds of delicious opportunities for adventure. Or not. You're their
chief role model for adulthood. When they look at you, what do you see?
Do they see an adult who makes adulthood look awesome? Or do they
see adulthood as a painful sacrifice filled with endless responsibility and
little pleasure?

Because our kids are with us all the time as homeschooled students,
how we live our adult lives is even more critical to how they envision

their futures. Do you relish your adult life? Or is it on hold until your kids are grown? Are you stretching yourself to have new experiences, learning for its own sake, talking about books and movies, exploring new places without your kids? If you have a paying job, do you share about it with pride or complain about it as tedious and stressful? Some kids resist growing up simply because the adulthood on display holds no magic for them—only weary responsibility.

For instance, when a teen is told that he must learn algebra to go to college and get a job, that proclamation may be a *disincentive* to ever studying advanced math if working seems like a bummer. On the other hand, if getting a job looks like the chance to live your best life—to get your hands on advanced tools; to work with smart, cool people; to earn money that can be spent on adventures—studying to get into college becomes meaningful.

Parents are quick to remind their teens that they have no idea what's ahead. They descend from Mount Parenthood shouldering two big slabs of "adult responsibility" and prophesy doom on the heads of their precious teens:

> *You think your boss is going to tolerate oversleeping and getting to work late every day? Think again!*
>
> *You've got it easy, bucko! The real world is demanding!*
>
> *Wait until you have to pay the bills. It's no picnic!*
>
> *If you don't pass chemistry now, no college will ever want you.*
>
> *What are you going to do with your life? Flip burgers?*

What a glum vision of adulthood! Who'd want to grow up with that nightmare looming? Better to be Peter Pan and play all day while they still can. No wonder some teens glue themselves to the computer—a last desperate attempt to cling to childhood joy and freedom!

One important part of parenting, then, needs to be *your ongoing self-education* that maximizes the opportunities and privileges of being an adult. Make adulthood look awesome and watch your children aspire to

great things. In fact, your strongest gift to your teens is taking real pleasure in *your* skills, hobbies, talents, and opportunities, not theirs.

✳ "I Don't Have Time for That!" ✳

You already feel maxed out by six kids and a baby. I get it. Homeschooling takes the lion's share of time and energy in every family. It's hard to
imagine adding anything to your overburdened life. That's okay! One of
the little-known secrets about homeschooling is that parents who begin
it for their children continue for themselves. Home education awakens
an educational renaissance for adults in their thirties and forties. The
place to begin putting the awesome into your adulting is indulging your
own academic appetite as it erupts—smack-dab in front of your kids.

✳ Nap Time Is Your Time ✳

One day when my children were six and under (I had three of them by
then), we read about the Battle of Little Bighorn and the courageous acts
of Sitting Bull. Not one of the children showed interest. Frankly, the
tragic history of US relations with Native American nations went right
over their heads. My toddler had long since collapsed on my breast. I
thrust the nearest scrap of paper (ever ready and willing on my living
room floor) into the book to hold my place and carried the big lug into
his bedroom. I hurried the more reluctant four- and six-year-olds to their
beds, flipping on the cassette player with Disney tunes to keep them
quiet.

Then, as a woman possessed, I raced back to the couch. I popped the
book open on my pregnant belly, laid my head against a pillow, and read
for an hour. I had to know what happened at that battle. I had to understand Custer's Last Stand and why the Sioux Indians were outraged
against our military. I was starved for intellectual stimulation—and here
it was, in a book I had checked out from the library for my kids.

Mind food. All those years of pregnancy, nursing, and baby care came screeching to a halt for an hour. I read with a voracious appetite about people and places that simply hadn't captured my kids' imaginations yet. They were too young to care. I was the exact right age to care. I finished the chapter before they woke up, deeply satisfied.

That's when I saw a truth: *I* wanted to be home educated. *I* wanted to know things. In a fit of amazement, I realized: I loved learning! We shifted from mom as homeschool teacher to mom as a partner in a shared learning adventure.

✳ Reviving Adulthood ✳

When I was a child, my dad used to say to me: "Enjoy playing now because when you're an adult, you'll be sorry you didn't take advantage of all this free time." It was impossible to appreciate free time in advance of losing it. That said, my parents' busy adulthood looked awesome to me when I considered their example.

My dad got his private pilot's license and took us flying. My mother became a freelance author. She traveled as a speaker all over the United States for a publishing company. My father, a trial lawyer, told us about his law cases at dinnertime, and I found them so compelling that I can still remember many of them today. Both of my parents played tennis. My dad also golfed and my mother took up running. They threw amazing themed parties for their friends (my siblings and I would catch glimpses of the guests arriving in costume).

My parents also threw parties for me and my friends to give a taste of their style of fun. They traveled to places like Tahiti. They were members of the Book of the Month Club and stocked a huge library. They held season tickets to LA Kings hockey games. When their friends couldn't go with them, my parents took us, their kids. My dad worked wood, and my mom sewed our clothes. They attended plays and symphonies together—and then found children's theaters and orchestras for us. As a child, I couldn't wait to grow up!

By the time I graduated high school, however, my parents' marriage shipwrecked. The glittering vision of adulthood I had cherished crashed into the brick wall of divorce. My desire to homeschool grew in the ashes of my shattered family of origin. I would be a committed mother, an educator, a person of self-sacrifice on behalf of my family. I would use my adult life in service of my children, not personal pleasure.

I dove into homeschooling—fully committed. I read books and articles, interviewed homeschooling friends. I was determined to do it right! But there was one popular homeschooling book that caused me to pause. This author described a fabulous vision of homeschooled children doing great adult things, like running for political office or joining the Peace Corps. Yet she also insisted that being a homeschooling mother was the top career choice for women.

I was a mother too—first and foremost. However, I started thinking about this idea that we were raising our kids to find their path of contribution to the world. I couldn't help but wonder: What if all girls grew up believing they should be mothers who homeschooled their kids? Could a girl aspire to also be a scientist if she was expected to pick the superior career choice of homeschooling her children? Would all future scientists (or fill-in-the-blank career options) only be open to men or unmarried women?

Let me tell you, that was *not* okay with me. As much as I loved home education, I also knew I had reached adulthood to be an adult—to find the unique contribution I could make (big or small) to the ongoing project of humankind—and not only through raising the next generation. I wanted my daughters to feel the same way: they mattered for who they are, not only for who they might raise one day.

Was it impossible to nurture children *and* pursue a vocation, hobby, passion, or career at the same time, if you were a mother? I considered what it might mean to be both a committed mother-educator and an adult who took advantage of the unique opportunities afforded to a person over thirty.

I began by indulging my craving to learn, on a parallel path to my kids'. As I taught my children to write, I built my writing career. I couldn't give more than a few hours per week to my goal, but the practice gave life to the rest of the days.

When I created Poetry Teatime, it was as much about my love of poetry as it was about my hope to inspire that same love in my children. I shored up my literary education by listening to books on tape every night while making dinner. I watched films in the afternoons, kids underfoot, some watching with me. As a result, Johannah became so enamored with all things Jane Austen that we read several books together, she took up vintage dance, and she wrote a fan-fiction novella based on *Emma*, set in the Civil War era.

Jacob discovered an affinity for classical music after I brought home the *Sense and Sensibility* soundtrack and played it during copywork. He went on to study and play saxophone in a high school orchestra. I couldn't have planned these outcomes. They were the overflow of my own learning adventure.

I watched this phenomenon each week at our local homeschool co-op. Parents brought passions and skills to our children and sparked all kinds of learning journeys. Our homeschool co-op biology classes were taught by two nurses—homeschooling moms who moonlighted as RNs. Their passion for science meant that my kids got to participate in ten dissections that year (unlike the local public high school that had recently moved to computer models for safety's sake). Kids would much rather slice open an earthworm or frog than see it on a screen. Dissection is *real* and it's also dangerous, adult, and exciting.

Sign language and photography, debate skills and Tae Kwon Do, calculus and advanced composition—skilled adults (parents) showed off! They modeled an awesome adult experience for our students. Homeschooling parents demonstrated every week to me that it was possible to blend the uniqueness of their talents and interests with educating their kids. Not only could it be done, it significantly enriched the learning experience for those children.

✳ More Ways to Be Awesome ✳

A deepening appreciation for school subjects is one way adults show up as awesome. Pursuing new interests is another. If you've always wanted to draw realistically (I did), now you can. Rather than requiring your kids to learn to draw so that you feel justified in learning yourself, forget them! Buy the videos, pencils, and sketch pad. Take time to follow the instructions. Practice—right in front of your kids, right in the middle of the day. They'll watch you struggle and redouble your efforts, and they will be impressed with your artwork. They may encourage you or praise you or remind you to keep trying when it doesn't go well. They may join you! An adult on a learning adventure is contagious.

One homeschool family I know "flipped houses" for fun. These parents taught their two boys how to hang drywall, rewire, paint, redirect plumbing, install cabinets and carpet, select hardware, and design landscape. Their sons got to wield tools, demolish walls, and lay wood flooring. What a huge gift from their parents: once grown, these sons can remodel their own homes, and these parents have a viable side business to continue together. Talk about awesome adulting!

✳ Family Culture ✳

One way to blend your homeschool efforts and the adventure of adulthood is to pay attention to your family culture. In our house, books, plays, and poetry dominated. My husband and I had a shared love of Shakespeare and became active volunteers for our local Shakespeare company. The kids wanted to be included in that experience—of course. That's what the cool adults in their lives were up to. All five of our kids have ushered at the theater and watched nearly every one of the bard's plays performed live. They became friends with the actors and two of my kids joined the acting company for teens.

Another friend of mine has a family culture of running. She and her husband met in college and ran together every week while dating. As a married couple, they've continued this tradition—on trails, in neighborhoods, on vacations. Predictably, their four kids grew up running too—joining cross-country teams and track. Running was what cool adults did! Now these adult children consider running one of the criteria for a future spouse. So awesome!

Sometimes volunteer work is how you expand your awesome into the community. I have a friend who worked in hospice. Her girls got to know the journey of life to death through the eyes of their mother, and this mother felt her worth as she gave support and love to the dying.

✳ Riding Solo ✳

Not all adult adventures need to be shared. When I developed a hunger to learn more about art, I took my kids to the local art museum frequently. But I also went on museum visits alone, or with friends and not a single stroller in tow. In fact, my first "grown-up weekend away" was in Chicago, where I met an Internet homeschool friend. We spent an entire Saturday luxuriously enjoying Georgia O'Keeffe and Marc Chagall at the Art Institute, chatting about paintings and literature without interruption. It was a glorious self-nurturing experience.

Sometimes self-care comes at a price, however. Johannah scored her first and only goal in a soccer game back in Cincinnati while I stood mesmerized, in front of Georges Seurat's famous painting *A Sunday Afternoon on the Island of La Grande Jatte*. When the text message arrived, I felt a pang of conscience. Had I put myself ahead of my daughter? Should I not have gone to Chicago? It's difficult to prioritize our own development when we're so willing to cheerlead every step our kids take.

A moment came when I could see that my presence at every soccer match was not essential to Johannah's healthy development. Johannah never cared much about soccer. My investment in myself, my friendships, travel, and art eventually made the more profound impact on her.

Today, she travels the world, puts her friends first, loves art, and is quick to take good care of herself and her needs. Sometimes modeling self-care *is* the healthiest part of the awesome adulting example.

Graduate school, starting a business, working part-time outside the home, running for political office—many home educators have paired homeschooling with these aspirations. The key is to recognize the balance between how much effort you put in now while homeschooling and how much more you can give once you reach the finish line. Keeping your foot in the door so you can swing it wide open later is good for everyone in the family.

✳ Your Kids Want to Be Proud of You Too ✳

No matter how well they conceal their true feelings, your kids want to be proud of you. We all know that who we are is bits and pieces of each parent—and we want to believe that those two people are good, capable human beings. That means that even if you never hear the words directly from your children, your kids do talk about you with their friends, and they want to brag about you behind your back. They feel pride in who they are when they have pride in who you are.

Have you completed a half marathon? Did they cheer you over the finish line?

Did you enter a painting in an art show? Have they seen it hanging among all the other paintings, with a price stuck to the corner?

Do you still surf at age forty-two?

Are you in grad school, writing papers and taking tests, nervous about your grades?

Do you use tools that are "adult only"—like a chain saw or industrial sewing machine?

Perhaps you're studying to be a yoga or scuba instructor. Perhaps you have an Etsy shop. Perhaps you raise chickens to sell eggs to friends.

Have you traveled to faraway places?

Do you make time with friends a priority?

Are sporting events or musicals or lectures important to you?

Perhaps you've worked a political campaign or maybe you volunteer at the local animal shelter.

Do you ever take yourself out to a movie and dinner alone for a little "me" time?

There are dozens of ways to showcase the advantages of adulthood. Find the ones that put a smile on your face. As you tap into your personal interests and aspirations, adulthood glitters with possibility for your kids too.

✳ Psst, ✳
It's Also a Good Idea to Like Homeschooling

You only get one life. One. If you choose to dedicate this sizable chunk of your adult years to homeschooling, it's important that you like it. In fact, it's no service to anyone if you feel trapped into homeschooling by poor public schools or the belief that you *should* want to home educate. Your kids pick up on that. No child wants to be the obligation that sucks life and joy from the person they love the most (their mom or dad). Homeschooling is a privilege and an opportunity—when it stops feeling like it, it's important to step back and ask yourself a few questions.

Is the life you're leading living up to what you imagined when you were a child, a teen, a young parent?

Are you doing the things you thought adults would get to do? If not, why not?

What can you add now, in a bite-size amount, to get started?

There are no do-overs. Life moves in one direction. That means, if you put your adult aspirations on hold until your children are grown, you may miss the moment. The computer programmer you wanted to be? No longer an option. Technology moves fast. Keeping up matters. The perfect program for your area of interest at the local college may no longer be offered when you're "ready." Alternatively, you might get the terrible diagnosis that changes everything: cancer.

Home education takes about ten to twenty-five years of your adult life. On the other side is an equal number of years (for most of us) waiting to be filled. When you make space for your passions now (even an hour a week), you help build the bridge to that new life when the last child leaves home. You keep a little kindling for your own fiery learning experience that helps enliven the education you are providing to your kids.

It matters! Knowing who you are and what brings you joy beyond your children provides comfort and optimism at the end of the homeschool odyssey. Not only that but homeschooling may lead you to the contribution you are destined to make.

If homeschooling stops being a source of joy, begin by shifting your attention to the awesome adult you want to be. Just that shift can inject energy into a flagging homeschool. I have several friends who've gone back to college or have pursued advanced degrees, others who've started careers or resumed them. Some have begun businesses; others have rekindled a hobby or passion. When I entered graduate school, my heart for homeschool surged. I regularly shared what I was learning with my kids. In fact, my thesis paper led Jacob to the key insight that drove his career choice in human rights law. That would not have happened had I put grad school on hold, waiting for the kids to all move out.

You may also notice that your empathy for the struggle to commit and follow through goes up. You'll know the contours of learning—the days when you just can't take another classic novel and need a break with *People* magazine; the moments when you shirk the responsibility of bookkeeping for your Etsy shop in favor of knitting more scarves. This kind of experience helps both you and your kids understand each other better.

If you find that homeschool has stopped being meaningful, and if you have no energy at all for expanding your adult life to include more wonderfulness, it may be time to take stock of the invisible education happening right now in your home. Let's find out what's draining the mirth and energy from your life. Before you move along to the next chapter, however, I've written a letter to you—homeschool mama to homeschool mama or papa. You can do this—for your kids, and for yourself.

✳ Letter of Encouragement ✳

My Dearest Awesome Adult,

The easiest thing in the world is to overlook your own needs: reasonable ones, like sleep, eating well, having fun, listening to music you like, exercise, good sex, and peace. In service of our sweet bunchkins, we skip what we want or need (or didn't know we wanted or needed).

What happens next? For me, when I shortchange my wellbeing, I take it out on the ones I love. I don't shout (at least, that's not my usual go-to). I expect. I expect my children to become the people I admire most so that I can live a little through them (since living through myself is off the table). I put my energy into shaping their character, their educations, their hobbies, their bright futures.

Until I run out. When they don't adopt my wonderful plans for their lives, I crash! Why aren't they cooperating with my brilliant design for their education or futures? Why don't they see my efforts to make their lives painless and fun? When will they realize that all I have in my heart is total, all-consuming, mad mad love for them down to their pudgy toes?

Alas, happy children don't notice all the good their parents give to them. They have the glorious gift of taking everything their parents do for granted—the sign of a happy, functional home. Deprivation leads a child to gratitude for the crumbs of kindness. Abundance leads children to the right and freedom to say, "No! I don't like that; I don't want that; that doesn't work for me."

You can unhook from the belief that your children's successful completion of childhood at your hands is the key to your ultimate fulfillment and happiness. It isn't. It can't be. You have one life and it isn't only in service of the lives of other people, even the amazing human beings living in your house.

Instead, you get to reclaim something of the person you still are—and to bring that fullness of self into your family and homeschool. *You get to show up too!* Remember: a stunning vision of you lived in your own mother's loving imagination. It's time for *that you* to come out and play.

May you rest, laugh, learn, and revive your optimism!

Be good to yourself,
Julie xoxo

PART FOUR

Breaking the Spell
and Rekindling the Magic

To truly be committed to a life of honesty, love and discipline,
we must be willing to commit ourselves to reality.

—JOHN BRADSHAW, *HEALING THE SHAME THAT BINDS YOU*

A young homeschooling mother confided in me a secret she couldn't share with friends. Her house was stuffed floor to ceiling with boxes, books, too many dishes, file folders, assorted hats, art supplies, toys, and random articles of clothing. Her kitchen table was piled so high with "stuff" that they ate dinner on a clear corner of a picnic table in the backyard when it wasn't raining. The hallways were lined with stacks of paper and magazines that she was sure she'd need some day. She cleared a narrow path down the hall to packed bedrooms. Her oven housed dirty dishes. Knickknacks, empty plates and glasses, and junk mail covered the countertops. To ask a child to complete a math page was impossible: there were no clear surfaces for writing. Ashley had been afraid to ask for help. One member of her community had already reported her to Child Protective Services. This precious mother's fear that CPS would take her children controlled every waking thought.

What courage she had—to reveal her deepest pain and shame to me.

What a thing to face squarely! I admired her. There's no way to fix an issue of that scale without honesty. She had hoped a new writing program might inspire her to get her house in order. Of course, I knew that my writing program would've found its way to the top of another stack of unused materials. We had to start where her pain lived, in all those boxes and piles and her fear of getting rid of them—so that's what we did. We started with reality.

CHAPTER 12

THE INVISIBLE EDUCATION

The Power of Family Dysfunction to Sideline Learning

> Education is an atmosphere—that is, the child breathes the
> atmosphere emanating from his parents; that of the ideas
> which rule their own lives.
>
> —CHARLOTTE MASON, *A PHILOSOPHY OF EDUCATION*

Education is an atmosphere—it isn't a house. It's not a program. Education is not accredited teaching. What our children learn at home is largely invisible to us—directly connected to their experience of well-being—the atmosphere of family life.

You can own a first-rate curriculum and transform your house into a fairyland of play and imagination—and still see homeschool fall to pieces. Invisible forces shape how your family experiences living together, which creates the core context for learning.

✳ THE REAL WORLD OF HOMESCHOOLING ✳

It's a delicate subject to address, but critical to the growth of homeschooling both as a movement and in our families. How children feel at home has everything to do with how well they're educated. Our kids spend all day every day with each other. If where they live is a hotbed of hostility, there's no bus to take them away for several hours a day. They must learn to cope without a break, without any other experience to compare to their own.

Homeschoolers are not immune to the dysfunctions that assail other kinds of families. They only expect to be—and that's the problem. Many homeschool leaders let us down. Some turned out to be violent parents or unfaithful in marriage. One famous family (television personalities) uncovered molestation between siblings.[1] Homeschool business leaders confess to neglecting their kids to travel all over the world hawking their curriculum and beliefs, yet living a lie—presenting a happy family life publicly, while at home, children and parents are at war.

Children raised in these families were taught to hide the dysfunction and suffered as a result. Today, recovery groups for homeschooled alumni address the unique trauma of having been schooled at home, pretending all was well when all was anything but well.[2]

✳ The Unhappy Homeschooler ✳

I hear from homeschool parents who are frightened by the unhappy home lives they lead. They worry for their marriages and their children. One woman wrote that she had lost her religious faith yet was married to a pastor and led their church's homeschool support group. That change created a crisis—as a family and as members of a tightly knit religious homeschool community. Could she still lead the homeschool group? Would the children be eyed with suspicion as "bad" influences on the other kids? Would her husband's profession be at risk?

When my friend's alcoholic husband lost his job, she wondered whether to leave him or stay, love, and support him. What about the children? Would she have to give up homeschooling if she got a divorce? No easy answers.

Another mom I know revealed that she couldn't stop screaming at her kids, just like her mother before her. She told herself every morning to stop yelling. By day's end, after succumbing to her out-of-control anger yet again, she'd sink to bed feeling like the worst parent ever.

Many mothers have shared that they work hard to nurture and support their children's interests and skill development, only to have the delicate burgeoning self-confidence of a child thrashed by a father's careless, unkind comments after work. How could these moms get their husbands to see that their cruel tone and flippant, critical speech in the evenings undermined their best efforts during the day?

What's worse is that some of these women were targets of verbal and emotional abuse by those same husbands. These wives brought their earnestness to the marriage and got accusations and rage in exchange. It's difficult to trust your hunches about your kids and their education when you're routinely denigrated for the decisions you make and you live in fear of angry outbursts.

Sometimes children present the challenge to the family dynamic through no fault of their own. If you have a child who is autistic, for instance, and needs twenty-four-hour care and supervision (including a wheelchair and special feeding apparatus), the other kids will experience the effects of that necessary yet unbalanced attention to the impaired child. It takes conscientiousness and creativity to ensure that your neurotypical kids get what they need too. No one to blame, yet a challenging circumstance to navigate, especially while homeschooling.

Fostering and adopting children can also impact how much attention and time a parent gives to home education—sometimes for a brief season, and sometimes for an entire childhood.

Occasionally one child in a family manifests the hidden anger of the home and acts out in belligerence and hostility. Blame is wrongly assigned to the "problem child."

Perhaps your marriage is on the rocks. When a couple decides to stay together after a husband's infidelity, for instance, the emotional drain on the homeschooling mother is profound. She's likely to be distracted, suffering from low self-esteem and coping with an impulse to spot-check her husband. One mom I know told me that the years following her husband's affair felt like walking as a zombie through life—hard for her to be all magical for her kids under those circumstances.

Another family I know got rid of their Internet connection because of a father's pornography habit. Their children were at a real disadvantage for their education while their mother attempted to control what was her husband's compulsion.

There are other impediments to homeschooling. If a parent gets a cancer diagnosis, homeschool is going to change dramatically during chemotherapy. Postpartum depression, a pregnancy that requires bedrest, surgery, chronic disorders like fibromyalgia and ulcerative colitis, learning disabilities, and natural disasters like tornadoes and mudslides all impact how well you homeschool, at least for a season.

A pregnant mother carrying twins? Life as she knew it is over. There's no way to homeschool with the same level of energy while raising multiples in the first two or three years of their lives.

You get divorced or an aging parent moves in; perhaps you enter therapy for childhood trauma; sometimes foreclosure or financial pressure requires you to earn money for a season. These life shifts demand untold quantities of energy.

Homeschooling is impacted by *all* these variables, and others you may be thinking about right now. The quick fix (new curriculum or new approach) is a Band-Aid over the deeper work that we need to do to make our homes healthy, whole, and functional.

✳ DYSFUNCTION-ALL ✳

American short story writer Flannery O'Connor said, "Anybody who has survived his childhood has enough information about life to last him the rest of his days."[3] I used to chuckle—we all have stories to tell. As I got older, I sobered up. That childhood may make for great short stories, but it also informs everything about our adult choices and dearest wishes.

Each family is made up of imperfect beings who knock into each

Characteristics of Dysfunctional Families

- One or both parents have addictions or compulsions (for example, drugs, alcohol, promiscuity, gambling, overworking, and/or overeating) that have strong influences on family members.
- One or both parents use the threat or application of physical violence as the primary means of control. Children may have to witness violence, may be forced to participate in punishing siblings, or may live in fear of explosive outbursts.
- One or both parents exploit the children and treat them as possessions whose primary purpose is to respond to the physical and/or emotional needs of adults (for example, protecting a parent or cheering up one who is depressed).
- One or both parents are unable to provide, or threaten to withdraw, financial or basic physical care for their children. Similarly, one or both parents fail to provide their children with adequate emotional support.
- One or both parents exert a strong authoritarian control over the children. Often these families rigidly adhere to a particular belief (religious, political, financial, personal). Compliance with role expectations and with rules is expected without any flexibility.[4]

other like bumper cars: jolting and jostling one another—sometimes to great joy, other times to the point of trauma. We all have pain. A dysfunctional family is in *chronic* pain.

Brown University cites the above characteristics of dysfunction commonly found in toxic families. Whether yours is chronically dysfunctional or merely crosses the line from time to time, it's worth it to glance through this list as healthy accountability. Use the information to face your truth squarely, so you have a chance to pivot and grow.

✳ When Being a Family Hurts ✳

Homeschooling thrives when kids live a life they take for granted—so naturally secure, they don't know how good they have it. Many of us have never lived in a home like that. Though my childhood memories were mostly the happy kind, I couldn't shake the feeling that all of it had been a mirage once my parents divorced. What constituted a healthy family life? What problems were the "ordinary" kind and which ones were dangerous to me, my marriage, and my kids? My therapist Sharon described a vision of a healthy family life that has stayed with me: an evening with her family.

My kids and I are in the house together. The boys are playing video games in the family room, and I've started dinner. I notice the clock: only ten minutes until their dad, my husband, gets home. I feel a little impatient. I'm tired from a long day and I don't have the energy yet to help the kids do homework or get cleaned up for dinner. I think to myself: When Dave gets here, we'll be complete. We'll get through all the family demands together.

Then Dave walks through the door and relief floods my body. My shoulders relax. I smile. He smiles and gives me a kiss. He waves to the boys and wordlessly joins me in the kitchen, picking up a knife. We finish making dinner together, catching up. When the meal is ready, Dave helps the boys wash their hands, I set the table, and we eat as a family, talking genially about the day's events.

After dinner, we clear the table and load the dishwasher as a family, chatting. Then my husband helps one child and I help the other with homework. We put the kids to bed as a team, and then relax to watch TV. The overarching feeling I have is this: everyone that is supposed to be here is home. We are better together.

I sat quietly as I listened to her—reflecting on my home, my life. An ache in my chest throbbed. For many families, this vision seems as believable as winning the lottery. I asked Sharon how a family like hers addressed conflicts and differences of opinion. She replied that in a healthy family, issues come up but they are a shared burden, without blame. When someone has an off day and mistreats another member of the family, the desire to resolve and return to peace is greater than the need to be right. Goodwill characterizes the relationships, and members are free to express their feelings, expecting to be heard and understood.

I allowed myself to imagine a life that peaceful—that free of eggshell walking. I wondered how many families I knew lived like Sharon's. I wondered how many didn't.

Reflection Activity

Pause now. Either in your mind's eye or on a sheet of paper, take a few minutes to think or write about how you *felt* in your home growing up. Peace? Anxiety? Pressure? Unsafe? Supported? Think of a memory where you felt loved and understood. Now consider one where you felt overlooked or demeaned.

Describe to yourself what it was like to come home after being away. Did you look forward to it? Did you worry about the mood of the family upon reentry?

Consider each parent: Did you prefer one to the other? Why? Identify one or two memories that help you characterize your relationship with each of your parents.

Did you feel close to or threatened by your siblings?

Which event was the biggest hurdle in childhood? Which one was your greatest joy? Who noticed in both cases? How did they enhance or hurt those experiences?

What do you want your home life to feel and look like now?

Add any other thoughts as they come to you. Get it all down and let your mind and pen go where they want to.

It's okay. I'll wait.

✳ Family 2.0 ✳

When we build our new families, we subconsciously react to our childhoods—the experiences you just described for yourself. We want to ensure an upgraded version of family—we'll be attentive, we'll provide structure. We'll keep house and give freedom. We'll require obedience and have a great marriage. We'll travel or stay home. We'll devote ourselves to religion or leave oppressive religion behind. We'll help or give independence; we'll cheerlead or provide respectful distance. We'll shout less and cuddle more. We'll read books and build bonfires. We'll stay current with technology or get off the grid. We'll eat healthy foods or permit orgies of sugar. Our decisions are driven by a desire to prevent the pain we suffered, or to secure the positive experience we had as kids—and even better.

The catch? We partnered up with someone else also reacting to a childhood, and we gave birth to a slew of "not-me's"—children with their own outlooks, personalities, dispositions, wants, needs, and aptitudes. This bundle of humans lives in a brand-new era with a changing technological, political, social, and economic landscape. Their ideas of happiness and yours are not identical.

Yet to get to the life we imagine, we use unhelpful strategies. For instance, to secure peace and joy, we shout it into existence. We say we want to earn our children's trust, and then eye them with suspicion. We celebrate the idea of a "love of learning," and then reject the subject our child loves to learn.

It's as if we're designed to notice what's missing rather than being delighted by all the good happening in front of our eyes. As my friend Dotty used to say to me: "When I see my kids outside playing, I think: *Why aren't they inside reading a book?* When they are inside reading, I think: *Why don't they go outside to play?* I'm never happy." And that's just it: that happy vision of family life exerts daily pressure. We're so worried we're going to make a mistake or miss it, we resort to coercion, pressure, and control—the very things that undermine what we want.

✳ A Poisonous Pedagogy ✳

In my twenties, I worked hard to understand what it meant to be a healthy parent. Yet I still fell into the trap of trying to control my children's behavior from time to time. Alice Miller, bestselling author of *The Drama of the Gifted Child*, defined a phrase that has been meaningful to me over the years: "the poisonous pedagogy." She explains it this way:

> *Poisonous pedagogy is a phrase I use to refer to the kind of parenting and education aimed at breaking a child's will and making that child into an obedient subject by means of overt or covert coercion, manipulation, and emotional blackmail.*[5]

Her work focuses on helping parents understand the importance of seeing and validating a child's emotional life—recognizing children's need to be known as themselves, not as extensions of their parents. The temptation is to emphasize obedience over cultivating a child's self-awareness, control over supported exploration, and accountability to adult standards over protection of childlike wonder. Homeschooling thrives when we shift from power *over* our kids to power *with* them—building empathetic relationships where the parent and child are partners in learning.

✳ Let's Talk About Yelling ✳

My friend Eileen and I were walking two strollers and ten kids to the farmers' market one sunny Southern California morning. The older boys kept running ahead on the curbs of the busy street, making Eileen and me uncomfortable. She'd call to her son, "David! Slow down." I'd shout to Noah, "Hey, don't walk on the edge of the road! There are cars whipping by!" The strollers could not keep up with our speedy ten-year-olds, who appeared to be minutes from death. Finally, in a moment of exasperation, Eileen looked at me and I looked at her. She declared: "If you weren't here, I'd be yelling at them right now!" I burst out laughing because I had had the same thought. We were holding back—giving the illusion of restrained parenthood when in fact, we were at our wit's end.

True enough: I had let my kids have it at home from time to time. And so had she. The crazy part? If you had asked me, I would have told you that yelling was an unacceptable way to parent. Yelling is the tactic we use when we feel tired, discouraged, and powerless. It's the last stand before we dissolve into a puddle of disheartened tears. Yelling is a tool of desperation.

✳ Padunk-adunk ✳

Let me share a story. My kids have a term they use to describe me when I get out over my skis. A busy day might spin out of control—too many activities, not enough evidence of education, silliness, a husband who throws me shade, and no food in the pantry to make dinner. Suddenly, the shoes strewn down the hall bait me into an explosion. "Get these shoes picked up! And who left their coats on the couch? Hang those up too. Now!" I let all my pent-up anxiety and hurt roll over the room in a tide of anger.

My kids told me later that under those conditions, they'd say to each other, "Don't worry. Mom's *padunk-adunking*. Just clean up. She'll be okay in a minute." They made up a code name for my outburst behavior—they saw it for what it was. I allowed my frustration to froth over the sides of my ordinarily composed person like boiled milk. They knew it was temporary and not about them (so healthy!). Yet they didn't deserve it—at all.

Parents justify yelling all the time, but they fail to appreciate the impact it has on their kids. Think of it like this. Imagine that you're happily walking along the street, and out of the blue, you hear a voice through a bullhorn: "Stop walking. This is the police."

Without a single additional word, your body will go into what I call "tuning fork mode." The volume and authority of the speaker will cause your nervous system to ping with electricity and anxiety. You'll feel like you're in trouble, even if you're not. This is how our kids feel when we yell at them. When we raise our voices, we put our children's nervous systems on high alert. Naturally. Automatically. We're big and powerful; they aren't. Yelling is a toxic management tool. We must do better.

We all "padunk-adunk" occasionally. A healthier way to express our frustration, however, is to *own* it. We're so quick to cover it up or assign it to someone else. Instead, I learned that I had to tell the truth—or I'd hurl my anger on others.

I could say to myself: "Shoes in the hallway again. I'm angry! I nearly broke my ankle. I feel powerless. No one cares about me. I want control! I want to be noticed and mothered. It's not fair."

My anger nearly always surfaced when I'd lost touch with my needs. Owning my anger returned my power to me. My choices rose to greet me: I could pick up the shoes, I could ask for help, I could sit in another room until I calmed down, I could make a cup of tea, I could fire off a self-pitying angry text rant to my best friend for first-class commiseration! I didn't have to turn the strewn shoes into evidence that my children didn't love me or that I was raising slobs.

✳ RESPOND IN THE OPPOSITE SPIRIT ✳

Years ago, a friend shared a principle with me to help de-escalate that building negative emotion. She suggested responding in the opposite spirit. One day, in the middle of my children's wriggly silliness that had my nerves jangling, I paused. I wanted to weep at my inability to stifle their misbehavior; I had wanted cooperation. I already knew yelling would only make everyone mad at me.

Helpless, I walked to the center of the living room, lowered myself to the floor, and crossed my legs. I sat without saying a word. I held back tears. I breathed in, out, in, out. I petted the dog. I waited. Five minutes went by. Glances in my direction became quieter voices. My children looked at me, puzzled. Sheepish smiles bloomed. Little stories dribbled from their mouths as they walked toward me. The whole atmosphere reset and I didn't say a word. We got on with the day, from the center of the floor and my silent truth. Dropping my need to get them under control ironically led my kids to quieting themselves.

✳ TELL THE FREAKING TRUTH ✳

If you're like me, when invited to tell the truth, you grab a polishing cloth and find a way to tell it that isn't so stark and distressing. It's tempting to put a positive spin on pain: "They're just being little kids. I know they don't mean to upset me." It's equally tempting to put the blame squarely on them: "They're trying to upset me, those insensitive beasts!"

Neither of these "truths" consider *your truth* in that moment. Tell the *freaking* honest truth—the raw, unedited, unpolished version that gets at your despair. "I feel abandoned and unappreciated. I feel afraid of failure. I feel inadequate." To identify your own freaking truth takes practice. Initially the annoyance or anxiety feels like it's located in someone else's behavior or attitude. We try to control the external environment to get quiet inside. That effort leads to escalation of conflict, however, since other people can never bring us the peace we crave. Instead, when I have the bandwidth, I challenge myself to take an "emotional selfie"— flip the camera around and ask myself, "What behavior or attitude is inside me that I haven't identified yet? What can I do to take care of myself? How would I like to feel right now?"

In the heat of the moment, it may be too difficult to pause and prevent the outburst. But it's never too late to take that internal inventory. We get endless chances for the pause—we can pause before, during, after, after, after, and after again. There's no expiration date on revisiting what was going on with *me* when I flew off the handle or dumped my anxiety on the heads of my children.

✳ What's the Weather? ✳

If the blaming habit is persistent, it's time to take a more deliberate look at the culture of the family—its habit of being. "Most teachers and most parents know that every child is a complex weather system of emotions, yet it used to be thought, and most educators believed, that understanding and feeling were very separate. In part this was because, while clinical psychology placed emotion front and center, other branches of psychology that have a significant impact on education largely discounted the role of emotion in thought and action," explain the Caines, our brain-researching friends.[6]

When we school our children at home, emotion and education are more obviously linked. Our kids act as emotional weather vanes of the family culture. How they feel necessarily impacts how they learn. The Caines go on to explain in the eleventh of their twelve principles of brain-based learning that "complex learning is enhanced by challenge and inhibited by threat."[7] Do you remember the optimal condition for learning? We discussed "relaxed alertness" in Chapter 5. It's impossible to get to that state when living with chronic stress. If your kids exhibit fluctuating moods and capacities for concentration, rather than reevaluating the program, check the emotional weather vane—your children's moodiness. What's prompting their out-of-sorts condition? What can bring them back to relaxed alertness?

A few years ago, my team and I held a retreat for Brave Writer mothers. I gave a talk called "The Invisible Education," during which we looked at our childhoods—the pain resulting from trauma like sexual molestation and violence, neglect, and verbal abuse—and how this legacy impacted our experience of parenting and homeschooling. One courageous mother shared with me privately a year later that she felt sucker punched during that session—imagining the impact of her unhealed self on her children's experience of home and family. Unwelcome memories of her childhood flooded her, yet in the year that passed, her healing and transformation had begun.

She emailed this story to me (I share it with you with her anonymous permission):

I am a yeller. Not always, not even often, but when I am triggered in just the right way, my anger and frustration and hurt and all the rest come out in yelling. I hate it. I loathe that about myself and I've worked so hard to overcome it. It's what I learned but it's no excuse. I know better, I should do better. My husband is a yeller too. This is what I got out of the retreat that was life-changing. My homeschool didn't need to change; I was doing fine in that regard. . . . What I did need to change was me. I am the reason I felt like I was failing [my kids]—because I was!

When we were with our small groups on the last day [of the retreat] somebody said, "What is the weather at your house?" On the plane home, I was thinking about the "weather" in our home and trying to record a few things in my journal. It occurred to me that I could track the atmosphere of our home using weather icons and it would be a discreet way to record the atmosphere and hopefully gain insight to ways we could have more sunshine days.

My basics are:

- *Blue skies and sunshine = the best day. Everyone is happy, their needs are being met, there is a positive vibe, relationships have been nurtured.*
- *Partly sunny = all is well, but maybe someone needs a little something extra.*
- *Lightning bolt = tension in the air.*
- *Rain = tears.*
- *Windy = a "storm" is brewing/blowing in.*
- *Cloudy = nothing wrong necessarily, but no joy that day either, just sort of meh.*

I've been able to see patterns and triggers and mentally note a storm blowing in and do what I can to avoid it. On the note of avoidance, it has also been really helpful for me to face the storms some-

times. I have a peacemaker personality and I need peace at all costs—but I'm learning that isn't always best, and sometimes I just have to weather the storm in order to yield blue skies/sunshine.

I recorded in my journal every day what "the weather" was at our house with these little weather icons. I've worked on me. It's been a rough road. I've had to go down paths I didn't want to go down—I wanted them left in the past. I am trying to heal, and through this healing, I hope that we can have the home I dream of. I take comfort in your words: "Anything you've damaged can be fixed." We've come far. We are far better now than we were a year ago and hope that we will continue down this path of growth and trust and emotional safety. That talk saved me and laid a path for me to journey down so I can finally heal and be the mom my kids deserve.

Powerful—yet such a simple tool.

Each member of the family contributes to the overall weather of the home. Tracking the emotional climate is a gentle form of accountability that helps establish awareness and creates the opportunity to pivot to new behaviors. I love this idea!

✳ Manage the Damage ✳

Most of us work hard to make sure our children don't swallow a Tide laundry pod or drink the bleach. Yet we sometimes forget about their emotional safety. Home should be the place where each person shows up as they are, without worry that someone else will belittle or take advantage of them.

That said, every parent blows it. Our kids blow it. Storms brew and unload their buckets of rain, followed by rejuvenation and new growth. Good enough families thrive because there's space for recovery from those ugly weather moments. Any damage you've done to your children in the name of self-protection and fear can be repaired.

Thank goodness. Because I've had to repair some pretty big mistakes.

That Time When . . .
We Sunk to Our Lowest Parenting Moment

I believed I would escape the challenges of parenting teens because I had found the golden key to a close, bonded relationship with my young children. We were oh-so-connected—on-demand breastfeeding, co-sleeping, homeschooling. I would always know my children's thoughts, and they'd always want to share their dreams with me.

When Noah, my oldest, turned fourteen, I discovered the failure of my belief system—the inscrutable truth that this gangly, pubescent, young male had rapidly become himself, differentiating away from me. That self had thoughts I couldn't pry open, ideas and opinions of his own.

Noah became enamored with heavy metal music—Metallica, Rage Against the Machine. Our family culture had not yet made the journey from Raffi to loud scratching guitars and aggressive lyrics. Noah's dad and I prohibited listening to certain bands. We also limited which books Noah could read based on our belief that he wasn't ready for what we considered "adult content."

No matter our restrictions, however, Noah found ways to read books and listen to music that fed *him*, despite the threat of punishment. One day, we reached a tipping point: we discovered he was listening to a prohibited audiobook. Our anxiety that Noah had gotten too far away from us in his choices rattled me and his father. That day, we sunk to our lowest parenting moment, propelled by fear.

We blindsided our smart, curious teen with loud accusations and angry shouts, echoing through the house, waking the other children who we shooed back up the stairs to their beds. We forecast doom over our beloved son—how could we trust him to drive a car or to come home sober from a party if he couldn't be trusted not to listen to a song or read a book we had banned? How would he ever learn to respect his boss at work if he couldn't follow our oh-so-reasonable limits as his parents?

Noah's response (in hindsight) seems so pure: *Of course, he'd be reliable with a car and wouldn't drink and drive. Why wouldn't he work hard at a job? How did that relate to listening to music or reading a book?* He appealed to our better angels: "Mom, you'd love the lyrics," and "Dad, this book has incredible philosophical themes." He couldn't understand our poorly designed limits on his rapidly expanding brain.

The dressing-down continued unabated for thirty minutes as our desperation escalated. Noah showed no sign of "getting it." We went too far—Jon hurled the player at the wall and it shattered into shards. A grave empty silence followed. We crushed Noah's last defense, leaving him wordless, in tears, and wounded. I'll never forget the chilling realization that dawned on me: "Control is an illusion. Noah is his own person. We've savaged him." I felt utterly beat, scared, and so ashamed. The irony didn't escape me—we'd done far more harm to Noah than any book or song could ever do.

It didn't take more than a day of conversation between us (Noah's dad and me) to realize we'd done great damage to our relationship with our precious firstborn child. We were out of our depth! It became instantly clear that parenting a teen needed an entirely different approach than littler kids. Together, Jon and I brainstormed ways to repair that damage. We fumbled into an apology. It wasn't enough. Noah needed us to change course—to join him on his passage to adulthood rather than controlling it. And so, we did.

It was time to know our teen on our teen's terms. This journey was not about his growing up, but our letting go. I squared my shoulders and mustered *interest* rather than judgment. I listened to Noah's music with him and read the lyrics of his songs. I wasn't comfortable. I pressed in. That's when I noticed the fist-pumping political themes and the powerful poetry. I asked curious questions. Noah talked animatedly about politics, identity, and music. He analyzed those lyrics every bit as well as the Shakespeare plays and poems we'd enjoyed at teatime. I grew to appreciate Rage Against the Machine; I now know Metallica songs and like them—they remind me of those years and Noah.

Jon took a different tactic. He bought tickets to a heavy metal concert for Noah's birthday, and surprised Noah by going with him—listening to loud music in a smoky stadium for five hours.

These two acts brought about a shift—they didn't eliminate the impact of all that parental laser-focused anger (that's what therapy's for), but they reset the gauge and allowed us to rebuild together, one conversation at a time. In the end—I discovered that there's no system that protects my children and teens from encountering a world tainted by violence, atrocity, and impurity. What protects them is not restriction, but connection—not co-sleeping when little, but co-creating an awesome teen life as they grow up—one into which the teen invites the parent.

If only we had actually *listened* to those Raffi lyrics all those years ago:

Everything grows and grows, sisters do, and brothers too, everything grows—Mamas too and Papas too: everything grows.

I'm grateful that Noah's allegiance to himself required us to let go of that control and learn how to connect around his burgeoning self. Otherwise we would have missed so much.

Some of today's homeschools are toxic not because of poor curriculum choices, but because of how we parent. John Bradshaw, famous for his work on shame in families (*Healing the Shame That Binds You*), reminds us that the real work of parenting is learning how to cope with our children's independent emotional lives—helping them to know their full range of feelings, how to avoid denying them (or pretending them away), and then how to integrate them meaningfully:

You can tell kids not to do things. And you can scare them, and you can punish them . . . Goleman [researcher] and his colleagues have gotten absolute clinical evidence showing how much better families

function, and really how much more control children have over emo-
tion, when they are dealt with right while the child's having them.
When they're talked about. When parents sit down with their chil-
dren.[8]

Jon and I could have had a completely different experience with
Noah and his excursion into music and books had we taken the time to
be *curious* rather than alarmed. We could have shared the journey from
child to teen, rather than trying to wrestle him into a shape that made
us comfortable. It takes cojones to do it! We had to become brave learners ourselves.

All of us harbor hurts and insecurities. What we want to do is find a
way to live alongside those pain points—not allowing our hurts or insecurities to control us (and by extension, our children) now. The key feature of our homeschools must be connection—connection never fails.
Your children deserve parents who are well and able to give the gifts of
presence and love.

CHAPTER 13

THE DISENCHANTING POWER OF DOING IT RIGHT

The Dangers of Ideological Alignment and True Belief-ism in Home Education

A person who never learned to trust confuses intensity with intimacy, obsession with care, and control with security.

—JOHN BRADSHAW, *HOMECOMING: RECLAIMING AND CHAMPIONING YOUR INNER CHILD*

Brave learning is all about the magic of trust—trusting yourself, trusting your kids, trusting the process. Trust implies not knowing the outcome in advance. The ordinary magic at work in your family is felt, more than seen. Trust allows for changes midstream, for revising a strategy, for accommodating a need.

Trust is letting go of the side of the pool to see if you'll swim. It's believing that a lifesaving ring will appear if you need it. It's accepting that you can climb out of the pool too. No one is forcing you to stay in the water.

Most of us don't come to homeschooling with that level of trust shored up inside. We look for fail-safe strategies and shortcuts. We want guaranteed outcomes. And so, we become intense, obsessed, and controlling.

✳ Ideological Purity ✳

Lots of parents latch onto a cure-all philosophy for living—a method to ensure their children will be spared the slings and arrows of growing up. Human beings *love* systems. We think to ourselves: *If I apply the system correctly, I get a guaranteed outcome.*

Most homeschooling moms (over 99 percent of home educators are women) start with an idealized view of motherhood. Jennifer Lois, author of the book *Home Is Where the School Is* and sociologist at Western Washington University, cites research that the culture in the United States "has raised the standards of good mothering to unprecedented intensity levels."[1] Today's mother feels dual pressures—to be utterly attentive to her priceless children, while also fulfilling the dream of feminism that is self-realization as a woman. Homeschooling *is* a powerful cultural solution to satisfying both aims.

Lois explains it like this: "Protestants used homeschooling to integrate their traditional gender ideologies with the more contemporary definitions of 'ideal womanhood,' whereas more liberal mothers used homeschooling to come to terms with staying out of the workforce. Homeschooling allowed both groups to be more than 'just' stay-at-home mothers."[2]

Yet such a massive task—the mothering *and* complete education of one's children (usually without training in either parenting or teaching)—is daunting! To find support for this task, we huddle together in ever-narrowing circles of rules we write for ourselves, hoping to secure a bright outcome for all that effort. Pema Chödrön, in her marvelous book *Living Beautifully with Uncertainty and Change*, says it so well:

> As individuals we, too, have fundamentalist tendencies. We use them to comfort ourselves. We grab on to a position or belief as a way of neatly explaining reality, unwilling to tolerate the uncertainty and discomfort of staying open to other possibilities. We cling to that position as our personal platform and become very dogmatic about it.[3]

✳ True Belief-ism ✳

I'm a sucker for strong ideologies. A true believer! Maybe you are too. Home births, breastfeeding, babywearing, religious fervor, staying married, veganism, unschooling, rural living, single-income family life, atheism, adopting special-needs children, screen-free/wooden-toys lifestyle, homeschooling, organic gardening, fostering—these are examples of commitments and belief structures that fly in the face of conventional modern life. To choose to live in a countercultural way requires devoted energy. The underlying assumption is that strenuous, unfailing commitment to the precepts of an ideology will result in a spectacular, happy, healthy family life—which will be on display for the world to see.

When I was a new mother, for instance, I caught a vision for breastfeeding: nursing a baby would lead to natural immunity, mother-child bonding, and good nutrition. Over time, I became dogmatic; I rejected all bottle-feeding. I thought mothers who used bottles were "less committed" to their children than I was. I became so passionate about breastfeeding, I never left my babies with a sitter and never used a bottle. I felt responsible to prop up the reputation of breastfeeding in mainstream society by absolute loyalty.

When one of my friends adopted a baby and bottle-fed her, I had to reconsider. Had I really believed that her adopted baby would have an inferior relationship to her mother because of a bottle? I have fond memories of breastfeeding and would do it again in a heartbeat. Yet I've had to ask myself: What drove this doubling down on breastfeeding as an ideology rather than enjoying it as a wonderful choice for infant nutrition?

It would take me another fifteen years to discover the danger of ideological purity: the absolute commitment to a belief system no matter your personal needs, experience, or changed circumstances. Homeschool parents seek like-minded friends to provide shelter from scrutiny. True believers latch onto the dogma with absolute commitment. They see any poor outcome as failure to practice *correctly* (worried that the belief system will be shot down by errant, less devoted practitioners).

Homeschool superstars are held up as role models of this fantasy life. When followers run into obstacles, the adherents from the group (keepers of the dogma) remind those who struggle to apply the practices and principles *more* perfectly or the fruits of that system won't be theirs. The failure is not in the system, but in the people living it out, so they say. Eventually, one of the role models is shown to be a hypocrite and the ideology shatters. The followers? Left wondering what went wrong and where to go next. Ideological nomads often swap one belief system for another.

You know that a group is entangled in the trap of ideological purity by how they treat nonmembers or members who fail to live up to the standards of the system. Are the true believers and leaders exclusionary and harsh? Do they focus on the rules of the system (or even the "un-system") more than each person's needs, personality, and contributions?

✳ Cruel to Be Kind ✳

One of the most startling experiences I had online was in an email group dedicated to helping parents become kind and gentle toward their children. The premise was that children needed to be loved and known *as they are*, trusting that children had their own wisdom. Parents were urged to take their children seriously, to adjust the lens of their perspective to see from behind their children's eyes, to tolerate childishness and mishaps in a spirit of loving support. The tools? Noncoercion and collaboration. I loved these principles.

Yet the group itself was a swirling stew of anger and hostility between the adult members and leaders. Word choices were routinely scrutinized under the harshest light; members who posted their struggles were blamed and shamed for not knowing better yet. Eruptions led to hurt feelings and members exited the list in droves every few months. Philosophy apologists railed against new members, defending the disrespectful tone of the leaders. It struck me as so odd! A child's perspective was never questioned while an adult's viewpoint was routinely denigrated. Somehow the kindness being promoted between parent and child was never on display in the group between members and leaders. I found it puzzling—how could that be?

I realized later that when people attach to a *philosophy* more than they focus on *connecting* in relationships, they become cruel—even if what they're promoting is kindness. Ironic! Not only that: when an environment becomes ideologically controlled, members stop feeling free to tell the truth about their experiences. They move from aspiration to pretense—hiding what isn't working, sharing only what they believe the group wants to hear. I noticed that I resented my family members for not living up to the ideals of the group. I worried that I'd lose my right to participate if the leaders knew that I hadn't adopted the principles perfectly in my own family.

When membership and participation depend on "doing it right," flaws, failures, and differences of opinion are driven underground. The glossy curated image that devoted members depict becomes more important than being real—than *telling the freaking truth*. In the end, the reason the philosophy appears to work is that no one is permitted to share the messy, imperfect practice. Let that sink in for a minute. The ideal models you follow? They may be phony—or at best, they likely exclude failures and doubts.

Worse—all that stress of living up to a model leads to tension in the home—between spouses who may not agree, between parents and children, and even between siblings. This happens even when the system declares it is *not* a system. Sometimes the effort to be hands-off is more paralyzing and confounding than any organized plan.

✳ Tell the Truth, Hold It Gently ✳

The first step out of a toxic ideological loop is to tell the truth. Pretending can't be an option. Instead, say what's so, and then reframe it gently.

See possibilities spring from your truth, rather than judging yourself harshly. Tell the truth, but *hold that truth benevolently*.

For instance, many home-educating mothers are crushed under the weight of doing it all perfectly. They want to be devoted mother-teachers, expert housekeepers, and intellectually adroit adults. They expect their own creativity, organizational skills, and intellects to meet every need. Mothers blame themselves when they can't.

Be courageous. Start with your limits, and then address them in your best mothering tone of voice—the one you wanted your own mother to use when you crashed her car. That's the voice—use it to help you face the truth with courage.

1. **Tell the truth:** *I wish I were the type of mother who could come up with creative ways to learn math. My kids hate math and I feel like it's my fault. I resort to nagging and arguing rather than inviting and inspiring.*

2. **Hold that truth benevolently:** *I lack mathematical training. Now's a chance to heal that sad history. What if I go on the journey to learn math with my kids? Who do I know that can help me grow and change my relationship to math?*

The place to begin is with the truth. Face your negative self-talk. Once you do (which may mean tears), shift gears to imagine how you might mother yourself in that moment. Let yourself off the hook. You can do that for yourself, for your child, and for how you see education. Start here:

1. **Make an honest appraisal of who you are today.** Who are you? Not, who do you want to be; not, who do you think you should be; not, who does your spouse expect you to be? What are your needs, desires, and abilities—today? Own them; be kind to them.

2. **Make a compassionate appraisal of your child.** Who is your child? See that child through loving eyes. Find all the ways to

describe your child's personality, strengths, and weaknesses with tenderness and empathy.

3. **Expand your choices in education.** What are your options? Put *all* the possibilities on the table. Let go of your need to prove anything to anyone—it is not on you to prove that homeschooling works. Be pragmatic, not idealistic. Include your child's desires in this equation.

Once you answer these questions honestly, give yourself time to live with the truths you've identified. Don't rush a solution. Allow yourself to linger. Once you put your mind on notice, your unconscious will take up the task of finding new-to-you ideas to explore.

In my experience, parents consider two of the three variables. They may look at their children and schooling options, but forget about their own needs or personality. For instance, a parent may read about the beautiful literature-rich, last-century education style of the Charlotte Mason philosophy of learning, ignoring the fact that the recommended books bore her. When the parent is out of sync with the learning model, irritation follows, and that irritation gets directed at the children.

Another example: some kids thrive on structure, yet they have a free-spirit parent. How do these get reconciled in a way that leads to a satisfying learning experience for everyone? Both factors matter for a happy homeschool.

Some parents may pay attention to their own needs and various schooling options, but forget to assess each child. One mother I met named Dana was frustrated with her daughter's active approach to learning (Casey hated seat-work). Dana put her little girl into the local elementary school halfway through the year to "teach Casey a lesson." Naturally, Casey struggled in that environment too. When I met Dana at a conference, I shared with her the power of collaboration. Dana had not considered that she was asking this active, social butterfly to learn by herself, dutifully.

The next day, when Casey began work on a school project, Dana joined her in the task that wound up taking five hours. At bedtime, her little girl hugged her mother tightly and whispered in Dana's ear, "I love you, Mama. Today was so much fun." Homeschool or traditional school, Dana discovered that the disordered relationship was not about an educational philosophy. Rather, collaboration and connection ensured the learning she wished for her daughter.

Finally, some parents never realize that more than one educational choice exists, and focus on parenting their children more and more exactingly to get them to cooperate with the parental choice. One homeschool discussion board I used to frequent was littered with posts like this one: "I don't take any guff. I just tell my kids—this is the assignment and you'd better get it done, or you won't go on the computer for a month. Works like a charm!"

But did it work like a charm? What lessons about learning, family, and relationship would a child under that system be getting? What invisible education?

The key to harmony at home, no matter which educational option you take, is ensuring that all three factors are a part of the educational and parenting choices—that you can dislodge your attachment to *proving* a method and instead attend to the people and possibilities in your immediate circle of concern.

✳ Sometimes You Can't ✳

There is another way to be faithful to the vision of mothering and educating our young that avoids the pitfalls of ideological attachment. When my friend Liz had her fifth baby, she experienced a health crisis—adrenal fatigue—for the first time. She and her husband had just moved to a new state and he had a new job. The third new thing—a new baby—put her over the edge. Liz and her husband were champions of homeschooling in their community and stood as role models to many. Yet when she became ill, Liz realized it was time to lay down her commitment to homeschooling to restore her health. It took courage to be willing to let someone else educate her children for hours a day. For the first time, all her kids would go to the brick building down the street. They'd bag lunches and risk being bullied; they'd bundle up in coats and boots at o'dark early every morning.

When we spoke on the phone, she explained, "I always thought we'd have a beautiful homeschool like the ones you and I read about in books. I kept thinking I could get there if I tried harder. But it's too hard now. I had to admit that I'm not equal to it during this season—that I could let someone else take the reins for a little while. Today I realized that we were writing our own school story for our family. It would look like us, not like anyone else."

What a powerful realization! Ideological attachment prohibits that kind of honest reflection. Eventually Liz brought her children home again, once she recovered. Today, some of her kids go part-time to the local high school and the others stay home all day. Her family story includes a variety of educational choices, including learning Spanish in Costa Rica at a language school for a summer as a family! Truly: her family's education story is unique to them.

One of the dangers of ideological purity is that it excludes perfectly good options from the table. It is possible to both reject the fundamental strategy of the local public school, for instance, and to find that it also selectively offers advantages to your children. It's possible to recognize that what works well for one studious child (classical education, for instance) creates distress for the more unstructured child. Similarly, one method may work well one year, and another method in a different season of life. When we stay open to lots of options, we create space for each person to show up as a unique person with their *own* story. The goal isn't to prop up a specific version of home education by pretending it always works with all children no matter what the circumstances. Our goal should be tailor-made education that allows our children to be the best versions of themselves.

✳ A Tale of Two Schooling Styles ✳

I remember when I started graduate school, I had also coincidentally just begun to study the theory of unschooling for my children's education. My hope and wish was to see my kids discover their unique passions and then to have all the time they wanted to pursue them and grow into self-directed adept learners—and of course, any learning they managed to acquire on their own would automatically prepare them for four-year college with little involvement from me (the fantasy). Meanwhile, I attended classes twice a week with a professor who designed a syllabus, prepared lectures, assigned readings and essays, and offered us slide shows of historical artifacts.

During those years, it dawned on me: I *loved* graduate school. I adored the feeling of showing up to a class where a PhD had prepared lessons for me. I had studied my field on my own for fifteen years and it felt like a relief to be in a community of learners where my only task was to follow along.

Yet at home, as I fumbled to apply the unschooling model, I felt guilty about preparing anything for my children—asking them to read a book or offering them a lesson based on my more complete education. I worried that I was interfering—that they would never catch fire for their own passions if I guided them in any way.

There was a moment when it all gelled for me. I saw that education came in a variety of methodologies, each one replete with specific advantages and limits. Sometimes it's a real treat to simply "show up" after someone else has done the preparation for you. Other times, it feels marvelous to give unfettered attention to a subject without it being filtered through another person's agenda. Both are valid perspectives. The day I realized that I loved traditional learning in graduate school was the day I let go of my educational ideological attachments, and the wind of freedom blew through the house. Suddenly *all* educational options were on the table. When Johannah expressed interest in part-time public high school, I didn't take it as an invalidation of homeschool. It felt like variety! As my homeschooling friend Susie once said, "Variety is the spice of life. I never followed the same philosophy of education three years in a row. I liked to try new things and so did my kids."

The gift we can give ourselves is permission to experiment with education. Why not? You only live once.

✳ Us-schooling ✳

One Brave Writer mom shared with me that during a challenging season of life, she turned to our program to support her in teaching writing to her girls. The next thing you know, her unschooling community declared that she was not a "real" unschooler because she had purchased a curriculum to help instruct her children in writing. She wrote in a fit of brilliance, "I wanted to say to them: We aren't unschoolers. We're 'us-schoolers'—we homeschool in a way that suits *us*."

When you can't give your kids the education you want to due to cancer, divorce, depression, or hoarding, or because you're sick to death of homeschooling, it's critical that you allow yourself the freedom to look at other options—even those that you ruled out when you started. To exit the box of ideology means pulling up a seat to the table marked "All options." The tools we need to create a "good enough" family life and education can only be developed with full conscious sight. We make choices in the light of our honest appraisal of who we are, not in the darkness of our anxiety about who we don't want to be.

✳ Disrupt Your Story ✳

Years ago, I read an interview with legendary rocker Bruce Springsteen in *Rolling Stone* magazine. His new album at the time had been a departure from what he had written before, and he wanted to account for it. "I didn't know what I wanted to do. I had to break the narrative that I was in, break the context and move to L.A. for three or four years, get away from all things connected to myself."[4] That idea of "breaking" your narrative stayed with me. We don't always know what we want if we are afraid to explore the edges of our options.

Springsteen went on to describe what that process felt like. "So you realize you've got to make your own map, and in so doing, you honor your parents by taking the good things they gave you and carrying them forth, and taking burdens and weights and putting them down so your children don't have to run with them."[5]

When we examine our educational options with our own personalities and our children's uniqueness in mind, we allow the fresh wind of possibilities to waft through the room. The best education we can give our children is the one that says: *There are unlimited ways to get to where you want to go; I'm here to help you find your way.*

Sometimes you must disrupt your *own* narrative: how you thought it all should go, how it should look, how it should feel. Sometimes the best educational choice you can make is the one you never in a million years considered. In fact, isn't that how some of us came to homeschooling?

CHAPTER 14

REVERSE THE CURSE

How to Rekindle the Magic

The Type B Checklist, Surprises of Happy, Paydays, and Becoming Wise

Please love your child unconditionally and give him a super-abundance of eye contact, physical contact, and focused attention.

—DR. ROSS CAMPBELL,
HOW TO REALLY LOVE YOUR CHILD

Once you've assessed your family dynamics honestly, it's time to dig out a new book of matches to reignite the love of learning in your family. The number one task of parents is to protect both the physical and emotional welfare of their children. You're on task if you're doing that.

What can any of us do when faced with family crises? Fortunately, lots of things. Being a native Californian, I've been a fan of talk therapy for as long as I can remember. I used to tell my kids that even if I couldn't pay college tuition, they could count on me to contribute to their therapy costs. I've kept that promise.

That said, too often parents want to fix their children rather than the problem. If you're facing a challenge with any of your children (or all of them), go to therapy as the *parent*. Get perspective, tools, and strategies for how to be a better mother or father to that "problem child" first. The issues in your kids are often a mirror to blind spots in you.

Not only that: if you send a child to therapy before you've been for yourself, the child rightly discerns that you consider the child the problem. If, however, you've used therapy in your life before asking a child to go, she learns that therapy is a natural choice for people who want to lead conscious, healthy lives. Therapy is good emotional and mental hygiene—just as teeth cleanings and going to the gym are good for physical health. Nothing to be ashamed of! Not only that, you are paying someone to listen to you. You don't have to reciprocate!

Support groups exist for addiction, codependency, domestic violence, divorce, grief, and eating disorders. Books and online communities are available for every dysfunction under the sun. Educate yourself, get help, grow. Your children will thank you.

✳ Garden-Variety Ups and Downs ✳

For the rest of the time when you face the usual challenges to parenting and educating, I've got three easy-to-use tools to help you get back on your feet after the wind gets knocked out of you.

Type B Checklist

Type A parents tell me they need to put check marks next to their to-do lists. They freak out when they hear "let inspiration lead you." They want to be able to make a list like this one:

* 6 pages read
* 12 problems of math completed
* Asian history project finished

These same parents tell me they couldn't possibly trust a "natural learning" style of homeschool because they are type A people. They need to know the plan, follow the plan, check off the plan. Checklists are great—it's up to you what goes on them. Strike the match: change the categories! Presenting the "Type B Checklist":

To-Do

* Make eye contact with each child.
* Listen—without distraction.
* Give a hug after an achievement.
* Jot down a little narrative that one of the kids spontaneously shared.
* Sit with a struggling child.
* Add a treat to a challenging activity.
* Spend a whole afternoon playing.
* Notice improvement and comment out loud.
* Chat about the book being read.
* Find a real-world application for today's math problems.
* Hold back angry words.
* Be curious about the interest that makes you uncomfortable.
* Use a brain break during the lesson.
* Skip the hard part for today.
* Smile.
* Share your child's success with the other parent in front of the child.

What Other Items Can You Add from the Lessons of This Book?

* Do one new thing today: prepare, execute, enjoy, reminisce.
* Use surprise, mystery, risk, or adventure to enhance how you present a subject.
* Apply one of the four doses of vitamin C (curiosity, collaboration, contemplation, celebration).
* Activate the mind, body, heart, or spirit in the lesson.
* Make a mess and let it stand.

* Connect to the child rather than shouting.
* Participate in the child's hobby to know and understand it.
* Reflect on the weather of the home today.
* Do one activity that helps you be an awesome adult.
* Go to talk therapy for a little self-care.

Be a type A person with a type B checklist!

Surprise of Happy

Sometimes life is underwater. You stare at the sky through wiggly lines of suffocating liquid weight wondering if you'll ever breathe the oxygen of happiness again. Gratitude lists feel like punishment, rather than liberation. At one such moment in my life, my friend Sherri told me to stop trying to be happy. It was too big a burden. Instead, she suggested foisting that responsibility back on the universe. Rather than conjuring up gratitude, I could simply be alert for a moment of the day that surprised me into happiness.

I woke the next morning and said into the air: "I can't feel joy. If there's happiness to be felt, come find me." I was alert in a passive way. Later that day, glinting light filtered through the blinds. Startling sunshine. I felt relief—a flicker of hope. Staying open to a "surprise of happy" has become my sacred practice.

When all else fails, let moments of joy find their way to you. Jot them down, or at minimum, pause. Notice. Feel. The Scatterbook is a great place to store these surprises of happy.

Paydays

This same wise friend, Sherri, listened to the news that my daughter had been accepted to Ohio State University for college. She declared, "Payday!" I laughed and said, "What?" She responded: "We don't make money homeschooling. We get paid when our kids achieve or do something wonderful. This is your payday." I *loved* that!

Paydays abound. Here are a few examples:

* A child comforts you when you're distressed.
* The first time your child reads aloud.
* A sixteen-year-old passes the driving test.
* Your child gets cast in a play.
* The gaggle of kids team up to clean the art table on their own initiative.
* Poetry Teatime happens every week and everyone loves it.
* Your college student decides to study abroad and wants you to visit.
* You overhear your twentysomething-year-old bragging about having been homeschooled.

Paydays are those moments when all your heart and hard work pay off. Our Brave Writer community uses the hashtag #payday on Instagram and Twitter to celebrate the realization of their dreams. Paydays accumulate and matter. Note them, count them, record them.

✳ You Only Have to Get It Mostly Right ✳

There's no way to fix every problem in a family or homeschool. Sometimes, we hit the ball out of the park. Others, the ball dribbles off the glove and rolls to the outfield into the weeds. A good enough homeschool and family life means that you are *conscious*—making choices, acting with goodwill, open to change and growth. Your children will forgive your mistakes if they know that they can name them and be heard, if they know you're trying, if they feel your earnestness. You can forgive yourself for your failures if you make friends on the journey, find tools for growth, and have reasonable expectations. This book is designed to help you with the tools and expectations. Come find me on social media and I'll introduce you to the friends.

✳ Becoming Wise ✳

Wisdom is not the gathering of more facts and information, as
if that would eventually coalesce into truth. Wisdom is a way
of seeing and knowing the same old ten thousand things but
in a new way. As my colleague Cynthia Bourgeault often says,
it's not about knowing more, but knowing *with* more of you.

—RICHARD ROHR, "LIVING IN THE NOW: PURE PRESENCE"

The beginning of wisdom is the recognition: "Hey, I need wisdom!" We become wise through our collective experience, our shared memory, and the same old ten thousand things that we understand together, in a new way, with *more* of ourselves each year.

It matters to pause occasionally and take stock. Most of us walk around embedded in whatever family system we've inherited, unaware that it needs examination and overhaul. I read about shame and parenting for the first time in 1989, when Noah was two years old. I swore I would never use coercion, control, or blame to raise him. Twelve short years later, I saw in the rearview mirror the ways I had failed to live up to that ideal. How inexperienced was I! I couldn't possibly appreciate the thousands of ways my heart would be twisted into a pretzel of fear, worry, and my own limitations. I couldn't see what I couldn't see; I couldn't know what I didn't understand. Reminds me of that saying: "You can't read the label when you're inside the jar."

The first step to wisdom is to become a brave learner. We embarked on this journey to give our kids an education. It's ironic that their learning journey is, in fact, contingent on ours. We need to acknowledge that we're out of our depth when we create new families. Every one of us has some dysfunction—how willing are we to name it and work with it? To disembed requires stepping outside our familiar family experience to reflect on its meaning and impact on our current lives. We do it again and again—there is no "once for all time" cleansing. It's an ongoing project, lived in a family.

The goal can't be to create a perfect homeschool. A healthy family and homeschool foster a space where routines, habits, aspirations, and lifestyle adapt to the changing needs and wants of each member, despite occasional lapses of anger or hurting one another. Paying attention to the ordinary magic in our day-to-day lives can light up learning for everyone—parent and child. When we tap into that slipstream of connection and joy, we discover that life and education are the same. All we need can be found in that cocoon of love and learning. It's a process—a bumpy, unpredictable, yet wonderful one.

One day I was talking with Johannah on the phone while she was away at college. She felt hurt that I hadn't called recently. My life was overfull with three kids still at home, their soccer practices and home education consuming my attention. Noah lived locally and needed my support and outreach too. She felt neglected.

As we talked, however, a realization dawned on her: I was mother to five children. In a burst of insight, she said: "Wait. I see. You rotate your attention. You can't care about each child at the same level every day, so you rotate through us depending on what we need." I paused, about to defend my devotion to all five equally—and then saw what she saw: it was true. I did rotate through my five kids.

We cycle through all kinds of needs and demands every day of our homeschooling years, all while hoping to achieve the dream: raising well-educated, emotionally whole, responsible adults. The illusion is that there is a day that result arrives and we can say, "There it is! My achievement!"

Nothing lasts. Even graduations and weddings, new jobs and grandbabies—these are moments too, and they're fleeting. We do the best we can, we show up, we celebrate, we love, we try, we keep going.

I was on the phone with my mother a few weeks ago. My sister, Erin, is in her early fifties and my mom sees her several times a week. Erin has a lot on her plate—kids living at home, an exchange student, a grandchild, working full-time. My mom worried about her to me, wanting my sister's life to be calm, at peace. As my mom talked, I suddenly cut her off with a shocking realization. "Wait, you mean I will still be worrying about my kids' well-being when they are over fifty years old!?"

My mom cracked up: "Yes. It never ends."

And honestly, that's good news. I wanted a rich *life* with my kids, not just their college-ready education, and I have it. The bonds I forged with my children are deep; I care, no matter how old they are. Even with our own brand of family pain, we experienced real pleasure in homeschool and beyond. It brings me relief and joy to know it now.

That monumental commitment included six philosophies of education and a couple shots at unschooling. We participated in two different kinds of co-ops, we used public high school for part-time and full-time enrollment, and we hired a slew of math tutors. Four of my five kids graduated from college, while one made three attempts and quit, finding his own way into his satisfying career. One graduated from law school and moved to Thailand. They all either studied abroad or traveled to visit siblings who lived in other countries.

During the growing-up years, we shared countless Poetry Teatimes and counted hundreds of birds. I read the *Harry Potter* series aloud— twice. We visited Italy on a "trip of a lifetime," which caused eight-year-old Caitrin to declare: "I don't care if I never see another painting!" A decade later, she and I toured Monet's gallery together in Paris. My kids and I threw parties, took nature walks, and went skiing. We studied Latin roots and Shakespeare, French and Greek. I attended hundreds of baseball, lacrosse, basketball, and ultimate Frisbee games, as well as soccer and chess matches. I gave standing ovations at plays and ballet performances.

I forgot to teach US government.

No one became proficient on the piano.

We never figured out a once-and-for-all housekeeping system.

Life rolled forward and some of what I took for granted shattered. Jon and I are no longer married. We continue the project of loving and serving our adult kids, as best we can. We found a way through our version of pain and heartache, we made tough choices, and we adapted. We keep forgiving ourselves and each other for being oh-so-very human.

Homeschooling—hell, parenting—is a journey of courage into the unknown with an audacious belief that you will be enough for your children: the ultimate brave learning adventure. It can't be any other way. Whatever you offer your kids—your best and your worst—they take it and turn it into fuel for their own blazing fires of blinding beauty. They astonish us every day, even as they terrify us too. You're doing it right if you stay connected, and every now and then pause in awe. Look! Those are *my* amazing human beings!

Keep going. I'm rooting for you.

ACKNOWLEDGMENTS

Like any good student, I've built my philosophy of learning and loving from the research, writings, and examples of countless people I've studied and admired. My hope is that I've captured the essence of their brilliance while offering my own spin and interpretation. Any omission or misrepresentation is on me.

At my stage of life, it's easy to look back and regret choices made in ignorance or with too much idealism and not enough life experience. One choice I have not regretted, even once, is the decision to homeschool my kids. The rewards keep coming and my tender memories are more precious to me with each passing year. Thank you to homeschool pioneers, the Easley and Withers families, for being the first to show me an attractive picture of homeschooling back in the 1980s—joy in family and learning, capable mother-educators.

Thanks to my agent, Rita Rosenkranz, who took a chance on this book's theme. Rita gave me the precise insight to shift the focus of the book to the right target. I appreciate how she championed the message even as she helped me to clarify it. I would also like to thank my editor, Joanna Ng, at TarcherPerigee for both catching the vision and ably honing it to the well-edited book you have in your hands today. I cannot imagine a better publishing experience than working with Joanna and her team.

Brave Writer, my writing company, has provided me the platform for this book. That little kitchen-table enterprise took leaps forward when I brought on two key staff members. To Cindy Clark: Brave Writer quite simply would not be what it is today without your skilled attention to every detail I overlook. You are the best! To Jeannette Frantz: our long-term friendship and haggling over homeschool ideas has bloomed into a working partnership. Thankful for you.

Thank you to the rest of the Brave Writer core team, especially: Kirsten Merryman, Tia Levings, Stephanie Elms, Jeanne Faulconer, Dawn Smith, Beth Miller, Paula Horton, Mary Wilson, Sue Antczak, Richard Powell, Tom Davies, and Bill Barkalow.

I deeply appreciate our Brave Writer community of parents and the members of the Homeschool Alliance, especially those of you whose stories appear in this book, both by name and those who appear anonymously. Thank you for your enthusiasm and participation in this project!

A special shout out to the Trapdoor Society women who were my best friends and chief dialogue partners in my formative years.

The following friends have made important contributions to this book. I'm glad for the deep and abiding friendship I've shared with Dotty Christensen and her family for more than thirty years. Thankful to my ally and dear friend Sherri Miller for her key concepts (*payday*, and *surprise of happy*), and to Beth Crews for, well, everything, but especially the plunge into taking our children seriously. I couldn't have written this book without the support of my marathon partner, Patrice Mosby, who tallied thousands of miles listening to my ideas. I've got a cherry-flavored Life Saver for you!

When I broke my ankle right as I began writing the manuscript, my sweetheart Jim Schaefer made it possible for me to write every day (he kept food in my pantry, ice on my incision, and a smile on my face).

Thank you to Dr. Curt Spear who gave me key insights into family dysfunction and how to build emotional health.

I'm grateful for colleagues: Melissa Wiley (author of *The Prairie Thief*)—my quick-witted sidekick on Slack and like-hearted educational visionary. Dr. Peter Elbow (author of *Writing with Power*) taught me the power of freedom to risk in writing and education. Dr. Susan Wise Bauer (author of *The Well-Trained* Mind) has been a friend on the journey as entrepreneur, home educator, and writer. Our conversations leave me with more questions than answers, which I love. Rita Cevasco from Rootedinlanguage.com offered invaluable insight into learning challenges, while Debba Haupert of Girlfriendology.com brainstormed a thousand ideas with me over glasses of wine and steak salads. A glad happenstance introduced me to the talented Dr. Barbara Oakley (author of *Learning How to Learn*), whose books and courses have expanded and reinforced my ideas.

I would never have attempted this dodgy educational practice in 1992 had it not been for the unwavering support of Jon Bogart, my children's father and my husband of twenty-five years. Jon's heart for people around the world, his deep love of literature, and his big juicy conversational style shaped our family culture. I'm indebted to him for allowing me to share our story (both the pretty and not-so-pretty moments) for the benefit of others.

Each of my children has given me permission to tell their stories as well. Noah, Johannah, Jacob, Liam, and Caitrin are the epitome of life-long learners. I'm grateful for their open hearts and precise opinions. They are, quite simply, the loves of my life.

Lastly and mostly: thank you to Karen O'Connor. My mother, an award-winning author, guided me gently in this publishing odyssey, believing in my book from its inception. She gave frank, helpful edits to my book proposal. She read the final version of the manuscript and celebrated it with specific, highlighted passages. What I love best is that my mother was also a kind of home educator before such a thing existed— her enthusiasm for books, discovery, and partnership in learning were evident throughout my childhood, and those passions found their full expression in me, as a homeschool mother. "Thank you" is not enough. I love you, Mom.

NOTES

CHAPTER 1: ENCHANTED LIVING

1 Kelly Barnhill, *The Girl Who Drank the Moon* (Chapel Hill, NC: Algonquin, 2016).

CHAPTER 3: MAGIC DOORS

1 William Reinsmith, "Ten Fundamental Truths About Learning," *The National Teaching and Learning Forum*, v2 n1–6 1992–93, https://files.eric.ed.gov/fulltext/ED360897.pdf, 45.

2 Geoffrey Caine and Renate Nummela Caine, *The Brain, Education, and the Competitive Edge* (Lanham, MD: Rowman & Littlefield Education, 2005): 39–40.

3 Caine and Caine, *12 Brain/Mind Learning Principles in Action* (Thousand Oaks, CA: Corwin Press, 2008), 145.

PART TWO: CASTING THE SPELL

1 William Reinsmith, "Archetypal Forms in Teaching," *College Teaching* 42, no. 4 (Fall 1994): 131–136.

CHAPTER 4: THE FOUR FORCES OF ENCHANTMENT

1 Jim Collins, "BHAG—Big Hairy Audacious Goal," http://www.jimcollins.com/article_topics/articles/BHAG.html.

2 "Brandon Stanton, NYC Photographer, Rallies Strangers to Send Little Boy on Wild West Adventure," *Huffington Post*, August 2, 2013, https://www.huffingtonpost.com/2013/08/02/brandon-stanton-nyc-wild-west-adventure_n_3695583.html.

CHAPTER 5: THE FOUR CAPACITIES FOR LEARNING

1 Arthur L. Costa (ed.), *Developing Minds: A Resource Book for Teaching Thinking* (Alexandria, VA: Association for Supervision & Curriculum Development, 2001), 85.

2 Aly Weisman, "Meet Steven Spielberg's Parents in This Revealing '60 Minutes' Profile," *Business Insider*, October 22, 2012, http://www.businessinsider.com/meet-steven-spielbergs-parents-in-this-revealing-60-minutes-profile-2012-10.

3 Renate Nummela Caine, Geoffrey Caine, Carol Lynn McClintic, and Karl J. Klimek (eds.), *12 Brain/Mind Learning Principles in Action: Developing Executive Functions of the Human Brain* (Thousand Oaks, CA: Corwin Press, 2008), 8.

4 Caine et al., *12 Brain/Mind Learning Principles in Action*, 7.

5 Caine et al., *12 Brain/Mind Learning Principles in Action*, 4.

6 Taina Rantala and Kaarina Määttä, "Ten Theses of the Joy of Learning at Primary Schools," *Early Childhood Development and Care* 182, no. 1 (January 2012): 99.

CHAPTER 6: THE FOUR PORTS OF ENTRY

1 Charlotte Mason, *A Philosophy of Education: The Home Education Series*, vol. 6 (Jilliby, Australia: Living Book Press, 2017), xxix.

2 Howard Gardner, "On Failing to Grasp the Core of MI Theory: A Response to Visser et al.," *Intelligence* 34, no. 5 (September–October 2006): 503–505, https://www.sciencedirect.com/science/article/pii/S0160289606000328?via%3Dihub.

3 Georgia Garvey, "Exercise Balls in the Classroom?" *Chicago Tribune*, November 2, 2009, http://www.chicagotribune.com/sns-health-school-bouncy-balls-story.html.

4 The Student Coalition for Action in Literacy Education, "Behavior Management: Important Facts," http://www.unc.edu/depts/scale/Member/trainings/BehaviorManagement-ImportantFacts.pdf.

5 Joshua MacNeill, *101 Brain Breaks and Brain Based Educational Activities* (2017), 8.

6 Michael Maloney, "The Role of Practice in Learning: Directed Practice," *The Maloney Method*, July 15, https://www.maloneymethod.com/resources/the-role-of-practice-in-learning-directed-practice/.

7 Costa, *Developing Minds*, 396.

8 Richard Weissbourd and Stephanie Jones, "How Parents Can Cultivate Empathy in Children," Making Caring Common Project, https://mcc.gse.harvard.edu/files/gse-mcc/files/empathy.pdf.

9 Paul Tournier, *The Adventure of Living* (New York: HarperCollins, 1979), chapter 2.

10 "What Is Hygge? Everything You Need to Know About the Danish Lifestyle Trend," *Country Living*, January 6, 2017, http://www.countryliving.com/life/a41187/what-is-hygge-things-to-know-about-the-danish-lifestyle-trend/.

CHAPTER 7: APPLYING THE SUPERPOWERS

1 Chauncey Monte-Sano, Susan De La Paz, and Mark Felton, *Reading, Thinking, and Writing About History: Teaching Argument Writing to Diverse Learners in the Common Core Classroom, Grades 6–12* (New York: Teachers College Press, 2014), 7.

2 Monte-Sano et al., *Reading, Thinking, and Writing About History*.

3 Peter Elbow, *Writing with Power* (New York: Oxford University Press, 1998), 15.

4 Barbara Oakley, *A Mind for Numbers: How to Excel at Math and Science (Even If You Flunked Algebra)* (New York: TarcherPerigee, 2014), 36.

5 "Why You Need a Teacher (even if you're sure you don't)," *Good Life Project*, Science update, January 18, 2018, https://www.frontiersin.org/articles/10.3389/fpsyg.2017.02253/full.

6 David L., "Gamification in Education," *Learning Theories*, January 26, 2016, https://www.learning-theories.com/gamification-in-education.html.

CHAPTER 9: HOUSE-SCHOOLING

1 Anne Lamott, *Bird by Bird* (New York: Anchor Books, 1995), 28–29.

CHAPTER 10: THE PIXIE DUST OF REASONABLE EXPECTATIONS

1 Reinsmith, "Ten Fundamental Truths About Learning."
2 David Elkind, *The Power of Play: Learning What Comes Naturally* (Boston: Da Capo Press, 2007), 117.
3 National Novel Writing Month Young Writers Program, https://ywp.nanowrimo.org/.
4 Ron Gutman, "The Untapped Power of Smiling," Forbes.com, March 22, 2011, https://www .forbes.com/sites/ericsavitz/2011/03/22/the-untapped-power-of-smiling/#593c4cd27a67.
5 Costa, *Developing Minds*, "A Biological Basis for Learning," 240.
6 Costa, *Developing Minds*, "A Biological Basis for Learning," 241.
7 Costa, *Developing Minds*, "A Biological Basis for Learning," 241.

CHAPTER 12: THE INVISIBLE EDUCATION

1 Abby Ohlheiser, "Josh Duggar Molested Four of His Sisters and a Babysitter, Parents Tell Fox News," *Washington Post*, June 4, 2015, https://www.washingtonpost.com/news/acts-of-faith /wp/2015/06/03/what-to-expect-from-the-fox-news-interview-with-josh-duggars-parents /?utm_term=.51a8e11900eb.
2 Homeschoolers Anonymous, https://homeschoolersanonymous.org/.
3 Flannery O'Connor, *Mystery and Manners: Occasional Prose* (New York: Farrar, Straus and Giroux, 1969).
4 "Dysfunctional Family Relationships," Counseling and Psychological Services, Brown University, https://www.brown.edu/campus-life/support/counseling-and-psychological-services /index.php?q=dysfunctional-family-relationships.
5 Alice Miller, *The Truth Will Set You Free* (New York: Basic Books, 2002): ix.
6 Renate N. Caine and Geoffrey Caine, *Natural Learning for a Connected World: Education, Technology, and the Human Brain*, (New York: Teachers College Press, 2011), chapter 3.
7 Caine and Caine, *Natural Learning for a Connected World*, chapter 3.
8 Janice and Dennis Hughes, "An Interview with John Bradshaw," *The Share Guide*, 2013, http://www.shareguide.com/Bradshaw3.html.

CHAPTER 13: THE DISENCHANTING POWER OF DOING IT RIGHT

1 Jennifer Lois, *Home Is Where the School Is: The Logic of Homeschooling and the Emotional Labor of Mothering* (New York: NYU Press, 2012), 7.
2 Lois, *Home Is Where the School Is*, 10.
3 Pema Chödrön, *Living Beautifully with Uncertainty and Change* (Boulder, CO: Shambhala, 2013), 7.
4 Joe Levy, "Bruce Springsteen: The Rolling Stone Interview," *Rolling Stone*, November 1, 2007, http://www.rollingstone.com/music/news/bruce-springsteen-the-rolling-stone -interview-20071101.
5 Levy, "Bruce Springsteen."

INDEX

Page numbers in **bold** indicate tables; those in *italics* indicate figures.

abundance vs. deprivation, 231

accessibility, critical to exploration, 193–94

accidental learning, 37, 38

activity, bodies craving, 109

adulting. *See* awesome adulting

adult vs. with child's flame, 14–16, 24, 28

Adventure (Force 4 of Enchantment), 59–63
   applying Superpowers, 125, 131, 132, 149
   away from home trips, 61, 62–63
   awesome adulting, 218, 219, 220, 222, 224, 225, 226
   Collaboration (Capacity 2), 75
   defined, xxii, xxiii, 30, 33, 37
   enchanted living, 8
   getting out into the big blue world, 59–60
   liberation from school, 173, 176, 181, 185
   performance, 60
   reversing the curse, 268, 274
   Risk (Force 3), 38, 54, 59, 131
   sparks fly, 13
   See also Forces of Enchantment

Adventure of Living, The (Tournier), 119

alcoholism, 236

allies, 113, 115–16

"always open for business" art table, 4, 5–7, 9–10, 189, 193, 270

American Girl, 95

Apple Watch, 156

applying the Superpowers (practical help in core subjects), 125–61
   Capacities for Learning, 125, 131, 137, 138, 142, 144, 152, 155, 156, 160
   Forces of Enchantment, 125, 128, 131, 132, 137, 138, 139, 142, 149, 157
   playing games, 154–61
   Poetry Teatime, 130–32, 224, 273

   Ports of Entry, 125, 128, 132, 135, 137, 138, 156, 159
   thinking like a . . . , 126–29
   See also casting the spell (Superpowers); *specific subjects*

archaeologist, digging like an, 127–28

art, xvi, 19, 25, 28, 41–42, 47, 60, 61, 95, 125, 133, 185, 189, 192, 226–27

Art Institute in Chicago, 226

art table, 4, 5–7, 9–10, 189, 193, 270

Ashley (dysfunctional parent), 233–34

Asia, 51–52

attention, sustaining by Mystery, 45–46

attention span, focused, 107–8

audiobooks, 133, 135

auditory intelligence, 101

Austen, Jane, 55, 224

awakening to the need to know, 23–28

away from home trips, 61, 62–63

awesome adulting (expanding our horizons), 218–31
   family culture, 225–26, 247
   Forces of Enchantment, 218, 219, 220, 222, 224, 225, 226
   "I don't have time for that!" 221
   letter of encouragement, 230–31
   more ways to be awesome, 225
   nap time is your time, 221–22
   perks of being an adult, 219–21
   Ports of Entry, 222, 229, 230
   psst, it's also a good idea to like homeschooling, 228–30
   reviving adulthood, 222–24
   riding solo (self-care), 226–27
   your kids want to be proud of you, 227–28
   See also sustaining the magic

Aztecs, 127

back-to-home surprises, 43–44

baking tips and tricks, 82

Bapa Was My Champion, 215–16

Barb (homeschooling friend), 148

"base twelve" times table, 90–91

bathtub stopper, 18

Battle of Little Bighorn, 221–22

Bauer, Susan Wise, xv–xvii

bellows or bucket of water? 13–16

benign indifference, 42

Big Hairy Audacious Goals (BHAG), 54–56, 59

big juicy conversations, 76–77, 212–13

big-sistering, 75, 79–80, 81, 83

biology, 17, 20, 147, 207, 224

birds, 8, 47, 86, 146–47, 148, 160, 182, 185, 193, 273

blaming, 118, 197, 199, 237, 241, 246, 247, 257, 259, 271

"blast off" practice, 109

board games, 154–55

bodily/kinesthetic intelligence, 101

Body (Port 2 of Entry), 106–12
    activity, bodies craving, 109
    applying Superpowers, 125, 132, 138, 156
    breaks, 77, 107–8, 112, 144, 169, 176, 216, 229, 268
    comfort, bodies craving, 109–11
    defined, 30, 99
    "Do, Be, Do," 111–12
    hygge and, 123
    invisible education, 240, 244–45
    liberation from school, 169, 174, 176, 186
    magic doors, 22
    Mind (Port 1), 99, 100–102, 107, 108, 111
    reasonable expectations, 205
    reversing the curse, 268
    Risk (Force 3), 58, 98
    See also Ports of Entry

Bogart, Jon, 66, 137, 251, 252, 253, 273

Bogart, Julie, xix–xxiii, 130, 230–31, 247
    See also brave learners

book club parties, 160, 207

boredom with curriculum, 203

Bradshaw, John, 252–53

brain-based learning, 22

brain breaks, 108

brave learners, xv–xvii, xix–xxiii, 266–74
    See also Bogart, Julie; breaking the spell, rekindling magic; casting the spell (Superpowers); enchanted education;

enchanted landscape of learning; sustaining the magic; traditional school

Brave Writer, xxi, 77–78, 79, 94, 119–20, 128–29, 135, 139–40, 212, 247, 264, 270
    See also writing

breaking the spell, rekindling magic, 233–34
    traditional school vs., 263
    See also brave learners; disenchanting power of doing it right (dangers of ideological alignment); invisible education (family dysfunction sidelining learning); reversing the curse (rekindling the magic); *specific subjects*

breaking your narrative, 264–65

breaks, 77, 107–8, 112, 144, 169, 176, 216, 229, 268

breastfeeding, 256

Bridgett (Julie's friend), 110

Brown University, 239

Built to Last (Collins), 54

Caine, Renate and Geoffrey, 21–22, 65, 87, 247

Caitrin (Julie's daughter), 45–46, 55, 62, 78–79, 100, 112, 137, 273

Capacities for Learning, 30, 64–96, 99, 125, 186
    See also casting the spell (Superpowers); Celebration; Collaboration; Contemplation; Curiosity

Caps for Sale experience, 4, 8

caring, inability to coerce, 17

Carol (Julie's friend), 194

casting the spell (Superpowers), 29–31
    One Thing Principle, 30–31
    traditional school vs., 29, 34, 35, 37, 72, 80, 85–86, 88, 89, 90, 101, 102, 103, 104, 107, 111
    See also applying the Superpowers (practical help in core subjects); brave learners; Capacities for Learning; enchanted education; Forces of Enchantment; Ports of Entry; *specific subjects*

cat, petting while writing, 111

Celebration (Capacity 4 for Learning), 89–96
    applying Superpowers, 125, 131, 137, 152, 156, 160
    choice in learning, 90, 93, 94–95
    copywork, 78, **81**, 92, 93, 94, 110, 112, 158, 169, 176, 182, 185, 207
    Curiosity (Capacity 1), 74
    defined, 30, 64, 65
    dictation, 92, 112, 169, 182, 183

Forces of Enchantment, 44, 55, 90, 93
Heart (Port 3), 116
house-schooling, 194, 198
invisible education, 242
liberation from school, 176, 181, 186
pretty please? (motivation), 91–92
reasonable expectations, 205, 216
reversing the curse, 268, 270, 272
See also Capacities for Learning
challenge, competence, and meaning, 114
challenges, 65, 89, 93, 94, 198, 267–70
chemistry, 20, 72, **81**, 144
chess, 84–85, 87, 142
child-led learning, 17
See also brave learners
Child Protective Services (CPS), 233
Children Already Love Learning (Principle 2),
    20–21
children as persons, not adults-in-training, 98
child's mind at work, 105
Chinese language, 78–79
Chödrön, Pema, 255
choice in learning, 90, 93, 94–95
chores, 194–201
Christina's Blackberry Fool, 182–84
Cincinnati, Ohio, 60, 62, 146, 226
cityschool, farmschool, 189–91, 192
classical education in fall, 172
coaching, 113, 115–16
Coffee Break French (podcast), 80
Collaboration (Capacity 2 for Learning), 75–83
    applying Superpowers, 125, 131, 137, 138,
        144, 155
    big juicy conversations, 76–77, 212–13
    big-sistering, 75, 79–80, 81, 83
    Curiosity (Capacity 1), 77, 78, 79
    defined, 30, 64, 65
    disenchanting power of doing it right, 257,
        260–61
    Forces of Enchantment, 75, 76, 82
    independent learning, 76–82, **81**
    learning vs. exploring, 79
    liberation from school, 176, 183, 186
    Mind (Port 1), 77, 79, 102, 105
    reasonable expectations, 210, 214
    reversing the curse, 268
    spark or fizzling flame? 77–79
    See also Capacities for Learning
college, xvi, xxii, 17, 21, 54, 60, 85, 103, 121,
    129, 132, 138, 157, 174, 175, 180, 204, 205,
    220, 229, 263, 269, 270, 273

Collins, Jim, 54
comfort, bodies craving, 109–11
Common Core, xxi
companions and champions, 214–17
complex learning enhanced by challenge,
    inhibited by threat, 247
computational capacity, intelligence, 101
computer games. *See* gaming
concentric circles, thinking like a historian,
    149, 150–53
connection, connection, connection, xxii,
    xxiii, 112, 122, 123, 124, 157, 159, 175, 176,
    209, 212–13, 214, 217, 252, 253, 258, 261,
    269, 272, 274
Contemplation (Capacity 3 for Learning),
    84–89
    applying Superpowers, 125, 131
    chess, 84–85, 87, 142
    Curiosity (Capacity 1), 67, 84,
        86–88
    dedication to one skill transfers to another,
        85–86
    defined, 30, 64, 65
    Fruits of Contemplative Learning, 86
    liberation from school, 176, 186
    reversing the curse, 268
    silent, invisible partner, 86–87
    valuing what your children value, 70, 85,
        87–88, 90, 91
    See also Capacities for Learning
context for magic in our homes. *See* enchanted
    living
Continent of Learning, 24–27, 27, 75,
    88, 122
conversations, 76–77, 212–13
cookie empire, 66, 174
copywork, 78, **81**, 92, 93, 94, 110, 112, 158, 169,
    176, 182, 185, 207
core subjects, practical help. *See* applying the
    Superpowers
Cornell Lab of Ornithology, 146
"cornucopia" of feelings, 100
Costa, Arthur, 72–73, 117
counting story, 157–58
creating the context for magic in our homes.
    See enchanted living
creativity, 101
cross-cultural study, 153
cruel to be kind, 257–58
cuddling, *hygge*, 123
"cultural cache," 148

Curiosity (Capacity 1 for Learning), 67–75
    applying Superpowers, 125, 131, 142
    Celebration (Capacity 4), 74
    Collaboration (Capacity 2), 77, 78, 79
    Contemplation (Capacity 3), 67, 84, 86–88
    curious until proven otherwise, 68–69
    defined, xxii, 30, 64–65, 67
    disenchanting power of doing it right, 250,
        251, 253
    Great Wall of Questions, 73–74, 142
    liberation from school, 165, 170, 174, 176,
        178, 186
    magic doors, 23, 24
    match.com of curiosity, 72–74
    outrageous curiosity, 70, 71, 74–75
    "outrageous presumption of curiosity,"
        68–69
    reasonable expectations, 210
    refining the question, 71
    reversing the curse, 268
    sparks fly, 14, 15
    Spirit (Port 4), 69, 122
    Surprise (Force 1), 64
    turn-taking, not the solution, 69–70
    when your kids are most curious, you may
        be most annoyed, 70
    See also Capacities for Learning

Dana and Casey, 260–61
dangers of ideological alignment.
        See disenchanting power of doing it right
daring to think differently, 56
dedication to one skill transfers to another,
        85–86
deepening the learning experience. See
        Capacities for Learning
De La Paz, Susan, 126
delight and Surprise, 39–40, 43
deprivation vs. abundance, 231
designing your house to play with your
        strengths, 190–91
dictation, 92, 112, 169, 182, 183
directed practice, 113
disenchanting power of doing it right (dangers
        of ideological alignment), 254–65
    Capacities for Learning, 250, 251, 253, 257,
        260–61
    cruel to be kind, 257–58
    disrupting your story, 264–65
    ideological purity, 255
    Mind (Port 1), 260

    sometimes you can't, 261–62, 264, 265
    tale of two schooling styles, 263–64
    telling the truth, holding it gently, 246,
        258–61
    true belief-ism, 256–57
    us-schooling, 264
    See also breaking the spell, rekindling magic
Disney, 11–12, 76–77
disrupting your story, 264–65
divorce of Julie's parents, 223, 240
"Do, Be, Do," 111–12
doing it right. See disenchanting power of
        doing it right
"do-it-yourself" model (chores), 197–99
"Don Rag" meeting, 180
doorways of discovery, 18
Dotty (neighbor and coconspirator in all things
        homeschool), 3–5, 8, 19, 36, 190, 242
Dotty's Enchanted Art Table, 4, 5–7, 9–10, 189,
        193, 270
Drama of the Gifted Child, The (Miller), 243
Drawing on the Right Side of the Brain
        (Edwards), 101
driving games, 142
Dutch, 94
dysfunction sidelining learning. See invisible
        education

eating schedule, 167–68
educational emergencies, none, 204
"educational intimacy," 29
education is an atmosphere, not a house, 235
Edwards, Betty, 101
Eileen (Julie's friend), 243, 244
Einstein, Albert, 99
Elbow, Peter, 137–38
election season, 154
Elkind, David, 206
Elms, Stephanie, 204
embracing our limits. See reasonable
        expectations
"emotional selfie," 246
empathy, 117, 121
enchanted education
    enchanted living, 3, 5, 8, 9, 10
    magic doors, 18, 19, 23, 24, 28
    sparks fly, 11, 12, 13, 14, 16
    See also brave learners; casting the spell
        (Superpowers); Forces of Enchantment
"Enchanted Education, The" (Bogart),
        xxi–xxii

enchanted landscape of learning, xxi–xxiii, 1
    traditional school vs., xx, xxi, xxiii, 17, 21,
        22, 23, 24, 25, 26
    See also brave learners; enchanted living
        (creating the context for magic in our
        homes); magic doors (lessons from
        monsters and maps); sparks fly (igniting a
        passion for learning); specific subjects
enchanted living (creating the context for
        magic in our homes), 1, 3–10
    Dotty's Enchanted Art Table, 4, 5–7, 9–10,
        189, 193, 270
    enchanted education, 3, 5, 8, 9, 10
    enchantment defined, 9–10
    everyday magic for learning and life, 10
    Forces of Enchantment, 3, 7, 8
    See also enchanted landscape of learning
enchanted principles, 19–21
enchantment in action, 13
encounter, learning method, 48, 49, 51–52
enjoyment (One Thing Principle), 31
en-magicked moments, 9
Erin (Julie's sister), 272
everyday magic for learning and life, 10
Everything Can Be Taught Through Anything
        (Principle 1), 19–20
evidence-based interpretation, 126
execution (One Thing Principle), 31
expanding our horizons. See awesome adulting
expectations. See reasonable expectations
experience, learning method, 48, 49, 51

Fagan, Mrs., 127, 128
fairy houses, 4, 5, 7, 8, 10
family
    conflict, addressing, 74
    doing chores as a, 198, 201
    thinking like a historian, 151–52
family culture, 225–26, 247
family dysfunction sidelining learning. See
        invisible education
Family Fun, 206
farmschool, cityschool, 189–91, 192
Faulconer, Jeanne, 212
Felton, Mark, 126
field guides, 48, 86, 147, 193
finding the right balance of challenge,
        competence, and meaning, 114
Finnish schools study, 91
fire as metaphor for enchantment, 11–12, 101
    See also sparks fly

fish, cross-breeding, 104
flashlight reading, 110, 134
flipping houses, 225
focused attention span, 107–8
following child as leader, 75, 79
food, hygge, 123
Forces of Enchantment, 30, 33–63, 99, 125, 186
    lifestyle, not a program, 34–36
    Pony Express, 36–37, 38
    See also Adventure; casting the spell
        (Superpowers); enchanted education;
        Mystery; Risk; Surprise
foreign language, 19, 25, 26, 61, 78–79, 79–80,
        94, 207
forms and formats, writing, 140–41
four capacities for learning. See Capacities for
        Learning
four forces of enchantment. See Forces of
        Enchantment
four ports of entry. See Ports of Entry
fragrance and sound, hygge, 123
freewriting, 95, 137–40, 185
French, big-sistering, 79–80
friends and Risk, 58
Frost, Robert, 18
Frozen (movie), 80
Fruits of Contemplative Learning, 86
fun aunt "Lady Inspiration," 1, 17, 19, 37, 38, 161,
        165, 168–70, 177–78, 182, 186, 187, 267
"fun" lessons, 21
fun + subject = learning, 206–7

gamification theory, 156
gaming, 84–85, 87, 93, 100, 104, 114, 142, 154,
        155–59
Gardner, Howard, 101–2
gasoline, drinking, 70
"getting behind," 167, 168, 170
getting out into the big blue world, 59–60
giver, being a, 121–22
giving vs. obeying, 200
giving your kids as much of what they want as
        you can, letting go, trusting, 57
global citizens, 126–27, 148
goals, setting measurable, 95–96
GoFundMe, 57
Gold Rush party, 159
Google, 49, 50, 51, 94, 153
grades vs. celebrations, 89
grammar, xv, xix, xx, 17, 23, 24, 25, 46, **81**, 88,
        128–29, 169, 170, 182, 190

Great Books program, 85
Great Wall of Questions, 73–74, 142
Greek, 78–79
Grun, Bernard, 153
Gutman, Ron, 211

Halloween, 9
Hamilton (musical), 80
handwriting, 93, 94, 95, 102, 110, 111, 137, 139, 169, 180, 181, 216
happy vs. cooperative, 18, 65, 96, 165
Harvard's Project Zero, 101
hawk, 48
Hawking, Stephen, 135
Healing the Shame That Binds You (Bradshaw), 252
HealthTap, 211
healthy family vision, 240
Heart (Port 3 of Entry), 112–16
    applying Superpowers, 125, 132, 137
    awesome adulting, 229, 230
    Celebration (Capacity 4), 116
    challenge, competence, and meaning (balance), 114
    defined, xxiii, 30, 99–100
    homeschool hand grenade, 113–14
    house-schooling, 187
    hygge and, 123
    liberation from school, 170, 174, 176, 186
    Mystery (Force 2), 45, 46, 48, 49
    reasonable expectations, 205, 212
    reversing the curse, 268, 270, 271
    See also Ports of Entry
heavy metal music, 250–52, 253
Help! I need somebody (chores), 199–201
hiking, 8, 123, 147, 172, 189
Hindi, 79, 94
hiring it out! (chores), 196–97
history
    breaking the spell, rekindling magic, 263
    casting the spell (Superpowers), 37, 41, 48, 50, 51, **81**, 87, 91, 100, 109, 119, 120, 121, 122, 125, 126–28, 130, 132, 144, 145, 146, 148, 149–53, 155, 159
    enchanted landscape of learning, xv, xix, xxii, 18, 19, 22, 24, 25, 26, 28
    sustaining the magic, 169, 174, 177, 182, 185, 207, 214, 221
home, not school, 166–67
home culture, thinking like a historian, 152
Home Educators Neglecting Science Education (HENSE), 104

Home Is Where the School Is (Lois), 255
Homeschool Alliance, xxi, 181, 182, 204, 212
homeschool hand grenade, 113–14
homeschooling. *See* brave learners
hospice, 226
house-schooling (recruiting your home to help you educate), 187–201
    Celebration (Capacity 4), 194, 198
    chores, 194–201
    designing your house to play with your strengths, 190–91
    essentials, 192–94
    farmschool, cityschool, 189–91, 192
    Heart (Port 3), 187
    mess, the, 187–88, 194, 196, 199
    moving, 191–92
    Risk (Force 3), 188
    See also sustaining the magic
Humans of New York (blog), 57
Hygge: The Danish Practice of Coziness, 122–24, 131, 140, 201

ideological purity, 255
    See also disenchanting power of doing it right
"I don't have time for that!" 221
igniting a passion for learning. *See* sparks fly
imagination, 13–14, 28, 38, 51, 69, 70, 101, 102, 118, 120–21, 155, 204, 212, 222, 231, 235
independent learning, 76–82, **81**
innovation, 102, 126, 127, 188
inspiration, 1, 17, 19, 37, 38, 161, 165, 168–70, 177–78, 182, 186, 187, 267
Instagram, 132, 188
intellectual growth, 213–14
intelligence, 101–2
inter/intrapersonal intelligence, 101
international travel, 62–63, 191
Internet Scavenger Hunt, 49–51
interval training, 170–72, 173
Introducing a New Idea/Subject/Interest, 74–75
intuition, 11, 21, 99, 101, 210
"Invisible Education" (Bogart), 247
invisible education (family dysfunction sidelining learning), 235–53
    Celebration (Capacity 4), 242
    dysfunction-all, 238–39
    family 2.0, 242
    let's talk yelling, 236–37, 243–45, 248–49
    managing the damage, 249–53
    padunk-adunk, 244–45
    poisonous pedagogy, 243

Ports of Entry, 240, 241, 244–45, 245–46
real world of homeschooling, 235–36
Reflection Activity, 241
responding in the opposite spirit, 245–46
Sinking to Our Lowest Parenting Moment, 250–52
Surprise (Force 1), 252
telling the freaking truth, 246, 258
unhappy homeschooler, 236–38
what's the weather? 247–49
when being a family hurts, 240–41
See also breaking the spell, rekindling magic
invitation, not insistence, 175–76
Italy "trip of a lifetime," 62–63, 84, 273

Jacob (Julie's son), 15–16, 24, 62, 66, 174, 224, 229
James, LeBron, 82
Jennifer, big-sistering daughter French, 79–80
Jill (Julie's friend) and Sara, 219
Johannah (Julie's daughter), 36, 40, 45, 54–55, 60, 62, 95, 112, 116–17, 137, 189, 207, 224, 226–27, 263–64, 272
John Rankin House, 51
jotting it down, 135–37
journaling, xxii, 105, 147, 181, 183, 184, 185, 189, 248, 249

"keep 'em busy, keep 'em alive," 10
Kennedy, John F., 54
kids, expectations, 213–17
kindling (fuel) for learning, 12, 13, 14, 28, 45
knowing the truth, primary quest, 72–73

ladybugs, 45
Lamott, Anne, 194
language, 18, 19, 25, 26, 40, 43, 46, 49, 61, 78–79, 94, 120, 128–41, 142, 153, 155, 169, 206, 207, 224, 262
Latin, xix, 26, 41, 43, 72, 81, 273
learning naturally, xxi, xxii, xxiii, 9, 17, 21–27, 27, 34, 36, 104, 188, 189, 267
learning vs. exploring, 79
lessons from monsters and maps.
    See magic doors
let's talk about yelling, 236–37, 243–45, 248–49
letter of encouragement, 230–31
Liam (Julie's son), 45, 60, 84, 85, 87, 89, 97, 98, 200
liberation from school (to schedule or not to schedule), 165–86

Capacities for Learning, 165, 170, 174, 176, 178, 181, 183, 186
Forces of Enchantment, 173, 176, 181, 185, 186
fun aunt "Lady Inspiration," 1, 17, 19, 37, 38, 161, 165, 168–70, 177–78, 182, 186, 187, 267
home, not school, 166–67
interval training, 170–72, 173
invitation, not insistence, 175–76
meaning-rich materials, 173–75
measuring progress, 176–86
Monthly Narrative Sketch, 181–84, 186
planning from behind, 177–78
Ports of Entry, 169, 170, 172, 174, 176, 178, 186
routine, not schedule, 167–70, 173, 175, 178
Scatterbook, 81, 184–86, 269
seasonal schooling, 172–73
sketching a narrative, 179–84, 186
See also sustaining the magic
life cycle, enchanted learning, 13, 14
lifestyle, not a program, 34–36
lifestyle of learning, 1
    See also enchanted landscape of learning
light and color, *hygge*, 123
lighting, 109–10, 193
limits, embracing our. *See* reasonable expectations
listening and writing, 135–36
"Literature and the Moral Imagination," 120–21
Little House in the Big Woods (Wilder), 51
Little Saigon in Orange County, 51–52
Little Town on the Prairie (Wilder), 126
Living Beautifully with Uncertainty and Change (Chödrön), 255
Liz (adrenal fatigue), 261–62
logical/mathematical intelligence, 101
Lois, Jennifer, 255
love of learning, xv, xix–xx, xxi, 10, 20–21, 22, 28, 29, 175, 206, 222, 242, 266, 272
    See also Heart
lowering the bar to experience success, 205
Lowery, Lawrence, 213, 214
Lowry, Lois, 177

machines to help with chores, 198, 201
MacNeill, Joshua, 108
magic, rekindling the. *See* breaking the spell; reversing the curse
magical assist (need to know), 23–28

magic doors (lessons from monsters and
    maps), 17–28
  Body (Port 2), 22
  Children Already Love Learning
    (Principle 2), 20–21
  Continent of Learning, 24–27, 27, 75, 88, 122
  Curiosity (Capacity 1), 23, 24
  doorways of discovery, 18
  enchanted education, 18, 19, 23, 24, 28
  enchanted principles, 19–21
  Everything Can Be Taught Through
    Anything (Principle 1), 19–20
  learning naturally, xxi, xxii, xxiii, 9, 17,
    21–27, 27, 34, 36, 104, 188, 189, 267
  magical assist (awakening need to know),
    23–28
  Risk (Force 3), 22
  See also enchanted landscape of learning
managing damage, family dysfunction, 249–53
Mango app, 80
marathon runner training, 171, 172
marriage problems, 236–37
Mason, Charlotte, 20, 98, 260
match.com of curiosity, 72–74
math
  breaking the spell, rekindling magic, 259,
    268, 273
  casting the spell (Superpowers), 39, 41, 42,
    48, 49, 52, 71, 75, 81, 82, 84, 90–91, 94,
    101–3, 106, 107, 109, 114, 123, 125, 129,
    141–45, 155, 157–58, 160
  enchanted landscape of learning, xv, xx,
    xxii, 8, 18, 19–20, 21, 22, 23, 24, 26
  sustaining the magic, 169, 170, 171, 173–75,
    178, 182, 193, 204–5, 207, 220
"mathematic curiosity," 68
meaning-rich materials, 173–75
measuring progress, 176–86
Melissa and math collaboration, 144
mess, the, 187–88, 194, 196, 199
Metallica, 250, 251
micro-lessons, 176
Miller, Alice, 243
Mind for Numbers, A (Oakley), 145
Mind (Port 1 of Entry), 99–106
  applying Superpowers, 125, 132, 135, 159
  awesome adulting, 222
  Body (Port 2), 99, 100–102, 107, 108, 111
  busy place, mind is, 104
  Collaboration (Capacity 2), 77, 79, 102, 105
  defined, xxiii, 30, 99

disenchanting power of doing it right, 260
hygge and, 123
invisible education, 241
liberation from school, 172, 174, 176, 178, 186
multiple intelligences, 101–2
"nth" degree, 105
program expectations and, 102–4
reasonable expectations, 213–14
reversing the curse, 268
Risk (Force 3), 58, 100
sparks fly, 13
Surprise (Force 1), 40
See also Ports of Entry
Money (no object), what would you do? 54–55
Monsters, Inc. (movie), 18
Monte-Sano, Chauncey, 126
Monthly Narrative Sketch, 181–84, 186
moral development. See Heart
moral imagination, 118, 120–21
"more, different, better" cycle, xxi
mothering and homeschooling, 255
Mother Jones, 18
motivation, 91–92
moving, house-schooling, 191–92
Mulan (movie), 100
multiple intelligences, 101–2
Multiplication Mastery Chart, 158, 158–59
music, 19, 25, 26, 89, 108, 110, 153, 156, 157, 160,
    197, 198, 207, 214, 224, 230, 250–52, 253
my book, by me, 40
Mystery (Force 2 of Enchantment), 44–53
  applying Superpowers, 125, 128, 131
  defined, xv, 30, 33, 37, 63
  enchanted living, 8
  Heart (Port 3), 45, 46, 48, 49
  Internet Scavenger Hunt, 49–51
  liberation from school, 176
  perception, xvi, 46–48, 101
  reversing the curse, 268
  Surprise (Force 1), 38, 44, 45, 131
  See also Forces of Enchantment

Nadine, math, and tea, 145
nap time is your time, 221–22
narrate child's accomplishments, mind, 105
narrative, breaking your, 264–65
narrative sketch, 179–84, 186
NASA, 54, 62, 66
National Novel Writing Month Young Writers
    Program, 207
National Teaching and Learning Forum, 19

naturalist intelligence, 101
natural learning, xxi, xxii, xxiii, 9, 17, 21–27, 27, 34, 36, 104, 188, 189, 267
nature, 8, 45, 105, 123, 125, 131, 145–48, 155, 172, 189, 190, 193, 273
Neurologic, 108
new information and ideas. See Ports of Entry
Noah (Julie's son), 18, 35, 36, 55, 60, 62, 90–91, 102–4, 142, 159, 250–53, 271, 272
notice/note child's accomplishments, 105
no two years of homeschooling are ever the same, 203
"nth" degree, Mind, 105
Number the Stars (Lowry), 177
nutrients of brave learning, 64, 66
    See also Capacities for Learning

Oakley, Barbara, 145
observation of parents, learning from, 117
O'Connor, Flannery, 238
Olympics, 153
101 Brain Breaks and Brain Based Educational Activities (MacNeill), 108
One Thing Principle, 30–31
online games. See gaming
options, staying open to, 261–62, 264, 265
oral narratives, 180
outdoors, hygge, 123–24
outdoor trips tips, 147
outrageous curiosity, 70, 71, 74–75
owning your anger, 245

padunk-adunk, 244–45
parents' beliefs, modeling, 119
partnering. See Collaboration
party school, 159–61
passion for learning, igniting. See sparks fly
peaceful, easy feeling, 208–9
People for the Ethical Treatment of Animals, 116
Pepys, Samuel, 130
perception, xvi, 46–48, 101
performance, 60
perks of being an adult, 219–21
Phineas and Ferb (cartoon), 25, 28
phonics, 8, 41, 82, 169, 170, 172, 173, 207, 215
physics, 20, 26, 33
piano, Continent of Learning, 24–27, 27
Pixar, 18
pixie dust of reasonable expectations. See reasonable expectations
places, exploring, 51–52

planning from behind, 177–78
play and learning, 205–6
playing games, 154–61
pleasure from overcoming struggle, 113–14
poetry, 89, 125, 148
Poetry Teatime, 130–32, 224, 273
Poetry Teatime Companion (Bogart), 130
poetry vs. math test, 102–3
points, badges, leaderboards, 157, 158
poisonous pedagogy, 243
political science, 148, 154
Pony Express, 36–37, 38
Ports of Entry, 30, 97–124, 125, 186, 187
    See also Body; casting the spell (Superpowers); Heart; Mind; Spirit
Potpourri of Possible Coffee-Table Items, 42–43
powerless and loving it, 209
power of play, 205–6
practical help in core subjects. See applying the Superpowers
practicing, 30, 55, 82, 83, 84, 85, 88–89, 113, 115, 141, 171, 215, 225, 257, 258
Prelutsky, Jack, 131
preparation (One Thing Principle), 30–31
pretty good homeschool is good enough, 204, 270
pretty please? (motivation), 91–92
Pride and Prejudice (Austen), 55
principles for math and science, 143–45
"problem child," 237, 266–67
"problem-solver" vs. "right-answer-getter," 144
problem-solving vs. character development, 69
provoking outrageous curiosity, 74–75
psst, it's also a good idea to like homeschooling, 228–30

quarterly deep cleans (chores), 196–97

Rage Against the Machine, 250, 251
rational mind, 99, 101
reading
    breaking the spell, rekindling magic, 242, 250
    casting the spell (Superpowers), 37, 39–40, 48, 49–51, 53, 58, 64, 71, 78, 79, 81, 85, 88, 94, 95
    enchanted landscape of learning, 17, 19, 24, 25
    sustaining the magic, 172, 173, 181, 183, 186, 190, 192, 203, 204, 205, 214–15
Reading, Thinking, and Writing About History (Monte-Sano, De La Paz, Felton), 126

reading aloud, 4, 39, 40, 41, 110, 119–20, 131,
    132–34, 136, 166, 169, 193, 200, 216,
    270, 273
reading to self, 134–35
real life, intruding, 203–4
real world of homeschooling, 235–36
reasonable expectations (embracing our
        limits), 202–17
    Capacities for Learning, 205, 210, 214, 216
    homeschool, expectations, 204–8
    homeschool sanity principles, 203–4
    kids, expectations, 213–17
    Ports of Entry, 205, 212, 213–14
    yourself, expectations, 208–13
    See also sustaining the magic
reciting facts, 126, 127
recruiting your home to help you educate.
        See house-schooling
refining the question, 71
Reflection Activity, 241
Reinsmith, William, 19, 29, 205
rekindling the magic. See breaking the spell;
    reversing the curse
"relaxed altertness," 87, 247
religious faith, lost, 236
reminiscing (One Thing Principle), 31
Renaissance Faire, 159
research for risk-taking, 55
resentments, addressing, 74
responding in the opposite spirit, 245–46
re-upping moment, 207–8
reversing the curse (rekindling the magic),
        266–74
    becoming wise, 271–74
    Capacities for Learning, 268, 270, 272
    Forces of Enchantment, 268, 274
    garden-variety ups and downs, 267–70
    paydays, 269–70
    Ports of Entry, 268, 270, 271
    surprise of happy, 9, 269
    Type B Checklist, 267–68
    you only have to get it mostly right, 204, 270
    See also breaking the spell, rekindling magic
reviving adulthood, 222–24
rewards vs. celebrations, 89
riding solo (self-care), 226–27
right outside the front door, Mystery, 45
Risk (Force 3 of Enchantment), 53–59
    Adventure (Force 4), 38, 54, 59, 131
    applying Superpowers, 125, 131, 138, 139,
        142, 157

awesome adulting, 218
Big Hairy Audacious Goals (BHAG),
    54–56, 59
Body (Port 2), 58, 98
Celebration (Capacity 3) and, 55, 90, 93
Collaboration (Capacity 2) and, 76, 82
daring to think differently, 56
defined, 30, 33, 37, 63
enchanted living, 8
house-schooling, 188
liberation from school, 176, 186
magic doors, 22
Mind (Port 1), 58, 98, 100
reversing the curse, 268
sparks fly, 14
Spirit (Port 4), 98
trusting your kids, yourself, process, 57, 254
    See also Forces of Enchantment
road-schooling, 52
Rolling Stone, 264
Rosetta Stone, 78, 79
routine, not schedule, 167–70, 173, 175, 178
Rumi and the horse, 57
running, 225–26

"sanding the edges" of personalities, 60
sanity principles, homeschooling, 203–4
"scaffolded learning," 157
Scandinavian studies of nature, 145–46
Scatterbook, 81, 184–86, 269
schedule or not to schedule. See liberation
    from school
science, xv, 19, 20, 25, 26, 48, 49, 73, 91, 104,
    113, 121, 125, 141–45, 153, 155, 169, 174,
    176, 180, 183, 185, 224
"science of relations," education as, 20
seasonal schooling, 172–73
self-awareness, 77, 102
self-care, 226–27
self-motivation, 91
self-regulation, 77
self-sufficiency, testing, 60, 62
Sense and Sensibility (movie), 224
September 11 terrorist attacks, 46–47
Seurat, Georges, 226
Shakespeare, William, 49, 55, 60, 62, 86, 104,
    131, 182, 185, 191, 225, 251, 273
shaming, 69, 77, 107, 118, 175, 180, 197, 199,
    216, 252, 257, 271
Sharon (therapist), 240, 241
Sherri (Julie's friend), 269

silent, invisible partner (Contemplation), 86–87

Silverstein, Shel, 131

Singer, Marilyn, 131

Sinking to Our Lowest Parenting Moment, 250–52

Sister Wendy, 146

60 Minutes (TV show), 107

sitting with feet on the floor, 106–7

sketching a narrative, 179–84, 186

smile, and the world smiles back, 211–12

social sciences, 19, 25, 148, 154

sometimes you can't (options), 261–62, 264, 265

sounding out words, 78–79, 172, 180, 215, 216

Space Camp, 15, 62, 66

spark or fizzling flame? (child's interest), 77–79

sparks fly (igniting a passion for learning), 1, 10, 11–16
    adult vs. child's flame, 14–16, 24, 28
    bellows or bucket of water? 13–16
    Curiosity (Capacity 1), 14, 15
    enchanted education, 11, 12, 13, 14, 16
    fire building 101, 11–12, 101
    Forces of Enchantment, 13, 14
    Mind (Port 1), 13
    See also enchanted landscape of learning

special-needs children, 203, 205, 237, 256

Spielberg, Steven, 75, 76

Spirit (Port 4 of Entry), 116–24
    applying Superpowers, 125, 128, 132, 137
    Curiosity (Capacity 1), 69, 122
    defined, 30, 99
    Hygge: The Danish Practice of Coziness, 122–24, 131, 140, 201
    invisible education, 245–46
    liberation from school, 174, 176, 186
    moral imagination, 118, 120–21
    reading aloud, 4, 39, 40, 41, 110, 119–20, 131, 132–34, 136, 166, 169, 193, 200, 216, 270, 273
    reversing the curse, 268
    Risk (Force 3), 98
    teaching your children well, 117
    treating your children well, 118
    what if I don't like their "cause"? 119
    See also Ports of Entry

spoiling vs. valuing child's curiosity, 70

Springsteen, Bruce, 264–65

St. John's College, 180

stamina and competence, 170–72, 173

standards, differences in, 198–99, 200, 201

Stanton, Brandon, 57

starter questions, driving games, 142–43

Star Wars (movie), 80

STEM, 141

Story of Painting, The (Sister Wendy), 146

"strewing," 43

strong-willed mother, 202–3

Student Coalition for Action in Literacy Education (SCALE), 107

Sunday Afternoon on the Island of La Grande Jatte, A (Seurat), 226

Superpowers of Brave Learning. See casting the spell

Surprise (Force 1 of Enchantment), 39–44
    applying Superpowers, 125, 131, 137
    back-to-home surprises, 43–44
    Celebration (Capacity 4), 44
    clear the coffee table, 41–43, 74, 156
    Curiosity (Capacity 1), 64
    defined, xxii, 30, 33, 37, 63
    delight and, 39–40, 43
    enchanted living, 3, 7, 8
    invisible education, 252
    liberation from school, 176, 186
    Mind (Port 1), 40
    Mystery (Force 2), 38, 44, 45, 131
    reversing the curse, 268
    See also Forces of Enchantment

Susic (Julie's friend), 264

sustaining the magic, 161, 163
    traditional school vs., 18, 166, 167, 204, 205, 213, 214, 216, 224
    See also awesome adulting (expanding our horizons); brave learners; house-schooling (recruiting your home to help you educate); liberation from school (schedule or not to schedule); reasonable expectations (embracing our limits); specific subjects

tabletop games, 154–55

taking a brain break, 108, 112, 268

"talent," 100–101

tale of two schooling styles, 263–64

"teacherly" parenting style, 40

teaching your children well, 117

Tea Times Two, 145

TED Talk, 211

telling the truth, 246

therapy for parents, 266–67

thinking, development of, 213

thinking like a . . . , 126–29
Timetables of History, The (Grun), 153
tireless learning, 65, 85, 87, 89
tone of voice, 209–10
Tournier, Paul, 119
traditional school vs. brave learners
    breaking the spell, rekindling magic, 263
    casting the spell (Superpowers), 29, 34, 35,
        37, 72, 80, 85–86, 88, 89, 90, 101, 102,
        103, 104, 107, 111
    enchanted landscape of learning, xx, xxi,
        xxiii, 17, 18, 21, 22, 23, 24, 25, 26
    sustaining the magic, 166, 167, 204, 205,
        213, 214, 216, 224
    See also brave learners
traffic light game, 142
transportation for risk-taking, 55
treating your children well, 118
"triangling in" experts, 60, 175, 208
true belief-ism, 256–57
    See also disenchanting power of doing it right
trusting your kids, yourself, process, 57, 254
Tubman, Harriet, 51
"tuning fork mode," 245
turn-taking, not the solution, 69–70
Twin Towers, 46

Underground Railroad, 51
understanding vs. rote training, 141, 143
unhappy homeschooler, 236–38
unit studies in winter, 172
unity through shared mutual understanding, 56
University of California, Berkeley, 211, 213
University of California, Santa Cruz, 180
University of Massachusetts Amherst, 137–38
University of Pittsburgh, 79
unschooling, xx, 23, 35, 43, 165, 166, 169, 172,
    173, 204, 263, 264, 273
Urban Homesteading movement, 189
us-schooling, 264

value and real learning, 19–20, 22–23
valuing what your children value, 70, 85,
    87–88, 90, 91
VanDerwater, Amy Ludwig, 131

veganism, 116, 119
verbal/linguistic intelligence, 101
video games, xix, 15, 17, 18, 22, 29, 41, 42, 69,
    112, 125, 156, 169, 182, 200, 206, 240
Vietnam, 51, 52
vintage dance, 55
visual/spatial intelligence, 101
volunteer work, 226

wasting time and Risk, 58
"way leads on to way," 18
Western Washington University, 255
what if I don't like their "cause"? 119
what's the weather? 247–49
when being a family hurts, 240–41
when the tears come, the lesson's done, 216
when your kids are most curious, you may be
    most annoyed, 70
wigglers and wrigglers, 106
Wilder, Laura Ingalls, 51, 126
wise, becoming, 271–74
world, thinking like a historian, 152–53
"world-schooling," 191
World War II, 177
writing, 135–41
    breaking the spell, rekindling magic, 264
    casting the spell (Superpowers), 36, 37,
        39–40, 73, 76, 85, 86, 91, 92–95, 102, 105,
        106, 107, 110, 112, 113, 114, 117, 133–34,
        158, 161
    enchanted landscape of learning, xix, xxi, 6,
        7, 12, 13–14, 19, 23, 24
    sustaining the magic, 169, 173, 174, 175,
        179–84, 186, 206, 207, 223–24
    See also Brave Writer
Writing with Power (Elbow), 138
written narrative evaluations in college, 180

yelling, 236–37, 243–45, 248–49
Yolen, Jane, 131
younger children and housework, 198, 201
your kids want to be proud of you too, 227–28
yourself, expectations, 208–13
YouTube, 55, 67, 80, 85, 146, 153
you've got the power, house-schooling, 195

Julie Bogart is the creator of the award-winning, innovative Brave Writer program, teaching writing and language arts to thousands of families each year. She's also the host of the popular podcast *A Brave Writer's Life in Brief*. Bogart homeschooled her five now grown children for seventeen years and is the founder of the Homeschool Alliance, which supports homeschooling parents through coaching and teaching. She is also the creator of Poetry Teatime, a joyful practice that launched a global movement fostering in children a love for poetry.